SMUGGLED IN
POTATO SACKS

In tribute to the courageous parents and rescuers
of the hidden children.

In memory of Ilana and Ariela.

Smuggled in Potato Sacks

Fifty Stories of the Hidden Children
of the Kaunas Ghetto

Edited by
S. ABRAMOVICH AND Y. ZILBERG

VALLENTINE MITCHELL
LONDON • PORTLAND, OR

First published in 2011 by Vallentine Mitchell

Middlesex House,   920 NE 58th Avenue, Suite 300
29/45 High Street, Edgware,   Portland, Oregon,
Middlesex HA8 7UU, UK   97213-3786 USA

www.vmbooks.com

British Library Cataloguing in Publication Data

Smuggled in potato sacks : fifty stories of the hidden
children of the Kaunas Ghetto.
1. Jewish children in the Holocaust—Lithuania—Kaunas—
Biography. 2. Holocaust, Jewish (1935–1945)—Lithuania—
Kaunas—Personal narratives.
I. Abramovich, Solomon. II. Zilberg, Yakov.
940.5'318'0922'4793–dc22

ISBN 978-0-85303-824-5 (Paper)
ISBN 978-0-85303-814-6 (Cloth)

Library of Congress Cataloging-in-Publication Data

Printed by Good News Digital Books, Stevenage

Contents

PART 2: MEMOIRS OF THE ACTIONS

PART 3: PLACES OF REFUGE

PART 4: IN THE COUNTRYSIDE

PART 5: SMUGGLED IN A SACK

PART 6: REUNIONS AND LOST IDENTITIES

Figures

Jacket photo: First row from left: Noemy Gurvich, Dr Gurvich's adopted 'hidden' child, Michaela (Michka) Karnovsky, Ariela Abramovich, Esia Elinaite, Dalia Judelevich. Second row: second from left, Mika Rosenblum, first from right, Kama Ginkas.

Foreword

I immediately recognized my mother, but was still afraid to show it. Before going into hiding they had instructed me to deny knowing my parents if I was questioned. So when the director of the orphanage asked if I knew this woman, I said no. Then I asked, 'Is it safe to know her?' Only when I was assured that it was, did I jump into Mother's arms.

Shalom Peres

Approximately 5,000 children were among the imprisoned Jews in the Kaunas Ghetto. Some were smuggled out of the ghetto and were hidden by Gentiles. Between 250 and 300 in all, survived. Ariela Abramovich Sef and Ilana Kamber-Ash, both born in the Kaunas Ghetto, initiated the collection of personal testimonies of other children who, like them, had been rescued. Ilana and Ariela felt strongly that now that we, children of the ghetto, were growing older, there was an increasing urgency to preserve our stories for the future generations.

Figure 1. Ariela Abramovich Sef.

Figure 2. Ilana Kamber-Ash.

We compiled a list of our friends and acquaintances who were under 12 years old in June 1941 when the Germans occupied Lithuania. These individuals are the very last living survivors and witnesses of the Holocaust. Each testimony led us to another survivor among their friends, schoolmates, and colleagues. Some of the contributors are speaking about their ordeal for the first time in this book.

The stories trace the histories of the families before the war and of life in the ghetto. They describe how the children were rescued, their experiences with the Gentiles who sheltered them, the reunions with their parents for the fortunate ones whose mothers and fathers survived, and of life with adoptive parents or in orphanages after the war. We learn what subsequently became of the child survivors and where they are today.

This book cannot be a strictly factual document. The majority of our heroes were very young and the information in the testimonies comes from what the contributors can recall and what they were told by their parents, relatives or family friends. Sadly, few of us have any childhood photos in our albums; we did not grow up in normal circumstances. Photography was forbidden in the ghetto. To our regret, as adults we had no desire, were not interested or did not dare to ask our parents what had happened there in those war years. This collection is an attempt to preserve the little we do know.

This book is a tribute to those heroic parents who, despite the enormous pain of separation, made every possible effort to rescue their children and place them in the hands of Gentiles, and to those Gentiles who, risking their own families' lives, gave shelter to Jewish children during this darkest period of the twentieth century.

Ilana's daughter, Judith Ash, provided much assistance to Yakov Zilberg in collecting and translating many testimonies from Hebrew to English. Financial support for preparation of the book came from Ariela's Trust, and her brothers Ben Brahms and Solomon Abramovich, who helped with translation of the stories from Russian to English and the editing and publishing of the memoirs, which allowed the fulfilment of Ariela and Ilana's project. We wish to thank Heather Marchant who edited the manuscript and made many useful suggestions, giving the book its final shape for publication.

We are grateful to Mrs Danute Selcinskaja from the Vilnius Gaon Jewish State Museum for her assistance. Profound thanks must be given to all participants for their readiness to open old wounds and to record their experiences.

'…my mind, still lost in flight, once more turned back to see the passage that had never let anyone escape alive before.'

Dante Alighieri, Inferno *(translated by Michael Palman)*

Historical Introduction:
The Origins of Lithuanian Jewry[1]

By the tenth century a settlement had been established on the site of the contemporary Kaunas at the confluence of two rivers, Neris (Vilija) and Neman. The name 'Kaunas' first appeared in the chronicles in 1280, while Vilnius, the capital of Lithuania, was mentioned only about forty years later.

The presence of Jews in Lithuania was recorded as early as the eighth century, and it is believed that the first Jewish immigrants arrived from the south and east, probably as refugees from Babylon, Palestine and the Byzantine Empire. In the twelfth century a much larger wave of immigration moved from the west to the Grand Duchy of Lithuania, an eastern European state founded by the Lithuanians, one of the pagan Baltic tribes.

Under the tolerant rule of Grand Duke Gediminas (1316–41) and his grandson Vytautas (1401–30), to whom the Jews owed a charter of privileges, the Jews of Lithuania reached a level of prosperity unknown to their Polish and German neighbours at that time. The Jewish communities in Lithuania rapidly grew in wealth and influence, but as the power of the church grew, the position of the Jews weakened and in 1495 Lithuania expelled its Jews. However, eight years later, in 1503, the Jews were permitted to return.

In the middle of the sixteenth century, anti-Jewish feeling, fostered by the clergy, who were then engaged in a crusade against heretics, found definite expression in a repressive Lithuanian statute of 1566: 'The Jews shall not wear costly clothing, nor gold chains, nor shall their wives wear gold or silver ornaments...they shall be distinguished by characteristic clothes...in order that all may be enabled to distinguish Jews from Christians'.[2]

In 1569 Poland and Lithuania formed a new state, the Polish–Lithuanian Commonwealth, which lasted for more than two centuries. There were almost a hundred years of prosperity and relative safety for the Jews in both Lithuania and Poland until the invasion of the Russian and Ukrainian Cossack army during the Khmelnicky uprising (1648–1654). This was followed by mass pogroms and the expulsion of Jews from cities captured by the Cossacks.

In 1795 neighbouring czarist Russia annexed Lithuania, which became one of the provinces of Imperial Russia. As a result of annexation there were Lithuanian uprisings in 1830/31 and 1863/64 against the Russian Empire; the town of Kaunas was one of the centres of these uprisings. In order to suppress the local population, the Russians built several military fortifications and established a huge military garrison. About a hundred years later these fortifications became the sites of massacres of Jews during the tragic period of the Nazi occupation of Kaunas.

Since the sixteenth century Jews were involved in the trade between Kaunas and Polish and German cities, and their competition provoked opposition from the Christian merchants. Jews were forbidden to settle in Kaunas on numerous occasions, and only by the eighteenth century were Jews permitted to reside in two streets and to engage in trade. In 1753 and in 1761 they were repeatedly expelled from land belonging to the municipality, but they found refuge in the suburb of Slobodka (Vilijampole in Lithuanian) on the other side of the Vilija River, where a Jewish settlement had existed long before that of Kaunas. In 1782 the expelled Jews were permitted to return to Kaunas. Restrictions on Jewish settlement in Kaunas were again introduced in 1845 but abolished in 1858.

There were 2,013 Jews living in Kaunas in 1847; 16,540 in 1864; 25,441 in 1897 (30 per cent of the total population); and 32,628 in 1908, comprising 40 per cent of the population. A Russian Empire Census of 1897 census revealed the ethnic composition in the city: out of 70,920, the Jews comprised 35 per cent, Russians, 26 per cent, Poles, 23 per cent and Lithuanians only 6 per cent. From the second half of the nineteenth century Kaunas became a centre of Jewish cultural activity in Lithuania, and the *yeshivot* of Slobodka were regarded as some of Europe's most prestigious institutions of Jewish higher learning.

Whereas in the provinces of Russia in the seventeenth, eighteenth and early nineteenth centuries there were episodes of pogroms, the Jews in Lithuania were reasonably safe. The eighteenth century was comparatively more prosperous for the Lithuanian Jews, although several anti-Jewish riots took place. The majority of the commerce and industries of Lithuania were in the hands of the Jews, and many of the estates and farms were managed by Jewish leaseholders.

Lithuanian Jewry was particularly oppressed during the First World War, as the attitude of the Russian military authorities toward the Jews was one of suspicion and hostility. Rumours were spread that the Jews were traitors, and in May 1915 Jews from several provinces, including Kaunas, were forced by the Czar's government to retreat, together with the Russian army. They were temporary settled in cities in Russia and Belarus.

JEWISH CULTURE IN LITHUANIA[3]

Following the expulsion of Spanish Jewry and the continued persecution of Jews in Western Europe, by the sixteenth century Poland and Lithuania had become the new cultural centres of Jewish life. The Jews of Lithuania had their own distinct and highly developed Jewish culture, including a special dialect of the Yiddish language. Lithuanian Jewry played a profound role in many Jewish ideologies, including the Jewish workers' movement, Zionism and rational religious thought.

In the eighteenth century a great genius emerged, Rabbi Eliyahu Ben Shlomo Zalman (1720–97), the 'Gaon of Vilna'. He became one of the most influential rabbinical authorities of all time and is the most widely recognized Jewish spiritual leader associated with Lithuania. Since then Vilnius became a recognized spiritual centre, known as the Jerusalem of Lithuania. By the mid-nineteenth century Lithuania had become one of the most important centres of the Eastern European Jewish Enlightenment, with Lithuanian Jews making a substantial impact on secular literature, music and art.

JEWISH POLITICAL MOVEMENTS[4]

Zionism had deep roots in the consciousness of the Lithuanian Jewish community. Theodore Herzl visited Vilna (Vilnius in Lithuanian) in 1903 and spoke to representatives of Jewish organizations from all over Lithuania, explaining the essence of Zionism and its meaning for the future of the Jewish people. In 1906 the central Zionist office for all Russia was moved to Vilna (Vilnius; we shall use Vilna when we are talking about events prior to the Lithuanian independent state) and later, in independent Lithuania, the Zionist organization's head office was located in Kaunas. The Zionist movement's branches spread quickly and were active even in small Lithuanian towns during the early 1920s.

Lithuania also became the cradle of Jewish socialist movements, the most important of which was the *Bund* (the General Jewish Workers Union in Lithuania, Poland, and Russia), which was founded in 1897 in Vilna and promoted cultural autonomy for European Jews in multinational states.

THE REPUBLIC OF LITHUANIA (1918–40)[5]

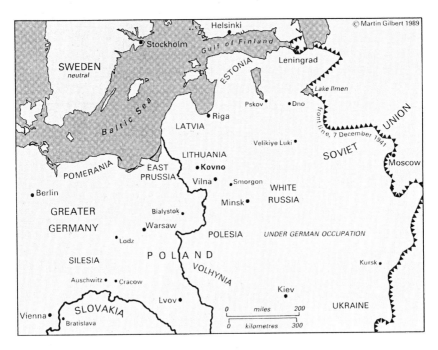

Figure 3. Eastern Europe in 1941.
(Courtesy of Sir Martin Gilbert.)

In 1917 the czarist government fell and the Lithuanian leadership met in Vilnius to organize a National Council, the *Taryba*, which declared independence on 16 February 1918, with Vilnius as its capital. In October 1920 Vilnius was captured by Polish legions and Kaunas became the capital of the independent Lithuanian state. Jews were invited to join the *Taryba*. The Jewish population supported the independence of Lithuania and when in December 1918, Lithuania's government called for volunteers to defend the State, among the 10,000 volunteers there were more than 500 Jews.[6] Altogether more than 3,000 Jews served in the Lithuanian army between 1918 and 1923.[7] Jews saw in the Lithuanian Republic an opportunity for stability and hoped that the new State would defend Jews from extreme nationalism; consequently Jews exiled by the Russians in 1915 began to return to their home towns.

In the following years relations between Lithuanians and Jews were on the whole tolerant, and the period between 1919 and 1924 is sometimes referred to as the 'Golden Age' in the history of Lithuanian Jews. Jews participated in the elections and several Jewish representatives served in all four *Seimas* (the Lithuanian parliament).

Jewish cultural autonomy was authorized by the Lithuanian government in the early 1920s, and the Ministry for Jewish Affairs, the Jewish National Council, and other central Lithuanian Jewish institutions were established in Kaunas. At the beginning of the 1930s five Jewish daily newspapers were published, the oldest being the Zionist daily, *Yidishe Shtime*, founded in 1919. The city now contained almost 100 Jewish organizations, forty synagogues, a Jewish Hospital and many Jewish-owned businesses. It was also an important centre of Zionism. The social and economic life of Lithuanian Jews flourished, and many Jewish families moved from the suburbs to the central streets of the city; there were many Jewish-owned apartments and shops on the main street of Kaunas, Laisves aleja (Laisves Avenue, 'Avenue of Independence').

The educational system in independent Lithuania was one of the most important achievements of Jewish national autonomy. Teachers in the Jewish elementary schools received their salaries from state funds. The three Jewish school systems were: *Tarbut* ('Culture' in Hebrew), which was Zionist-orientated; 'Yiddishist'

schools, with a socialist trend; and *Yavneh*, the traditional religious schools.[8] Besides the schools where the language of
instruction was Yiddish, the network of Hebrew educational
institutes included kindergartens, elementary and high schools.
Because of this large number of Hebrew schools for all grades,
Lithuania acquired a reputation among Jews as the second 'Land
of Israel'.

This golden era, however, did not last long. Anti-Semitism in
Lithuania grew in the 1930s, especially during the second half of
the decade. It was conditioned by domestic circumstances: the
impact of the world economic crisis on the Lithuanian economy,
and competition between Jews and Lithuanians in the sectors of
industry, crafts and commerce, as well as by external influences,
such as anti-Semitic and racist propaganda originating from
Germany. Mounting tension between Lithuanians and Jews was
provoked both by contemporary anti-Semitism, and traditional
anti-Judaic attitudes. Although practically all Jews spoke
Lithuanian, it was not adopted as their customary language,
since working-class Jews and those in commerce mainly spoke
Yiddish, while the professional class and the intelligentsia chose
to speak Russian. Lithuanian nationalists therefore inflamed anti-
Semitic sentiments, blaming Jews for their non-acceptance of the
Lithuanian language.

In 1923, as the influence of the Christian Democrats gained
strength, the autonomy of the Jews began to weaken. The cleri-
cal groups prevailing in the *Seimas* felt that they did not need
the help of Jews either at home or abroad. At first covertly and
later openly, they launched a campaign against Jewish autonomy and business interests. The new Lithuanian cabinet,
formed in April 1924, included no minister for Jewish affairs.
Consequently, a feature of Lithuanian Jewish national-cultural
autonomy, which distinguished it from Jewish communities in
neighbouring states, was lost. All that remained in terms of
autonomy were the Jewish people's banks and the Hebrew-
Yiddish school system. The Jewish secondary and
pre-secondary schools had to be maintained largely by the
parents, as the Ministry of Education reduced its subsidy to
Jewish educational institutions year by year.

The military coup d'état of 17 December 1926 put an end to
democracy in Lithuania. The Lithuanian National Union, the

most conservative party at the time, came to power and introduced the conservative authoritarian government led by A. Smetona. The parliament was dissolved in 1927 and the nationalistic Lithuanian government began to create all kinds of hurdles in the path of the Jews in national and civil service; anti-Semitic incidents started to occur. The number of Jews in intellectual professions continually decreased, and their positions were taken by Lithuanians. Jews were essentially treated as second-class citizens, and, in general, were excluded from positions in government and municipal offices, in cultural agencies, the military academy and the diplomatic corps, and in university departments, despite laws mandating equality. One example of anti-Semitism is seen in the admissions policy of Kaunas University, which in 1922 had 1,168 students, of whom 368 were Jews (31.5 per cent); by 1935 the student body numbered 3,334, among them 591 Jews (16.4 per cent). A '*numerus clausus*' was unofficially introduced in the medical faculty during this period, and in 1936 not a single Jewish medical student was admitted.[9] Among the 411 professors, lecturers, and other members of the teaching staff of Kaunas University, there were only six Jews.

Figure 4. The Jewish students of the Kaunas Medical School, 1934 (Abram Zilberg far left).

The social and economic contrasts existing between the Lithuanians and Jews influenced their relationship. Economic anti-Semitism found its expression in the organization of Lithuanian traders and workers known as the *Verslininkai* (skilled workers). The organization was formed in 1930 with a slogan of 'Lithuania for Lithuanians'; its attitude toward the Jews became increasingly aggressive. Both open and unofficial measures aimed at ousting Jews from their economic positions led many Jews to emigrate. Between 1928 and 1939, 13,898 Jews left Lithuania for South Africa, which became celebrated as a haven for its Jewish population, and also to Latin America, the United States and Canada, and about 5,000 to the British Mandate of Palestine.[10]

Another contribution to the nationalistic and anti-Semitic policy of the governing parties was the comparatively active involvement of secular Jews in the Communist movement. Of the 1,120 members of the Communist Party of Lithuania (banned in Smetona's times), 346 were Jews. However, it should be noted that even during the years of Smetona's rule, Jews faced less anti-Semitism in Lithuania by comparison with other East European countries. Inter-war Lithuania did not witness any deaths caused by pogroms, as happened in Poland and Romania. Although anti-Semitic demonstrations occurred from time to time, they were suppressed, and not a single anti-Jewish law was officially adopted; Jews maintained their schools and social care agencies, and their religious life remained unrestricted. Jewish soldiers and officers served in the Lithuanian army (see Figure 5). Next to the chaplain stood the chief rabbi, who attended to the requirements of Jewish soldiers.

THE SOVIET OCCUPATION, 1940–41

A Treaty of Non-Aggression between the USSR and Germany, the so-called Molotov–Ribbentrop Pact, was signed in August 1939 by the foreign ministers of the two countries. The treaty included a secret protocol concerning the division of Eastern Europe into spheres of influence and territorial and political control, which were swiftly imposed.

The invasion of Poland by Nazi Germany began on 1 September 1939, only one week after the signing of the

Molotov–Ribbentrop Pact. It marked the outbreak of the Second World War. The USSR was not slow to follow and on 17 September invaded eastern Poland. By 6 October 1939 the whole territory of Poland was occupied. Immediately after this the Soviets forced Lithuania to sign a Pact of Mutual Soviet–Lithuanian Assistance. According to this agreement the Soviets returned Vilnius to Lithuania in exchange for stationing 20,000 Soviet troops within its territory.

Figure 5. Jewish officer Jakob Abramovich (centre) during his military service in the Lithuanian Army, 1938.

A year later, in the ultimatum of June 1940, the Soviets demanded that Lithuania form a new pro-Soviet government and admit to its territory an unspecified number of Russian troops. Lithuania had no other choice but to accept the ultimatum, since any effective military resistance to the Red Army was out of the question. Soviet troops were already located within Lithuania, according to the terms of the Pact of 1939. President

Smetona left Lithuania, as fifteen divisions comprising 150,000 soldiers of the Soviet military forces crossed the Lithuanian border on 15 June 1940. A new pro-Soviet puppet government was established, carrying out orders from Moscow. The *Seimas* was disbanded and new Soviet-style 'elections' were organized on 14/15 July 1940. Official results of the elections showed over 90 per cent support for the Communists. During its first session on 21 July the 'People's *Seimas*' unanimously agreed to send a petition to Moscow, pleading to be allowed to join the Soviet Union. On 3 August the petition was approved by the Supreme Court of the USSR and the Lithuanian SSR was accepted into the Soviet Union. This farce of the legitimization of the occupation was complete and the USSR annexed Lithuania. Exactly the same process was effected in Latvia and Estonia.

Immediately a rapid process of 'Sovietization' of occupied Lithuania began. All the land was nationalized and large farms were distributed among small landowners. All religious, cultural, and political organizations, with the exception of the Communist Party, were banned. An estimated 12,000 'anti-Soviet' elements were arrested; during the June deportation some 17,000 people (mostly former military officers, policemen, political figures, intelligentsia and their families) were deported to Siberia, where many perished due to inhumane living conditions.

Relations between Lithuanians and Jews turned very bitter during the two years of the Soviet occupation (1940/41). Anti-Semitism grew to a new, far more threatening level. The leadership of the Lithuanian Activists Front (LAF), a resistance organization established in 1940, issued the anti-Semitic proclamations that came from headquarters in Berlin. The LAF's appeal published in spring 1941, 'Let us Liberate Lithuania from the Jewish Yoke Forever', proclaimed: 'Russian Communism and its eternal servant, a Jew, are one and the same enemy... The elimination of the occupation by Russians and enslavement by the Jews is one and the same sacred task.'[11] LAF propaganda had a significant impact on the attitudes of Lithuanians toward Jews. Previous stereotypes of Jews, such as 'enemies of Christians' and 'exploiters of Lithuanians', were now, in the minds of many Lithuanians, overshadowed by the new image of Jews – 'the traitors of Lithuania'.

The dramatically increasing Lithuanian hostility against Jews during the first Soviet period was conditioned by a number of factors:[12]

- Contrasting geopolitical perceptions: for Jews, the Soviets represented 'a lesser evil' when compared with Nazi Germany, while many Lithuanians hoped that Germany would liberate them from the Soviet Union.
- Lithuanian Jews were accused of joyfully welcoming the Soviet Army when it marched into Lithuania. And there are those who say that on that night the fate was sealed for years to come not only of this tiny country, but also of the Jews within it. Lithuanians would never forgive the Jews for the relief they felt during the tragic days of the end of the independent Lithuanian State.[13]
- Because of the significant membership of Jews in the Communist Party, the Jew-Communist stereotype was established in the minds of many Lithuanians. Lithuanians considered the Soviets/Russians/Communists/Bolsheviks (and they identified Jews with all these terms) as the main enemy.
- A number of Jews served in the Soviet occupational administration, including the feared NKVD (The People's Commissariat for Internal Affairs), the public and secret police organization of the USSR, which directly implemented the commands of the Soviets, including political repressions. For Lithuanians it was a sufficient argument to believe that Soviet government was synonymous with government by Jews. Jews were regarded as being responsible for the deportation of Lithuanians to exile in Siberia and were also accused of being the NKVD's cruellest interrogators.[14]
- The Lithuanian Republic suffered several political and diplomatic defeats: Poland occupied Vilnius; the Klaipeda (Memel) region was annexed by Germany in 1939; the Red Army garrisons were located in Lithuania in October 1939 and, finally, came capitulation to the demands of the USSR in June 1940. All these caused a deep moral crisis in the Lithuanian nation which sought scapegoats for these failures, and which partly explains why the Lithuanian Jews came to be perceived as largely to blame for the misfortunes that befell the country.

Yet the reality is that the Soviet troops were met with flowers by both Jews and by the Lithuanian people; a fact known only to a few is that the first friendly faces to meet the occupying force were officers of the Lithuanian Army.[15] Furthermore, in 1939 Jewish Communists comprised barely 0.3 per cent of the Jewish community of Lithuania. Although many Lithuanians collaborated with the Soviet regime, Jews were far more conspicuous, as they were viewed through a magnifying glass.

Neither Lithuanian nor Jewish historians have found any particular Jewish role in the process of the 'Sovietization' of Lithuania and in the policy of Bolshevik terror.[16] In reality Jews did not play an especially significant role in the institutions of Soviet rule during 1940/41; like all the other nationalities in Lithuania, Jews suffered under Soviet rule.[17] Religious Jews and Zionists were treated harshly by the Soviet-imposed communist government in Lithuania prior to the German invasion. The number of Jewish high schools was reduced by half, the Hebrew language was no longer permitted, and Saturday, the Jewish Sabbath, was no longer a holiday. Nationalization of property caused the greatest harm to Jews. Nearly 500 Jews were arrested in one year, and a total of 2,600 Jews suffered Soviet repression.[18] Jews accounted for 13.5 per cent of the June 1941 deportees, while their share in the entire population of the country was about 7 per cent. Stratocide, the destruction of certain social classes, and not the genocide based on ethnic principles, was the Soviet policy in 1940.[19]

THE SECOND WORLD WAR AND THE HOLOCAUST

Without formally declaring war, Germany broke the Molotov–Ribbentrop Pact, and on 21 June attacked the Soviet Union. Within a few days the Germans occupied Lithuania's territory. At this time the Jewish population of Lithuania had grown to about 250,000 and comprised 10 per cent of Lithuania's population, due to an influx of refugees from German-occupied Poland and the migration of Jews from the USSR in 1940/41.

Only a small number of Lithuanian Jews succeeded in escaping to Russia. Even just days before the outbreak of war, the Soviet authorities accused anyone who planned to leave of 'dissemination of panic and disorder'. Although Jews had heard about the anti-Jewish campaigns of the Nazis, most of them refused to believe that the nation which had given the world Goethe, Kant and Beethoven would tolerate such barbaric destruction and killing. Jews also had never expected that among the Lithuanians, with whom they had lived for centuries, there would appear so many murderers.[20] After the German invasion, there were almost no means of transport available by which to escape. The Luftwaffe had bombed the trains and roads, and the 'White Armbands', *'baltaraisciai'*, participants in the uprising of Lithuanians against the Soviets in the first days of invasion, blocked the roads and either killed Jewish refugees or forced them to turn back to their homes, which in the meantime had been robbed and occupied by neighbours. Out of about 15,000 Lithuanian Jews who were either deported by the Soviets or managed to escape, about 12,000 survived. More then 5,000 fought in the Sixteen Lithuanian Division of the Red Army and about 2,000 fell in battles.[21] Local collaborators, incited by the LAF, took drastic measures against the Jewish population.[22] In at least forty Lithuanian settlements, before the Germans had even reached them, armed Lithuanians began, on their own initiative, to kill the Jews. By the end of August 1941, almost all of the Jewish population in Lithuania's provinces had been slaughtered by Lithuanians and the German *Einsatzgruppen* (mobile killing units).[23] The surviving Jews were eventually concentrated in the Vilnius, Kaunas, Siauliai, and Svencionis Ghettos, and in various labour camps in Lithuania. Living conditions there were miserable, with severe food shortages, outbreaks of disease, and overcrowding. By the end of the Second World War, around 200,000 – 94 per cent – of Lithuanian Jews were killed.[24] This was proportionately one of the highest rates of loss in the Holocaust.

The public institutions and political leadership, which claimed responsibility for the restoration of a liberated nation, did virtually nothing to relieve the ugly atmosphere of ethnic hatred and bloodshed. A public denunciation of mob brutalities could have persuaded at least some of the Lithuanians who had volunteered or been co-opted into participating in the killings to change their behaviour. A single voice within the Provisional Government circle, historian Zenonas Ivinskis, reportedly urged the Government to publicly disassociate itself from the massacre of the Jews, but to no avail. The Lithuanian intelligentsia had for the most part never been truly anti-Semitic, despised and condemned the Fascists, but had no influence at all.

KAUNAS – THE FIRST WEEKS OF OCCUPATION[25]

Following Germany's invasion, the Soviet forces fled Kaunas. Even before the Germans entered the city on 24 June 1941, many Jews had been killed by Lithuanian Fascists. Immediately after the German occupation, large-scale anti-Jewish pogroms took place, affecting some 35,000 Jews. Encouraged by the SS, ultra-nationalist Lithuanians, so-called 'partisans', carried out a most violent and barbaric pogrom in Slobodka (Vilijampole) in which 800 Jews were killed. Some were brutally tortured before their death.

On 27 June, sixty-eight Jews were killed in the Lietukis garage, in the city centre, a slaughter which became infamous around the world. It was committed in the presence of a crowd of local residents, including women and children, who gathered around to observe the spectacle of defenceless people being either battered to death with crowbars or wheel braces, or choked to death by having a hosepipe shoved down their throats and water pumped into their gullets. German soldiers and officers were also present, calmly watching and taking photographs of this dreadful event. Rounds of applause came from the crowd after each murder was committed. At the end, one of the bandits took out his harmonica and together with the assembled crowd sang the Lithuanian national anthem. In this act of barbarity, the Lithuanian mob shamelessly displayed its hatred and contempt for the Jewish population.

From the end of June until 6 July 1941 Jews were hunted down, arrested in various parts of the city and taken to the Seventh Fort, where between 6,000 and 7,000 of them were murdered. On 7 August 1941, 1,200 Jewish men were picked up in the streets and about 1,000 put to death. The arrest, robbing, torture and killing of the Jews were executed by the White Armband partisans and later by the members of Lithuanian military battalions.

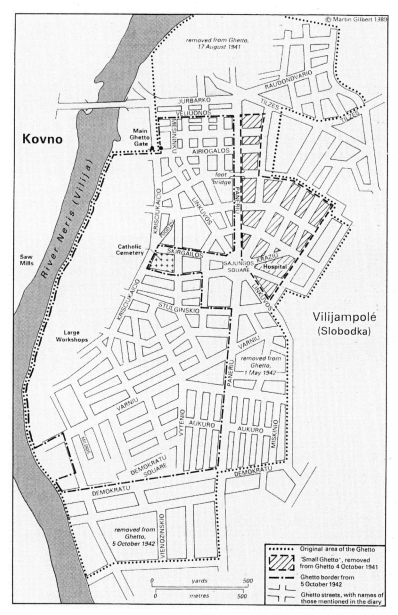

Figure 6. The Kovno Ghetto: streets and boundaries. (Courtesy of Sir Martin Gilbert.)

On 11 July 1941, instructed by the Germans, the Lithuanian military commander and the mayor of Kaunas issued an order stating that by 15 August all the Jews in the city and its suburbs were to move into a ghetto in Slobodka. The official purpose of this act was 'to defend' the Jews from further persecution by the local population. Some 29,000 people, who had survived the initial pogroms, were concentrated in an area of small, rudimentary houses with no running water. A part of Slobodka, allocated for the ghetto, had already been 'cleared' of its mainly Jewish inhabitants during the pogroms. Lithuanians residing in the ghetto area were evacuated to Kaunas and occupied the apartments of expelled Jews. As in all other ghettoes, the Jewish Council (*Aeltestenrat* or *Judenrat*, Council of the Elders) and the Jewish ghetto police were established.[27]

Figure 7. Example of the Identity certificate issued by the Jewish Police in the name of Jakob Abramovich and signed by Judo Zupovichius.

Dr Elkhanan Elkes, a highly respected physician, was elected to head the Jewish Council, and who reluctantly, under pressure from the Jewish community, accepted the position. Dr Elkes was born in 1879 in Kalvarija, western Lithuania. He graduated with distinction in Medicine from the University of Königsberg in East Prussia. During the First World War he served as a medical officer in the Russian Army, and after the war returned to Kaunas, where he became one of leading physicians in Lithuania. With his fellow doctors he built the Department of Internal Medicine in the Jewish Hospital and with Dr Moshe Schwabe and few others he established the Hebrew Gymnasium. Elkes was connected with the *Hehalutz* Zionist youth movement, and was also closely involved in Jewish cultural activities.

Dr Elkes, with all his intelligence, integrity and courage tried as hard as he could to fortify the endurance of the community and to defend their interests in the face of merciless killers. He is regarded as one of the most distinguished leaders to emerge during the horrors of the Holocaust, a man whose memory is revered for the dignity with which he led the Kaunas Jewry in their hour of greatest need, until he was deported in 1944 and died in Dachau.

The Jewish police numbered about 200 members. On the initiative of Dr Elkes and other members of the Jewish Council, many intellectuals, who had no skills for physical work, were recruited to the Ghetto police.[28] Most of the Jewish Polizei cooperated with the Ghetto resistance groups.

The ghetto provided forced labour for the German military. Jews were employed primarily as forced labourers at various sites outside the ghetto, especially in the construction of a military airbase in Aleksotas. The Jewish Council created workshops inside the ghetto for those women, teenagers and the elderly who could not participate in the labour brigades. These workshops eventually employed almost 6,500 people; they were a prerequisite for survival. Dr Elkes hoped the Germans would not kill Jews who were producing for the army.

The ghetto was divided into two sections, the 'Small' and 'Large Ghetto', separated by Paneriai Street and connected by a small wooden bridge over the street. Each ghetto was enclosed by barbed wire and closely guarded; both were heavily overcrowded. The Germans continually reduced the ghetto's size, forcing Jews to move from one place to another, time after time.

These were years dominated by vulnerability, fear and uncertainty. Gradually, all human rights were being stripped away from a community which had once felt safe and lived a

Figure 8. Example of the work card issued by the
Administrative office of the Jewish Community of the
Kaunas Ghetto.

prosperous life in this region. Conditions were deteriorating. It was forbidden to bring food into the ghetto, or coal and wood to warm the houses. Worst of all was living in the shadow of imminent 'actions', which everyone understood were no more than the prelude to the massacre of those who were taken away.

Selected sites (■) of Jewish slave labor outside the ghetto

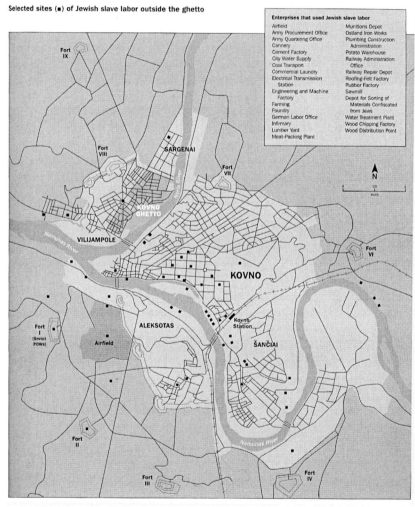

Enterprises that used Jewish slave labor

Airfield	Munitions Depot
Army Procurement Office	Ostland Iron Works
Army Quartering Office	Plumbing Construction
Cannery	Administration
Cement Factory	Potato Warehouse
City Water Supply	Railway Administration
Coal Transport	Office
Commercial Laundry	Railway Repair Depot
Electrical Transmission	Roofing-Felt Factory
Station	Rubber Factory
Engineering and Machine	Sawmill
Factory	Depot for Sorting of
Farming	Materials Confiscated
Foundry	from Jews
German Labor Office	Water Treatment Plant
Infirmary	Wood Chipping Factory
Lumber Yard	Wood Distribution Point
Meat-Packing Plant	

Figure 9. Map of Kaunas with suburbs, forts and sites of Jewish slave labour outside the Ghetto. (Courtesy of the US Holocaust Memorial Museum.)

In the middle of August the Germans called for volunteers to perform more skilled intellectual jobs. On 18 August, 534 men who responded to this call were taken to the Fourth Fort and killed there; 'The Intellectuals' Action' was the first mass shooting of the ghetto inhabitants. An SS officer from the *Einsatzgruppen* reported that units under his command shot more than 1,800 Jews at Fort Four on this date.[29]

On 26 September 1941, about 1,000 Jews were killed at Fort Four, in retaliation for the alleged shooting of Commander Kozlovsky, known as the 'Krishchiukaichio Street Action'. On 4 October 1941, the 'Small Ghetto' was liquidated, and almost all of its inhabitants killed at the Ninth Fort. The infectious diseases hospital, located in the 'Small Ghetto', was set on fire. All the medical personnel and patients trapped inside the hospital were burned alive.[30]

Later that same month, on 28 October, all the ghetto inhabitants were forced to assemble in a central square of the ghetto. SS-Rottenführer (master sergeant) Helmut Rauca, the head of the Kaunas Gestapo, personally conducted the selection for death of one third of the ghetto population. The next day 2,007 Jewish men, 2,920 women, and 4,273 children were shot at the Ninth Fort and buried in huge pits dug in advance. It was the largest mass murder of Jews in Lithuania in a single day, and known as the 'Great Action' of the Kaunas Ghetto.[31]

Besides Jews from Kaunas, thousands of Jews and their belongings were transported to the Ninth Fort from Germany, Austria, France, and other European countries for 'resettlement in the East' and murdered there.[32] Two such resettlement 'actions' took place in the Kaunas Ghetto as well: in 1942 about 350 Jews from Kaunas were transferred to Riga. On 26 October 1943, approximately 3,000 Jews, deemed fit to work, were deported to labour camps in Estonia. The Kaunas Ghetto was then converted into a concentration camp, and the SS assumed control of the ghetto. The Jewish Council's role was drastically curtailed. The Nazis dispersed more than 3,500 Jews to the sub-camps of Aleksotas and Shanchiai, where an even stricter regime than in the main camp governed all aspects of daily life. More tragic events in the ghetto were to follow.

Escapes and Deportations from the Kovno Ghetto, 1943–1944

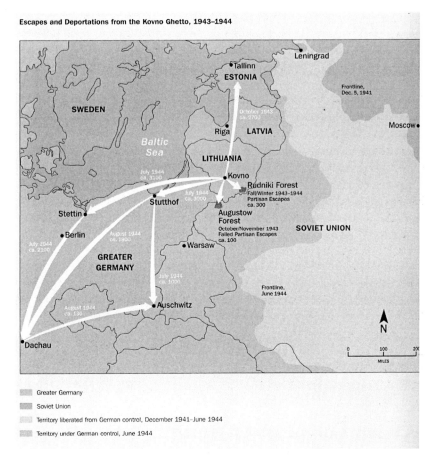

Figure 10. Escapes and deportations from the Kaunas Ghetto 1943–44. (Courtesy of the US Holocaust Memorial Museum.)

'FINAL SOLUTION'[33]

Hitler conducted a process of mass murder that was designed to exterminate European Jewry. The first step was to blame the Jews for all of society's ills, then to demonize them as a dangerous enemy, dehumanize them, and finally portray them as evil creatures that must be destroyed. The Nazi plan for the systematic genocide of all Jews, the 'Final Solution' of the Jewish question, was accepted at the Wannsee conference in Berlin on 20 January 1942, resulting in the final, most deadly phase of the Holocaust.

Mass killings of approximately one million Jews had already occurred prior to the plans outlined in the Final Solution. After the formal decision to eradicate the entire Jewish population, extermination camps were built and the mass slaughter of Jews was industrialized. It is arguable that the implementation of the Final Solution took its most dreadful shape in Lithuania. Mass executions occurred in various locations throughout Lithuania, most of them at the Kaunas Ninth Fort and in the forest of Paneriai (Ponary) near Vilnius. The liquidation of the Vilnius ghetto on 23 August 1943 signalled the last phase of the destruction of Lithuanian Jewry on the very soil on which they had lived since the Middle Ages.

RESISTANCE[34]

Several Jewish resistance groups were active in the ghetto from 1941. In 1943, under the leadership of Chaim Yellin (Elinas), the General Jewish Fighting Organization was established, uniting the major resistance groups, which numbered up to 800 fighters. The Jewish Council in Kaunas supported the ghetto underground movement. Moreover, a substantial part of the ghetto's policemen participated in resistance activities. The resistance acquired arms, developed secret training areas in the ghetto, and established contact with the partisan detachments concealed in the forests.

From autumn 1943 to spring 1944 the underground managed to send about 300 armed fighters to partisan units in the Augustow and Rudniki forests, located near Lithuanian border in Belarus. Through lack of experience and mainly because of the hostility of the local population, many of the members of the underground were killed or captured on the long journey to the partisan units. More than one third were killed in action against the Germans.

A group of sixty-four prisoners in the Ninth Fort, Russian POWs and Jews, employed by the Gestapo to burn corpses of the victims executed there, managed to escape on Christmas Eve 1943.[35] It was a most courageous escape, taking into account the Fort's structure and the extremely thorough guard procedures.

Thirty-seven were caught by the Gestapo, betrayed by the local population, nineteen reached the ghetto. They were then sent by the ghetto underground to the forests and absorbed into the Soviet partisan units. Among documents taken by the group to the forest was a copy of the act describing German atrocities in the Ninth Fort. In April 1944 Chaim Yellin was caught by the Gestapo, tortured and executed.

Throughout the years of hardship and horror, the Jewish community of Kaunas documented its story in secret archives, diaries, drawings and photographs. Hirsh Kadish (Kadushin) secretly photographed the trials of daily life within the ghetto with a hidden camera. Some documents, discovered after the war, provided evidence of the Jewish community's defiance, oppression, resistance, and death.

The rescue of the ghetto's children was one of the main tasks of the anti-fascist underground. The resistance members made contact with reliable people outside the ghetto, looking for safe places to hide children in Kaunas and the vicinities. Representatives the Lithuanian intelligentsia and clergy initiated assistance to inhabitants of the ghetto. They organized a well-coordinated network of rescuers. Extraordinary acts of bravery and compassion were exercised by honourable people including many ordinary citizens and peasants from the countryside, who thereby saved adults and children.

CHILDREN IN THE GHETTO

Adults did their best to preserve some kind of childhood in the ghetto. Birthdays and holidays, especially Hanukah and Purim, were somehow celebrated despite all the difficulties. During the autumn of 1941 the Jewish Council organized schools for children, but on 25 August 1942 educational instruction was formally banned. Limited elementary education continued in private homes, and the German authorities permitted the continuation of vocational schools set up for teenagers. In these schools Hebrew and Jewish history were taught in addition to crafts. Most children, however, did not go to school but either hid in the houses or wandered the streets aimlessly.

On 24 July 1942 the German authorities forbade pregnancies and births in the ghetto, declaring that women who were up to seven months pregnant would be shot if they did not terminate their pregnancies by mid-September 1942.[36] Despite the risks, some women carried to term and gave birth, assisted by courageous physicians and nurses, and then hid their babies from the Germans.

Figure 11. Underground school in the Kaunas Ghetto, 1942 or 1943. A teacher in the photo is Shmuel Rosental.

Children were especially vulnerable members of the Jewish population. There were about 5,000 children, up to age 12, in the ghetto by the autumn of 1941. Hundreds of children were killed in pogroms and 'actions'; 4,273 children perished in a single day during the 'Great Action'. Later most children suffered severe malnutrition and many died from various diseases.

In November 1943 fear for the safety of the remaining children in the ghetto mounted after a message was received of a 'Children's Action' that had taken place in the ghetto of Shauliai.

The underground organization massively increased its efforts to rescue children. Through the resistance's arrangements, as well as through private contacts with pre-war neighbours and colleagues, there were many more attempts to smuggle children and to transfer them to Gentile families.

Figure 12. Purim in the Ghetto, 1943. Two children are identified: second row fourth from right Gita German-Gordon; first from right (sleeveless dress) Sheinale Gordon who perished.

Saving children presented a special problem, as they could hardly be a part of the conspiracy to create a new identity. Parents and children had to separate, and perhaps never see each other again. Children old enough to distinguish between their natural and adopted parents had to erase from their minds the memory of their true parents and their own former names, forget their Jewish affiliation and religious customs and re-adapt to totally new relationships, new cultural and religious environments.

Many parents had hesitated to separate from their children, unable to contemplate turning over their child for an indefinite period for safekeeping and adoption in either a children's home or with a private family. Now they sought desperately for hiding places outside the ghetto. There were even cases when mothers in despair threw their little children over the barbed wire in the hope they would be picked up by somebody. Parents were now going to any lengths to save the lives of their children, even if it meant that they would eventually live as orphans or be converted to Christianity.

Figure 13. Moshe Levin, the commander of the Jewish police and his deputy Juda Zupovich, 1943. Both were executed in 1944 for refusing to disclose the hiding places of surviving children. Juda was brutally tortured before the death. The third policemen is Tanchum Arnstam, who was sentenced by the Soviet court for cooperation with the Germans and executed.

The Kaunas Ghetto 'Children's Action' took place on 27/28 March 1944. During the two-day 'action', German troops and Ukrainian auxiliaries went from house to house and rounded up the ghetto's children and the old and sick. About sixty children who appeared in the Germans' lists were not found. Furious SS suspected the ghetto policemen of participation in resistance activities and arrested many of them. Despite torture, most of the policemen refused to provide any information on the specially constructed children's hiding places. The SS killed 36 Jewish policemen, including Moshe Levin, the head of Jewish police, and his deputy Yehuda Zupovich.[37] However, a few could not withstand the torture and cooperated. The SS and its auxiliaries with dogs, accompanied by the Jewish policemen, went from house to house in the ghetto in a thorough search for the remaining children. Many infants were dragged out of the hiding places. About 1,300 children and the elderly (other sources say 2,000) victims of this, the most brutal 'action', were either taken to the Ninth Fort or deported to Auschwitz where they perished.

After this 'action' the Germans assumed there were no more children in the ghetto, so additional attempts to smuggle the few remaining were undertaken. Some children aged 12, and even younger, were registered for work, pretending they were 16.

THE RIGHTEOUS AMONG THE NATIONS

The Nazis warned the local population of dire punishment, including the death penalty, for any violation of regulations, forbidding aid to Jews. Yet in the midst of an ocean of hatred and bloodshed, hundreds of Lithuanians and Polish people risked their own and their families' lives sheltering the Jews. There were many cases when rescuers paid with their life for saving Jews. The Israeli Holocaust Museum, Yad Vashem, has recognized more than 723 Lithuanian Gentiles as 'Righteous among the Nations' for helping to shelter the Jews. This figure is far from complete as many cases were never reported. According to various sources, between 180 and 400 of the Kaunas Ghetto children were successfully hidden and survived the Holocaust.[38] No data exist, only suggestions.

During the past decade, the Vilna Gaon Jewish State Museum has unearthed the names of many more rescuers, and it commemorated their names in several books and exhibitions. In 2009 a deeply affecting exhibition was opened in the Museum, devoted solely to the rescue of children.[39]

THE FINAL DAYS OF THE GHETTO

When the Soviet attack began in July 1944, the Germans and their collaborators liquidated the Kaunas Ghetto and concentration camps in the area. On 8 July 1944, three weeks before the Soviet army arrived in Kaunas, the Germans and their Lithuanian collaborators razed the ghetto to the ground with grenades and dynamite in order to kill the Jews hiding in bunkers. As many as 2,000 people were burned alive or were shot while trying to escape the burning ghetto. Only about 500 had survived in forests or in a single bunker, which had escaped detection during the final liquidation.

Figure 14. The elderly Sira Abramovich with the empty food bowl and a piece of bread in her other hand. The queue for food in Kaunas Ghetto, winter 1944.

About 8,000 Jews were deported from the Kaunas Ghetto and satellite camps. Men were sent to Dachau and women to Stutthof concentration camp in Germany. Over 80 per cent of them died in these camps before liberation. Of the 37,000 Jews in Kaunas, only 3,000 survived the war.

THE SOVIET ERA (1944–1990)

Immediately after the Red Army had liberated Kaunas from the Nazis on 1 August 1944, a list of survivors and notes about the search for relatives were pinned up in the synagogue. The small Jewish community immediately set about establishing orphanages for the Jewish children.[40] In many cases, children were handed back by the Gentiles who had harboured them. Some Jewish activists travelled the villages, looking to reclaim hidden children.

The Soviets prosecuted a number of Lithuanians for collaborating with the Nazis. Sites of wartime massacres, such as the Ninth Fort, became monuments. Inscriptions, however, always read, 'here perished Soviet citizens', and the fact that almost 100 per cent of them were Jewish was omitted. Throughout Soviet rule, there was tension between the Jewish community and the authorities over how to properly commemorate the Holocaust.

Immediately after the war, there were hardly any Jews left in Lithuania, their cultural life was destroyed. Those who survived gathered in the larger cities. This created the illusion of a continuity in Jewish life. In 1945 the Jewish Museum was registered in Vilnius; Vilnius and Kaunas religious communities were formed in 1946. Jewish primary schools, children's homes for the orphan-survivors, and kindergartens were established in Vilnius and Kaunas. But in 1949 the Soviet government, which maintained anti-Semitic attitudes and policies, closed down the museum, schools and the kindergartens.

When the Soviet regime became slightly more liberal after the death of Stalin in 1953, there was a revival of Jewish cultural life in Lithuania. In Kaunas and Vilnius, amateur artists' collectives with a Jewish repertoire of songs and theatre in Yiddish were organized. These were the first such collectives in the Soviet Union, and came to be known in many regions throughout the country.

In 1963 the Jewish cemetery was ploughed up and Jews were ordered to bury their dead in the general cemetery. They were, however, at their request, permitted a separate Jewish section. Several incidents in which Jews were beaten up in the streets were reported in 1968.

Figure 15. Jewish kindergarten and the first class, Kaunas, Purim 1946. From left to right: first row: Nesia Aleksandrovich, Abrasha Levin, Tereza Smoliansky, Liuba Zakovich, Beny Ton, Sima Shenker, Rina Zupovich-Kaplan (white wig); second row: Alik Rubin or Chonke Gold, Sima, unknown, Boris Poger, Sergey Volensky, Elena Smerkovich, Benya Chaitas, Akiva Flier, Misha Fridburg, unknown, Frida Glazman; third row: Katia Berezin, unknown, Genia Smoliansky, unknown x 3, Liuba Peres, Gidon Sheftel, unknown x 3, Estera Elinaite; fourth row: unknown x 2, Julia Meltz, Roma Lafer, Vova Zivov, Svirsky, Misha Langevich, unknown, Salia Bychovsky-Broyeris, Anton Smoliansky, Anatolij Shimkovich, Busia Elin (Estera's mother); top row: Hindale Sherman; Roza or Tamara, Genia Chaitas (Benya Chaitas's mother); Shmerkovich (the manager and Elena Shmerkovich's mother), Rachel Kogan-Antanavichiene.

POST-WAR EMIGRATION OF THE LITHUANIAN JEWS

Most of the Jewish survivors of the concentration camps did not return to Lithuania. They were later followed by nearly 1,000 Jews who left Lithuania illegally after its liberation. In addition,

Jews originating from Vilnius were able to move to Poland legally as a part of its agreement with the Soviet Union over the repatriation of pre-war Polish citizens. Most of the emigrants reached Palestine, overcoming many obstacles, while others emigrated mainly to the United States.

Figure 16. Jewish orphanage, 1945. First row: first from right: Tamara Ratneryte-Kadishaite-Levy; third from right: Aharon Avidonis (?): sixth from right (with white ribbon): Dalia Hofmekler-Ginsburg. Second row: first from left: Rina Zupovich-Kaplan; sixth from left: Estera Elinaite (just above Dalia Hofmekler). Fourth row: fourth from left: Maxim Broyeris (?). Sixth row (teachers): first from left: Frida Kaplan (Rina Zupovich's adoptive mother); fourth: Busia Elin. Top row: sixth from right, Riva Taft, next to her (with white collar) Gurevich.

The majority of Jews who remained in Soviet Lithuania after the war could not leave and could never forget the genocide that had taken place, not least because many of the perpetrators still lived among them. After the most horrible experience during the war, those who previously were sympathetic to socialist ideas

and retained any Jewish consciousness, cultural heritage and
beliefs, were bitterly disappointed with Soviet policy towards the
Jews. Establishment of the State of Israel resulted in feelings of
pride in their Jewish heritage and hope in their hearts. For these
kinds of reasons, the desire of Lithuanian Jews to leave was deep,
grew constantly, and they took every opportunity to fulfil it.

The first, small-scale emigration from Lithuania to Israel
began in the early 1950s, reuniting separated families, but then
came to an abrupt halt until a new Polish–Soviet repatriation
agreement could be concluded. About 4,000 Jews, many thanks
to fictitious marriages with pre-war Polish citizens, left for
Poland between 1956 and 1959, and then made *Aliyah* (the return
of Jews from exile to Israel) in a wave known as 'Gomulka's
emigration'.[41] According to the 1959 census, about 25,000 Jews
lived in Lithuania, almost half of them coming from other parts
of the USSR, attracted by the more favourable economic circumstances compared to other Soviet Republics. The Jewish
population of Kaunas numbered 4,792 (2.24 per cent) in 1959.[42]

The desire to fulfil their Jewish aspirations within the Soviet
Union and to emigrate to Israel continued. Many Lithuanian
Jews were among the activists in the struggle to obtain exit visas,
and were refused. They alerted the West and the conscience of
the world to the abuses of human rights in the USSR and to the
plight of the 'refusniks'.[43] Eventually, in the early 1970s, about
200,000 Soviet Jews and, among them, the vast majority of
Lithuanian Jews, were allowed to leave; in addition, thousands
of Jews migrated to the United States, a wave of emigration that
lasted until 1979.

In the huge 'exodus' that followed the fall of the Soviet
empire, the proportion of Jews leaving from Lithuania was mini-
mal, because only a very few Jews remained behind. Today, there
is still a small Jewish community in Lithuania, of less then 4,000
people, about 0.12 per cent of the total population. Only some 500
Jews remain in Kaunas.[44]

THE SECOND REPUBLIC OF LITHUANIA

On 11 March 1990, following an unarmed uprising, Lithuania
became the first Soviet republic to declare its independence. With
the restoration of Lithuanian independence on 11 March 1990,

the prospects for Jews in the country improved, thanks to much-needed changes in legislation. The government approved and guaranteed equal rights for national minorities, the Jews included. Laws were passed abolishing discrimination against Jews and creating the conditions necessary for the remnants of Jewish cultural life to be resurrected from ruins. The Vilna Gaon Jewish State Museum was re-established, together with a Jewish state school, kindergartens and a Centre for Judaic Studies at Vilnius University.

The post-Soviet Lithuanian government has on a number of occasions stated a commitment to commemorate the Holocaust, combat anti-Semitism, and bring war criminals of the Nazi era to justice. On 20 September 2001, to mark the sixtieth anniversary of the Holocaust in Lithuania, the *Seimas* held a session during which the historian A. Eidintas delivered an address giving an account of the annihilation of Lithuania's Jews. In 1995, the president of Lithuania, A. Brazauskas, apologized in the Israeli parliament, the Knesset, for the Lithuanians' participation in the Holocaust.

However, contemporary Lithuanian nationalism still exists. It celebrates the acts of anti-Soviet resistance, even if many 'heroes' of the Lithuanian resistance against the Soviet occupation were also Nazi collaborators who had cooperated in the murder of Jews. These nationalists also put forward the theory of two equal disasters in Lithuania, the 'theory of two genocides': the mass killing of Jews by Nazis and also the mass repression of Lithuanians by the Soviets – by implication, the Jews. This theory is a cynical and thinly disguised attempt to find an excuse for the mass slaughter of the Jews, which was perpetrated by the Nazi collaborators. All right-thinking Lithuanian citizens deplore and condemn such attitudes, and all the more so when they clearly invoke the murderous history of anti-Semitism.[45]

S. Abramovich and Y. Zilberg

NOTES

1. Dov Levin, *The Litvaks: A Short History of the Jews of Lithuania* (London and New York: Berghahn Books, 2001); S. Dubnov, *History of the Jews in Russia and Poland. From the Earliest Times until the Present Day*, translated

by Israel Friedlaender (Philadelphia, PA: Jewish Publication Society of America, 1916–1920); S. Atamukas, *Lietuvos zydu keliais* (The Way of Lithuanian Jews) [Lithuanian] (Vilnius: Alma Literra, 2001); D. Levin, 'Lithuania', and 'Kovno', in *Encyclopedia of the Holocaust* [Hebrew] (Tel Aviv: Sifriyat Hapoalim, 2006), pp.636–9 and pp.1071–4.

2. The second Lithuanian statute of 1566, Paragraph 12.

3. Levin, *The Litvaks*; D. Levin, 'Lithuania', and 'Kovno', in *Encyclopedia of the Holocaust* [Hebrew] (Tel Aviv: Sifriyat Hapoalim, 2006), pp.636–9 and pp.1071–4; Atamukas, *Lietuvos zydu keliais*.

4. Levin, *The Litvaks*, p.160. S. Atamukas, 'The Hard Long Road Towards the Truth: On The Sixtieth Anniversary of the Holocaust In Lithuania', *Lituanus. The Lithuanian Quarterly Journal of Arts and Sciences*, 47, 4 (Winter 2001), pp.16–45; Atamukas, *Lietuvos zydu keliais*.

5. Levin, *The Litvaks*, pp.122–4; Atamukas, *Lietuvos zydu keliais*, p.124; Atamukas, 'The Hard Long Road Towards the Truth'; Levin, 'Lithuania', *Encyclopaedia Judaica*.

6. Atamukas, *Lietuvos zydu keliais*.

7. Ibid., pp.124f.

8. Levin, *The Litvaks*, p.146.

9. 'Jews in Lithuania – State of Lithuania 1919–1939', *Encyclopaedia Judaica* (1971), Vol.11, p.382.

10. Atamukas, 'The Hard Long Road Towards the Truth', p.148.

11. L. Truska, 'Preconditions for the Holocaust in Lithuania', in J. Levinson (ed.), *The Shoah in Lithuania* (Vilnius: The Vilna Gaon Jewish State Museum and Vaga, 2006), p.361.

12. Ibid.; Levinson, 'The Shoah and the Theory of Two Genocides', in Levinson (ed.), *The Shoah in Lithuania*, pp.322–53; V. Vareikis, 'Preconditions of the Holocaust. Anti-Semitism in Lithuania, 19th Century to Middle of the 20th Century (15 June 1940)'. Research work database of the International Commission for the Evaluation of the Crimes of Nazis and Soviet Occupational Regimes in Lithuania, Jews in Lithuania (Vilnius, 2000); 'The Nazi Occupation 1941–1944 and Other Nazi Crimes. The Preconditions of the Holocoust in Lithuania'. *International Commission for the Evaluation of the Crimes of Nazis and Soviet Occupational Regimes in Lithuania, Jews in Lithuania* (Vilnius, 2000).

13. S. Eilati, *Crossing the River* (Tuscaloosa, AL: University of Alabama Press, 2008).

14. Levinson, 'The Shoah and the Theory of Two Genocides'.

15. Ibid., p.328.

16. 'The Nazi Occupation 1941–1944 and Other Nazi Crimes'; Truska, 'Preconditions for the Holocaust in Lithuania'; Vareikis, 'Preconditions of the Holocaust'; Levin, *The Litvaks*; Atamukas, 'The Hard Long Road Towards the Truth'; S. Ginaite-Robinson, *Resistance and Survival, the*

Jewish Community in Kaunas 1941–1945 (Canada: Mosaic Press in Canada and The Holocaust Centre of Toronto, UJA Federation, 2005).

17. Truska, 'Preconditions for the Holocaust in Lithuania'; Atamukas, 'The Hard Long Road Towards the Truth'.
18. Atamukas, 'The Hard Long Road Towards the Truth'; Levin, *The Litvaks*; Ginaite-Robinson, *Resistance and Survival*.
19. T. Venclova, *Forms of Hope* (New York: Sheep Meadow Press, 1976).
20. Levinson, 'Foreword', *The Shoah in Lithuania*, p.13.
21. The Association of Lithuanian Jews in Israel, *Lithuanian Jewery. Vol 4. The Holocaust 1941–1944* [Hebrew] (Tel Aviv: Reshafim, 1984); Arad Ytzhak, 'The Murder of the Jews in German occupied Lithuania (1941–1944), in A. Nikzentaitis, S. Schreiner and D. Staliunas (eds), *The Vanished World of Lithuanian Jews* (Amsterdam and New York: Rodopi, 2004); Levin, 'Lithuania', *Encyclopaedia Judaica*, pp.1072–4.
22. L. Vildziunas (ed.), *Mano seneliu ir proseneliu kaiminai Zydai* (My Grand and Great Grand-Parents' Neighbours were Jews) [Lithuanian] (Vilnius: Garnelis, 2002).
23. A. Bubnys, 'Holocaust in Lithuania: An Outline of the Major Strategies and their Results', in Nikzentaitis, Schreiner and Staliunas (eds), *The Vanished World of Lithuanian Jews*, pp.205–21; Levin, 'Lithuania', *Encyclopaedia Judaica*, pp.1072–4.
24. Bubnys, 'Holocaust in Lithuania'; Michael MacQueen, 'The Context of Mass Destruction: Agents and Prerequisites of the Holocaust in Lithuania', *Holocaust and Genocide Studies*, 1 (1998), pp.27–48.
25. 'Kaunas', *Encyclopaedia Judaica* (1971), Vol.10, pp.848–9; Ginaite-Robinson, *Resistance and Survival*; D. Ghelpern, *Der Emes* [Yiddish] (Moscow: State Publishing House, 1948), C. Bargman – translator Yiddish–Russian, Robin O'Neil, translator Russian–English, *Kovno Ghetto Diary* (JewishGen, Inc.,1996).
26. Levin, 'Lithuania', *Encyclopaedia Judaica*, pp.1071–4; Ghelpern, *Der Emes*; Ginaite-Robinson, *Resistance and Survival*; Eilati, *Crossing the River*.
27. Ghelpern, *Der Emes*; J. Elkes, *Doctor Elkhanan Elkes and the Kovno Ghetto* (Brewster, MA: Paraclete Press, 1999).
28. Ghelpern, *Der Emes*.
29. Ibid.
30. Ibid.
31. A. Tory, 'The Great Action in the Kaunas Ghetto', in J. Levinson (ed.), *The Shoah in Lithuania* (Vilnius: Vaga Publishers, 2006), pp.78–93; A. Tory, *Surviving the Holocaust. The Kovno Ghetto Diary* (Cambridge, MA: Harvard University Press, 1990).
32. M. Elin, 'Kaunas Death Forts', in V. Grossman and I. Erhenburg (eds), *The 'Black Book' on Atrocities of the Nazis against the Jewish Population* [Russian] (Vilnius: Yad, 1993), pp.279–90; Bubnys, 'Holocaust in Lithuania'.

33. Konrad Kwiet, 'Rehearsing for Murder: The Beginning of the Final Solution in Lithuania in June 1941', *Holocaust and Genocide Studies*, 12, 1 (1998), pp.3–26; D. Porat, 'The Holocaust in Lithuania. Some Unique Aspects', in David Cesarani (ed.), *The Final* Solution: *Origins and Implementation* (London: Taylor and Francis e-library and Routledge, 2002), pp.159–74.

34. M. Elinas and D. Ghelpern, *Kaunas Ghetto and its Fighters* [Lithuanian] (Vilnius: Mintis, 1969); Ghelpern, *Der Emes*; Elin, 'Kaunas Death Forts'; A. Faitelson, *Nepokorivshiesia* (Not Defeated) [Russian] (Tel Aviv: DFUS Ofset Israeli Ltd, 2001); Aleks Faitelson, *Heroism & Bravery in Lithuania 1941–1945* (Tel Aviv: Gefen Books, 1996); Levin, 'Lithuania', *Encyclopaedia Judaica*, pp.1071–4; Ginaite-Robinson, *Resistance and Survival*.

35. Faitelson, *Nepokorivshiesia*; Faitelson, *Heroism & Bravery in Lithuania*; Grossman and Erhenburg (eds), *The 'Black Book' on Atrocities of the Nazis against the Jewish Population*.

36. Ghelpern, *Der Emes*; Elinas and Ghelpern, *Kaunas Ghetto and its Fighters*.

37. Faitelson, *Nepokorivshiesia*; Elinas and Ghelpern, *Kaunas Ghetto and its Fighters*.

38. Eliezer Zilber, 'A List (incomplete) of Jewish children Saved at the Kaunas Ghetto', in Levinson (ed.), *The Shoah in Lithuania*, pp.311–14; Elinas and Ghelpern, *Kaunas Ghetto and its Fighters*.

39. *Hands Bringing Life and Bread*, vols 1–3 (Vilnius: Vilna Gaon Jewish State Museum/Zara, 2005).

40. E. Oshry, The Annihilation of Lithuanian Jewry (New York: The Judaica Press Inc., 1995), pp.158, 164–8.

41. Gomulka, the Polish Communist Party Leader, during the upsurge of anti-Semitism allowed and actually expelled those Jews who wanted to leave Poland for Israel.

42. Department of Statistics to the Government of the Republic of Lithuania (Statistics Lithuania).

43. Y. Ro'i, *The Struggle for Soviet Jewish Emigration 1948–1967* (Cambridge: Cambridge University Press, 1991).

44. Ibid.

45. Venclova, *Forms of Hope*; Venclova, 'Jews and Lithuanians'; Truska, 'Preconditions for the Holocaust in Lithuania'.

PART ONE

BORN IN THE GHETTO

1. Right Meant Death, and Left, Life

Ariela Abramovich Sef[1]

Today is 9 May, celebrated as Victory Day in Russia. For me it is the most important holiday of all – more important than New Year or Passover. My father, Yakov Abramovich, had been on duty in an army hospital when the war began. When he heard that the Germans were marching into the town, he telephoned the director of the hospital and said, 'The Germans are coming and we need to do something with the patients'. The reply came back, 'Don't stir up panic, things will get sorted out without you'. Father never saw that doctor again, and he did not have time to get away himself. My parents were marooned in occupied Lithuania. Father and his brother, Beno Abramovich, were arrested as leftist sympathizers. Father did not think that he would get out alive. My mother Bronia (Bracha) gave him some gold jewellery to take with him, just in case. He gave it to his brother, hoping that Beno would manage somehow to escape, but he was convinced that he himself was going to be shot by the Germans. In the end everything turned out the other way round. Beno was led off and shot straight away in the Seventh Fort, but my father, thanks to the efforts of Mother, who ran round to all the Lithuanian army doctors she could find, and with help from Professor Zhilinskas, was released.

Before the war my father studied in France and Mother in England and they were brought up on German literature and culture, could recite the poetry of Heine by heart, and like many educated young Jews, knew Hebrew. They felt disorientated by everything that was happening.

While Father was still in prison, some Germans broke into our flat accompanied by some Lithuanians. A caretaker or servant must have tipped them off. They came in two lorries armed with a list. The list they had was very precise. Mother's belongings made the visit worthwhile. They took everything: pictures, silver, diamond necklaces, which she had inherited from her mother, Berta Maizel, who had only left Lithuania for Palestine in 1940.

Some Lithuanian had pushed his pistol up against my pregnant Mother's stomach and demanded she bring out all the items on the list. She did not resist. So they took literally everything, including the furniture. The lorries drove off crammed to the top.

When Father was released, the two of them were some of the last to set off to the ghetto, without furniture and without belongings. With 'luggage' like that, a small room in a communal flat was ample. When I was born, we were given a wickerwork cot – a leftover of bygone luxury. It was the main ornament of our room.

Figure 17. Ariela Abramovich, 2 years old. Near the house in the ghetto, 1943.

I was born at the end of October 1941. It was a premature birth at 12 Raguchyo Street, several days before a round-up in the Kaunas Ghetto, when the Germans were approaching Moscow. It was very bad timing, but there was nothing to be done and when I was only five days old I went, or rather I was taken, tied to my mother's breast, to the 'Great Action'.

Figure 18. Ariela Abramovich's Birth Certificate Nr 122 (in Lithuanian) in Ghetto.

All the Jews were driven out into Democracy Square, which was cordoned off. Before that Lithuanian volunteer policemen searched all the flats, every single cellar and attic, emptying the whole ghetto. SS officer Rauca had been in charge of the whole operation. He was standing on raised ground, so as to get a better view of the crowd: people were walking along in groups, in families, in households. The 'selection' began. Rauca pointed with his truncheon to indicate who should go to the right and who to the left. He was separating families. Relatives were pushing and straining towards each other. People did not yet realize that Right meant death and Left, life. It was very cold. People were becoming more and more agitated.

Our relatives clustered tightly around me and my mother. We managed to go to the 'good' side, the whole of our family except

Grandmother Sira. She was a wise little old woman, who understood everything that was going on: so as not to upset her family,
she had hidden in the crowd of those selected for death.
Everyone was very agitated. Then suddenly my father took three
leaps over to the right side, hunted out and literally dragged
Grandmother out of the crowd. Then he ran back with his mother
to the 'good' side. When they tried to stop him amidst the heart-
rending weeping, noise, barking of dogs, the curses and lashings
meted out by the Lithuanian Polizei, Father ran up to an officer
and explained to him in fluent German that he had been given
permission to go and fetch his mother. Before they had time to
realize what was happening, Father had brought Grandmother
back to the vital side.

Later my father used to be asked, 'How come you weren't
afraid? You could have been shot. You're a hero!' His reply was,
'Yes, I was frightened, more than anyone. That's why I ran.'
When life was calm and peaceful, my father was often plagued
by doubts, but in serious situations I don't really know anyone
who could be more decisive.

Father gradually came round to the idea of hiding me – come
what may. The other relatives regarded him as a madman. They
all decided he was out of his mind, paranoid, but he went on
saying, 'I'm going to throw her out of here'. Grandfather Shlomo-
Icik kept on saying, 'She's not just a baby. She's a picture. What
will happen to all of us? If something happens, perhaps God will
help.' Father replied that he could not take the risk, and nor did
he intend to start negotiating with God.

I spent two years in the ghetto. Our relatives and all the other
tenants of our communal flat used to feed and clothe me. By the
time I was 18 months old, I knew all too well which of the neighbours had their dinner where and when. I would make sure to be
in the right place at the right time and by the right door.

My father, being a doctor, could work actually in the ghetto,
but because of me he used to work with a special brigade out at
the airfield in Aleksotas, to which he and his fellow workers
would be sent out under escort. Initially his brother Ruvim was in
the same work team. The labour was physically much harder, but
there were far more 'perks'. The local inhabitants used to go over
to the Jewish prisoners and liked bartering with them. The Jews
risked being shot, but they had no choice and so they took the

risk. Father used to barter very honestly and quite successfully. Some people who were unable or unwilling to take risks gave him their belongings as well. Admittedly, there was one occasion when he was given a whole can of oil, which turned out to be motor oil, not cooking oil. Everyone in the house came down with diarrhoea.

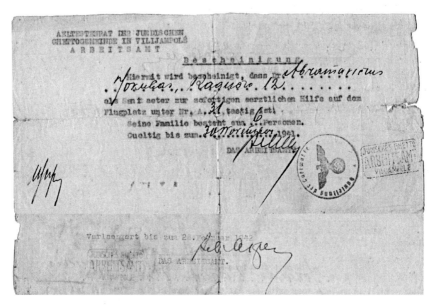

Figure 19. Certificate of employment of Jakov Abramovich,
30 November 1941.

Council of Elders of the Jewish Ghetto Community in Vilijampole
Works Department Certificate
Herewith is certified that Dr Abramavicius Jokubas of Ragucio 12
Is employed as first aider at the airport under Nr A.31. His family
consists of 6 persons.
Valid until 30 November 1941
Works Department signature
Stamp (German)   Stamp Jewish Ghetto
Airforce Building section   Works Department
Vilijampole
Extended until 28 February 1942

Most of the guards were old soldiers, who were not malicious in the least, and it was possible to come to an understanding with them, especially for those prisoners who had a good command of German. This applied in my father's case. They knew that he was the doctor in his work team who had studied medicine in Paris, and they were prepared to forgive him a good deal. One German officer even said to him, 'I'm ashamed to be a German now'. On one occasion, my father managed to come to the rescue of an unlucky barterer, a clumsy man in glasses. He became so carried away with his dealing that he would have been shot, if my father had not stepped in with some far-fetched explanation. The man in question, by the name of Jacob Rabinovich, became the editor of a German newspaper, the *Algemeiner Journal* in America, and he sent us a letter from Canada, after learning of my father's fatal accident, saying how grateful he had been to Father, who had helped him and other prisoners.

Before the war Father had never sold anything, let alone engaged in barter, despite the fact that he was descended from a family of merchants. My grandfather and two uncles had traded in fabrics, while my father, the youngest of seven children, had studied medicine in Paris and then started work as a junior hospital doctor. He had come back on a temporary visit to Lithuania for a short period of military service and had also worked as a doctor in the Lithuanian army. But when it came to practicalities, he could not even boil an egg.

Strange though it may seem, in the ghetto my uncles turned out to be less adaptable, less fit and older than their years. My grandfather was very old, and the only young and healthy member of the family to find his bearings was my father. He was, admittedly, the only one with a baby.

Our neighbours for the most part were educated people. My main friends and mentors were the neighbours' two boys, 11-year-old Beba and 9-year-old Veva Mintz. They completed their school syllabus at home. They worked away long and hard, as if they had been preparing for the entrance exams to gain a place in a gymnasium or at university, and not for the crematorium or the firing squad. They were fascinated by history. I used to repeat the names which impressed me from their lessons, such as Napoleon Bonaparte, Marshal Foch, Cardinal Richelieu and so on. When I was finally taken out of the ghetto, the boys wanted to come too.

But it would have been impossible to find anyone to take them in. So those perfectly innocent boys perished, along with the rest.

In 1943 people started digging a tunnel, a 'robber's hideout'. The Russians were already advancing westwards. People hoped it would be possible to hide there, when prisoners were being rounded up. Our family was not allowed in though, because of me, the small child, who might cry at the wrong moment.

In October 1943, the Germans took the whole of Uncle Ruvim's family out of the ghetto, along with about 3,000 other Jews. They were dispatched to Estonia. Uncle Ruvim Abramovich was already ill by then and his son, 12-year-old Borya, went along with him to the same camp. He was a remarkable boy with a real flair for poetry and mathematics, always thinking up devices for everyone in the ghetto to use; one of them was for stealing electricity. Borya used to spend all his time with his father, although he realized that his father was hardly likely to be selected for work and that his days were therefore numbered. Uncle Ruvim's wife Basia and daughter Myriam, however, survived and at the time of the liberation found themselves in the American Zone of Germany. Later they left for Canada.

Figure 20. Ariela's cousins Rivochka, Myriam and Josef (standing) survived the Ghetto and the concentration camps. Borya (first left) and Boris with grandparents Sira and Solomon-Itzik Abramovich all perished.

When everyone knew that there was going to be another 'action' my father said firmly, 'Ariela's not going to be rounded up'. Through a young member of the underground, Shimon Ratner, my parents learnt that it would be possible for a small girl, pretty and blonde, to be given shelter in an orphanage, where a certain Dr Baublys was director. Father had known him slightly before the war as a colleague, so the rest 'would not be a problem'.[2]

On 14 December 1943, Father gave me an injection to put me to sleep and after I had been dressed as a peasant child, he took me to that orphanage. He left me by the door in the porch in a sack with a label on it which read, 'I am an unmarried mother and unable to care for my child and ask for my daughter Brone Mazelyte to be taken into your care'. Mother's maiden name had been Bronia Maizelyte.

The rest of the family was in tears. How could he? Abandon a pretty little girl loved by everyone, virtually on the street, on a winter's night with temperatures of –25C. Apparently, when I woke up, I began to scream from fright and I was taken into the building. Through those same members of the underground, Father managed to let Dr Baublys know what the child's real name was.

For a time my parents did not receive any news about me. Father was still going outside under armed escort to work at the airfield, while Mother remained inside the ghetto. In December 1943 Uncle Max Abramovich was taken off with his son, pretty little daughter Rivochka (Riva) and his wife. Uncle Max's son, Boris, was mentally handicapped and the family was sent to Auschwitz, where he and his son in a short time perished. His wife and daughter, Rivochka, however, survived.

Mother used to tell me about all the very different kinds of people to be found in the ghetto. There was a famous Dr Elkes, whom the Germans had even been prepared to release initially. He and his wife, although far from young, had decided not to leave, and remained with their fellow Jews. Later Dr Elkes perished. My parents also mentioned a brave member of the underground, Dr A. Zilberg, with whom my father worked in Aleksotas. Then there was Dr Zacharin, who had been universally respected before the war. He had said to my terrified mother: 'If she dies, she dies. What difference does it make? What would become of her, after all, if she did survive? There would just be one more whore.' I survived and had the chance to grow up, while he met his end. He was called to account. (See Figure 21, Jakob Abramovich's Work Permit signed by Dr Zacharin.)

Figure 21. Jakob Abramovich's Work Permit.

Vilijampole 30.1.1942
Council of Elders of the Jewish Ghetto Community in Vilijampole
Health Office Certificate
We herewith certify that Dr. Jokubas Abramavicius is employed at the
Ghetto Hospital Outpatient Department as a locum doctor until
10.11.1942
Head of the Health service
Jewish Council of Elders   signed Dr B. Zacharin
Stamp Council of Elders of Jewish Ghetto Community in Vilijampole

One fine day Dr Baublys sent word that I was dying, and that if there was even the slightest chance, my parents needed to come and fetch me. It turned out that I had retained word-perfect everything our neighbours' sons had taught me. Well aware that this attracted attention, I started reciting the names I had learnt: Napoleon Bonaparte, Marshal Foch and so on. 'That can't possibly be an abandoned bastard child!' was the response. To make matters worse, when I cut my finger I asked for Streptocide! It had only just come out at that time. Soon, it was all too clear. A little Yid! 'Her eyes are brown, not a common phenomenon among Lithuanians'. That was what really worried the woman looking after me, not a great admirer of Jews. She was of the opinion that they should all be wiped out. 'We're having to look after little Yids as well! As if there weren't enough of our own kind . . .' She stopped putting my shoes on in the orphanage and I was made to patter about barefoot on the tiled floors. She often did not bother to dress me either. There was nobody to protect me. Dr Baublys could not give himself away. If he had, all the other Jewish children would have perished, and he too. The only thing that kept my tormentor from informing on me was that she felt sure I would die anyway.

My father began desperately searching for someone among the local inhabitants who would take in his child. A fisherman, Dovtort (Dautartas), turned up one day near where they were working and recognized Father from the days when he used to sell fish to people nearby in their summer cottages. Father began talking him round. The fisherman said he would have to talk to his wife and sons. My father gave him the only photograph that had been taken of me in the ghetto (photography had been strictly forbidden there).

I looked pretty enough and, most important of all, I was blonde. On the night of 3 January 1944 Father left the ghetto for good, taking Mother with him and, after saying goodbye to his elderly parents and his sister, Dr Rebeca Griliches, set off to persuade the fisherman's family to take me in. Mother was always very persuasive and in this case more so than ever, since she truly believed in the unique beauty and brilliance of her child! She described to them how clever I was, and all about the small blue vein on my forehead through which the blue blood flowed. In short, there was no better decision they could possibly take, although in fact the last thing the family needed was an extra member. Yet those people were deeply religious and their own daughter had died not long before. My parents succeeded in convincing them that it would be the right thing for the God-fearing to do. The idea appealed to them. After that Mama Julia, my future foster-mother, set off with her son Zigmas, an officer from the Lithuanian Army, to the orphanage to fetch their wondrous and beautiful little 'granddaughter'.

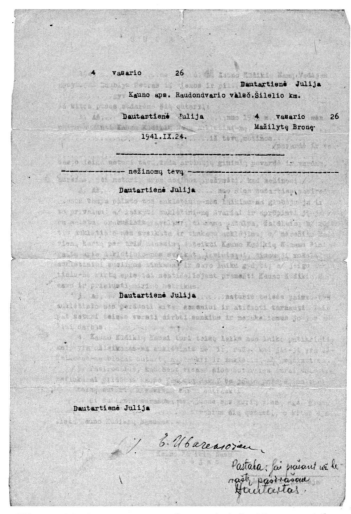

Figure 22. Agreement to foster Ariela Abramovich,
26 February 1944.

Agreement of 26 February 1944 between Kaunas Children Home
Director Doctor Petras Baublys and Julia Dautartiene of Kaunas region
Raudondvaris area Silelis Village to foster Brone Mazilyte 1941 IX.24

Signature E. Ubareviciene

(Note: Julia Dautartiene asking for her son Dautartas to sign as she
could not write.)

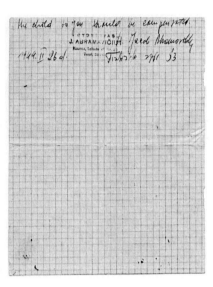

Figure 23. Testament dated 26 February 1944 written by parents (father) of Ariela Abramovich both in English and in Russian.

She was told that the little girl was very clever and blonde, but what was handed to them was a blood-stained mess. They brought me back to their home in a state of panic. They had been deceived. What kind of little blonde was this? What nonsense? This was a squealing creature, who must have been about to die. Their faith got the better of them and they started praying for me to recover, although their hopes were very slim. My parents meanwhile had decided to come and find out if everything had worked out all right. They came back to my new home, walking through the woods to stay there for several days in the bitter cold.

What a horrific sight greeted them! Mother's first reaction was that there must have been a mistake, and it was impossible to convince her otherwise. Then at last, when she recognized a mole somewhere on the bleeding piece of meat, she accepted that it must be her daughter after all. They begged the family to try and save me. My father promised that he would come over at night-time to help and that he would get hold of medicines and make me better.

Being homeless now, Father first of all disguised himself as a peasant and went into town. He started doing the rounds of the pharmacists whom he had previously known. Some of them shut the door in his face, but others gave him medicines and even let him and Mother shelter in their warm home for a few days, but no one could let them take refuge for long. With the medicines he could come by, Father went back to Shilielis (the name of the village) and worked his magic. The little walk there involved twenty kilometres and he did it night after night. Mama Julia knew a good deal about folk remedies, she made herbal infusions and cleaned my wounds. Indeed, in the village she had a reputation as a healer. They brought me back from the brink. Fast and faster than they would have thought possible, I regained consciousness and was on the mend. My hair started growing back. I started talking again, although only in Polish now, like Mama Julia and her husband. On his last visit Father brought my mother with him. It was cold and Mother was very tired. On the way they had seen a peasant with a cart. They waved him down, but after a mere two or three words the peasant whipped his horse and galloped off. My parents realized that he had guessed what kind of people they were.

After that they forgot about their tiredness and made their way to their destination as fast as they could. Zigmas and Juozas, the Dovtort's second son, hurried my parents into the shed and covered them with logs. The Germans came rushing over soon afterwards: they searched the whole house, jumped about on the logs in the shed but, when they failed to find anyone, they asked straight out whether the family had seen two runaway Jews. Tall, well turned out, dashing Zigmas said that some had run past and he pointed out the direction they had taken. When the Germans set off in hot pursuit, the brothers pulled my parents out from under the firewood. After that they did not come to visit me again until the liberation. Nor did I really need them then.

Mama Julia and 'Dziadunia' were very fond of me. People definitely believed that I was their family's child and they used to tell the neighbours a fairy tale to the effect that they had taken me in, after their daughter had apparently had a child by a German and died soon afterwards. They had me christened at the nearby church and used to take me to services every Sunday where I used to pray very earnestly. I even used to go with the other village children to the local SS head quarters, where the Germans used to give us chocolate. They say that I used to come away with more chocolate than anyone else. Yet, when the Germans came by, Vladik, the youngest son in the family, who later became the writer Vladas Dautartas, tried to take me away on a boat. He was 14 then and had no confidence in me; he thought I might give myself away again. Everyone would have long since forgotten about my past if it had not been for Mama Julia's third son, Lyonka. He was serving in the police, was already married, had children of his own, but had a terrible weakness for the bottle and used to get out of control. He used to try and wheedle money out of his parents all the time and threatened to give me away.

Figure 24. Ariela Abramovich with foster mother Julia Dautartiene who took her from Dr Baublys children's home, 1945.

When the Germans withdrew, he left with them, leaving his wife and three children behind. Many years later he wrote his parents a letter, thanking them for helping his children: he invited his family to join him in Canada and us to pay him a visit. He had settled down well. My parents did not write to him but via Vladik they relayed to him that they knew about his threats. In response Lyonka later wrote back, 'Yes, I did make threats, but I did not betray her'.

After long wanderings, my parents made their way to a farm near the village of Kulautuva where Father had rented a *dacha* in Lukshakaimis before the war, and Jurgis Kumpaitis, the head of the household, had driven them to his home from the town. He was German by descent. By then the Russians were already advancing in our direction. Father promised him a reward after the war (we would have to survive that long though!) and he let my parents live under the floor of a shed housing cows and pigs. They spent seven months there, only coming out for fresh air at night. If things had turned out badly, the Kumpaitis family would have been risking their lives, but they were convinced that my father would be able to help them after the war, and they were right to have done so. They had been prosperous peasants and they could easily have been sent to Siberia. When, later on in the 1950s, my parents rented a summer cottage nearby, they showed me that cowshed.

As they retreated, the Germans blew up and burnt the ghetto. My grandparents were led out of the ghetto, together with 2,000 old people and children, and perished.

My parents used to tell me that on the very first day after liberation they came and saw me in the garden. I was stained with juice and stuffing berries into my mouth. They were delighted. They did not take me back to Kaunas immediately because I did not want to go anywhere. I clutched at Mama Julia's skirt and said in Polish, 'Good day, Pan, good day, Pani'. As soon as people began explaining to me that I had other parents, I would start sobbing. Only after my parents had visited me several times was Mama Julia able to pull me away from her skirt.

I travelled to Kaunas on a boat with Mama Julia's husband and Vladik. In the flat, in the same house as before the war, to which my parents brought me, there were two mattresses in one of the rooms and in the other two, only polished parquet and three pictures by Remeris on the walls, but that did not worry them in the slightest.

I was brought along and then my parents had to help me get used to a new life. The war was still not over, but my parents had started 'living' again. They were so keen to make up for what they had lost. They used to go to a restaurant almost every evening, rather than cooking anything, and they would drag me along too to the *Metropole* and *Versailles*, which used to impress me far more – there was a revolving dance floor there. At any rate my parents used to dance there and, as it seemed to me, almost forgot their little girl sitting on the couch. Restaurants are something I loved from a very early age, and still love. Dining-room furniture appeared in our flat, which still stands in my brother Solomon's house in London.

People started coming back to town from wherever they had been evacuated. Families of the old intelligentsia began reappearing: the Pers, the Grodzenskys, the Judelevichs and the Ginks, the survivors. Then people from the forces started coming back: air-force officers, army surgeons. They would fly in, have supper with us and sometimes even spend the night. My father used to smoke very heavily. Everyone was smoking. It was all very friendly, although there were many heated arguments. The pilots would fly in and fly out again. The war was still going on.

Food appeared on the table again quite soon. Private patients used to come to see Father from the countryside and they would naturally bring food: eggs, pork fat, butter and even bread, which were all in short supply. Bread was extremely scarce and rationed. On one occasion my old nanny, Mariona, went out to exchange her ration cards for food and later came back without a single piece. She had given them to a German refugee with a babe-in-arms from Königsberg. They had no ration cards and those refugees, at their wits' end, were just following their noses. Mariona had been very worried that someone would start making a fuss, asking why she had given the ration cards to the Germans, but no one reprimanded her.

The pilots used to give me chocolate as well. Sweet things did not appeal though, all that I wanted was sausages, and they were hard to come by and very expensive. Sometimes, as a special treat, I would be given two skinny sausages. Those I ate with great gusto. I did not like anything about the town; understandably, I wanted to go back to the country.

Then my father started earnest discussions with Dr Ryabelsky and another officer 'behind closed doors'. They were organizing a whole 'gang' to rescue Jewish children, who were still in villages scattered throughout Lithuania. These young officers of Jewish descent were travelling from village to village at a time when that was still far from safe. There were *Zaliukai*, the so-called 'forest brothers', at large in the forests, and those Lithuanians would not be showing Soviet officers any mercy. That was how one of them fell by the wayside. Risking their lives as they did so, the officers would bring the children back from the villages. Some people would give them back joyfully and of their own accord. Others were loath to lose additional labour, and the officers would have to pay them for the children. Some children soon became truly fond of their adopted families.

Figure 25. Teacher Shmerkovich and Dr Jakov Abramovich with Jewish kindergarden, 1945. He was one of the organizers finding Jewish homes for rescued children and a trustee of the Jewish orphanage and kindergarden.

The children were brought to Kaunas, some of them to the recently opened Jewish Orphanage, of which Father was one of the trustees[3] and Mrs Abramovich was a teacher for a short time,[4] while others were adopted straight away. Orphaned children sometimes found parents among childless couples. Some became truly fond of the children.

Figure 26. Family Abramovich after the liberation in the garden of Kaunas War Museum 1944.

Immediately after the war it proved possible to send some of those Jewish orphans abroad. The pilots, with a good deal of help from my father (who used to devote almost all his energies and free time to this), would personally take the children or make arrangements with army trains to convey them to Poland. Once they were there, the Red Cross and other charitable organizations took over. Naturally all of these arrangements were illegal, everyone involved could have been sent to prison. Looking back, I feel that Father probably did not realize how dangerous that work had been. As a result of their efforts many of the children were lucky enough to reach America, Israel or Europe. For my father it was obviously a great happiness when he successfully completed such operations.

Father devoted a great deal of energy and time to the orphans. He treated countless children and took them into his own home in emergencies, complete with their snuffles and squints. Heavens alive! Somehow he found refuges for them all.

This work he carried out together with Dr Gurvichiene, reputed to be one of the best children's doctors in Lithuania, who was also a cousin and close friend of the children's writer, Samuil Marshak. There was no end to the stream of children passing through our house. My father helped innumerable refugees: he was obsessed with the Jewish cause by this time.

After his experience of the ghetto, his sense of Jewish identity became very strong, probably blotting out many other ideas. Almost every day he had the urge to adopt another child: one day it would be the young one-eyed rascal Tedik, and the next, a boy with the surname Gold, who went on to become a motor-cycle racer and drunkard. Mother put her foot down, otherwise I would have had a whole crowd of brothers. Thank Heaven, she managed quite soon to give birth to one of her own, my brother Solomon, and a few months later our little cousin Anya appeared.

Anya had been the daughter of Uncle Nyonya Maizel and had been born in prison. Her arrival had been a complete surprise to me. My Uncle Nyonya, of whom I had been very fond when he was still a bachelor, used to come from Vilnius to visit us, bringing presents and telling me fairy stories. One fine day he turned up with a woman and said that she was his wife, Lily. I was unable to find anything nice about her: she did not even speak Russian, only German and Polish. After returning from Russia, where he had been evacuated, Nyonya had encountered this girl who had survived in Vilnius. She was the daughter of a rich Leipzig furrier, who had fled with his family in 1933 back to his home country, Poland. When the Germans entered Poland, Lily's parents had been killed. In 1940 she found herself in Vilnius. She did not look Jewish, spoke both her native German and Polish very well, and thanks to that survived the Nazi occupation.

After the war, Lily was legally entitled to return to Poland or Germany, which she decided to do with my Uncle Nyonya. My parents were also keen to leave Lithuania, where everything reminded them of the recent genocide. Getting hold of the necessary 'Polish documents' was not difficult, and soon we managed to get our hands on some. My uncle and Lily, who was pregnant by this time, found an airman by the name of Volodya (or rather the airman found them), who agreed to transport them by air. My parents then also decided that was how they would like to travel, but Nyonya persuaded them not to leave at the same time, 'We shall fly first and let you know when we get there, and then you'll be able to arrange things with the same airman'. We were left with no news from them for a long time and Father was hurt by their behaviour. My parents decided to make the journey another way. That was when news came from our relatives, who by now were in Vilnius prison. As soon as they were airborne the pilot flew back down again: Volodya turned out to have been working for the NKVD. They took all the diamonds and money our relatives had with them and locked them up to start with in Vilnius prison as spies and traitors to the homeland. Lily was given eight years and my uncle ten. It was while Lily was in prison that little Anya was born. As a child of 'Enemies of the People' she was due to be sent to a special orphanage for such children. That was how our departure plans fell through. Sometimes God seems to be punishing us but then grants our desires. We should be grateful for the fact that our relatives had refused to take us with them.

My father got to know either the governor of the prison or someone from the NKVD. I remember clearly that the man in question had a shaven head combined for some reason with a moustache. Father explained to him that his relatives were in prison, and in response the man said, 'Do you realize what all this involves? They have been convicted under Article 58, Point 1a. Do you realize what that means?' Mother answered, 'Not really, before the War "1a" meant top quality, the very best'. The man eventually told them, 'Listen, stop trying to help them or you'll end up inside yourselves'.

The governors of the Vilnius men's and women's prisons were husband and wife. Papa operated very successfully on their son and treated the prison governor himself, who had something wrong with his ear. The governors did not send our relatives further afield, and for a whole two years, while they were in charge of the prisons, Nyonya and Lily were able to stay where they were, rather than being dispatched further east. The governors' appetites, meanwhile, were growing. The dinner service and the money Father was earning were not enough. By this time almost everything Father was earning went to them. My grandmother began sending us parcels from Palestine, mainly dress lengths. These parcels all went straight to the prison governors, as they were.

Mother used to go to Vilnius with parcels very often. She would stand in the queue: first at the men's prison and then at the women's. One day when she was in Vilnius she went into labour prematurely; that was when my brother Solomon was born. It took about two or three days before Father found out and was able to make the journey. I was left behind with a friend of the family, Grandad Malkin. I was very scared of him. He wanted me to like him and he used to tell me stories, which made me cry my heart out.

At last my parents reappeared with my little brother. Lord, what an unpleasant surprise! All the attention which once had come in my direction was now centred on him; I felt hurt by this, but that was only half the story. A few months later they brought home little Anya. That was a real disaster. Her appearance on the scene was a huge shock: a frighteningly ugly, squealing creature. She was covered in eczema from top to toe and howling all the time, always demanding things. Not only did I have to put up with a brother, but now a sister into the bargain. Was not that too much all at once? Solomon behaved quite calmly; he was always good, a child who did not cause any problems. Anya always needed medical care, and then she had to be taught to talk and be calmed down when she was hysterical. The two of them grew up like twins. Their age difference was just nine days.

Over the course of many years my parents used to send Lily and Nyonya ten-kilo parcels every single month to every possible corner of the Soviet Union. Mother would sometimes get dates muddled up, but Father never did. If Mother failed to have one of the parcels ready in time there would be fireworks at home. Father would get very angry and indignant, 'They're hungry out there and we aren't ready in time! We're just sitting here, eating ourselves silly.' I never remember my father becoming as angry about anything else as he did about those parcels.

At the age of 6 I learnt the truth, that Anya was not my real sister, but Uncle Nyonya's daughter. I was given strict instructions not to tell anyone about it; I duly promised. Indeed, I really did not say a word to anyone, even when provoked, because Anya was a very pretty child: plump, friendly with slightly pigeon-toed feet, a real charmer. By 8 or 9 though I was a very different proposition. I had acquired a bluish complexion by then because of my heart condition. Someone had heard something somewhere, rumours travelled fast and said, 'The older sister is probably not their child'. I endured it all. I never let myself say that it was not true and that I was my parents' daughter, even though I knew the whole story. Anya lived with us till the age of 9, when her parents reappeared. They say that there are two categories of people: givers and takers. My father was without doubt a giver.

After the war my father quickly built up a large private practice and he did a good deal of hospital work as well. He was soon heading his department. In the evening he would sometimes take me out for a walk, which gave him the chance to meet friends at the same time. We lived on the town's central street, Laisves Avenue. I shall never forget, when I was ill once and not allowed out, he stood me on the window sill (they were quite high in our flat) when I was still just a small girl and showed me through the window, 'There goes an NKVD officer'. We children had come to feel terrified at the mere thought of them by then. We were even told that, if we were naughty, the witch *Nevralka*, or a captain from the NKVD, would come and catch us.

My father, like his father before him, used not to go to the synagogue before the war. But immediately afterwards, being Jewish acquired a whole new meaning for him. Father now had a very strong sense of his Jewish identity. He used to listen to the 'Voice of America' and the BBC, which was not forbidden in those days. When Israel appeared on the scene, he began listening to '*Kol Zion la'Gola*' (Voice of Zion for the Diaspora). He did not listen to the programme in Russian, but in the foreign languages he knew. The radio, a cup of strong coffee and feeding the cats, those were his favourite moments in the morning, and this routine lasted for the rest of his life, even when they started jamming the programme.

As soon as it became possible, in 1973, my parents migrated to Israel, where they lived for the rest of their lives. After my father's fatal car accident, my mother came to London to be with my brothers. When I finished at high school, I went to Moscow where I studied French at the University. There I married a French citizen and moved to live in Paris. And now, I share my time between Paris and Moscow, where my second husband, Roman Sef, lives.

Paris-Moscow-London, May 2008

NOTES

1. Ariela Abramovich Sef died on 23 December 2008 in Paris and was buried in London. Ariela published her memoirs in Ariela Sef, *Rozdennaya v Getto* (Born in the Ghetto) [Russian] (Moscow: Olimp, 2009).
2. M. Gilbert, *The Holocaust* (London: Collins, 1986), p.231.
3. E. Oshry *The Annihilation of Lithuanian Jewry* (New York: The Judaica Press, Inc., 1995), p.164.
4. Ibid., p.158.

2. The Young Shoots of the Tree

Ilana Kamber-Ash[1]

Prior to the war, my mother, Judith Moses-Kamber, had worked as a nurse in the Jewish Hospital *'Bikur Cholim'* in Kaunas. My father, Marcus Kamber, was called up to serve in the Soviet Army on the first day of the war; he was an officer in the 16th Lithuanian Division. So my mother found herself in the ghetto alone. There she discovered she was pregnant.

I was born on 27 March 1942 and my mother, attended by Dr Elkes, gave birth in a cellar so that if she cried out the Germans would not hear her. My mother had been on friendly terms with Dr Elkes when they worked at the Jewish Hospital. He was later elected to lead the Jewish Council in the ghetto. It was Dr Elkes who insisted that I be given the name Ilana, which means 'tree' in Hebrew. He pointed out to my mother that the young shoots of the tree would survive while an old tree would die.

Once, while my mother strolled with me in the ghetto, a German officer approached us, took me in his arms and carried me to the commandant's office. My mother was convinced I had been taken away for good and ran around the building of the office completely frantic with worry. After half an hour he emerged with me, carrying a box of food for us. My blonde hair and blue eyes must have stirred some form of nostalgia in him.

In 1943 rumours were circulating about the possibility of a 'Children's Action'. A chilling message came from the Jews of the Shauliai Ghetto saying, 'Save your children'. Mother began considering desperate measures to save me. Her brother, Eliezer Moses, had connections with underground groups in the town. He obtained the name of a Polish woman who helped save Jewish children. Having bribed the ghetto guard with her wedding ring, Mother escaped with me and located this woman. She, however, refused to take me in, showing my mother a room in her house full of Jewish children, mostly boys. She told my mother that there was simply no room for even one more child, and taking another could endanger them all. With a feeling of relief that she would not be separated from me, Mother returned to the ghetto.

But the atmosphere in the ghetto was becoming more and more unsettling; Mother could no longer delay getting me out. Dr Elkes gave me a sleeping pill and helped my mother hide me in a potato sack. She decided to take me back to the home of the Polish woman but again she refused to help. This time, out of desperation, Mother put me down on the doorstep and said, 'So be it, let her die here, she will surely not survive the ghetto, and I cannot bear to watch her die'. The woman, convinced of my mother's resolve, took me by the hand and led me into her house.

My mother returned to the ghetto alone. During the 'Children's Action', she was to witness how the mothers of the murdered children lost their minds, having helplessly watched their children's fate. In this 'action' my 8-year-old cousin was murdered.

Thanks to my Aryan appearance, a Lithuanian family, living in a village not far from Kaunas, adopted me. Kazys and Brone Liutkus were a middle-aged childless couple. Naturally they had me christened and I was renamed Laimute Liutkute. During our first few days, Brone would take me to the ghetto fence so that my mother could see me. However, seeing me provoked too much distress in my mother, and Brone was obliged to cease this ritual, fearing that the Germans would discover what was happening.

When the ghetto was liquidated my mother, like all the women of the ghetto, was sent to the Stutthof concentration camp.

I was one of the lucky few to have ended up with caring adoptive parents. I was loved, fed and spoilt. During a walk with my adoptive mother, a German approached us and offered me a sweet; I thanked him in Yiddish. Brone froze in her tracks for fear that I had inadvertently disclosed my Jewish identity. However, the German was delighted at my response and wondered how I knew the German for 'thank you'. From then on, I was kept at home until I forgot Yiddish and started speaking in Lithuanian.

I read somewhere that ghetto children grew up fast. Once, playing in the yard, I noticed the Lithuanian policemen approaching our house. Two partisans were at the Liutkus household at the time. I must have understood the danger the police posed and ran to the gate to deter these guards and told them that my father was not home. They turned and left. Brone often used to recall this event.

At the end of 1944, after a serious injury and a lengthy stay in hospital, my father was discharged from the army. He returned to a liberated Kaunas. On his way from the railway station, he encountered my Uncle Eliezer Moses, who had fled the ghetto and joined the partisans. Eliezer told father he had a daughter born in the ghetto and this was how my father first learnt of my existence. He went straight to the Liutkus family home and announced that he was the father of the little girl. Still carrying his army kit bag, and with nowhere to go (the home they had left when they were forced to move to the ghetto had been occupied by Lithuanians), he wished to take me with him. Mr and Mrs Liutkus, to their credit, advised that he should first find accommodation and work, and they would then part with me.

At that time my father's friends, Maxim and Erica Levin, lived in a huge four-bedroom house. They gave my father a room, which was where he brought me. Finding work also posed no problems. A Lithuania in ruins was crying out for civil engineers. My father and Maxim would go to work, and Erica would look after me and Carmela, a little girl they had fostered from the Jewish Orphanage. Soon, I began calling Erica 'Mama'. I spoke only Lithuanian and this remained the language I would always speak with my father.

In 1945, survivors of the concentration camps were beginning to return. My father would inquire about his wife and discovered that she was in a transit camp already in Soviet territory, so he went to look for her.

I remember nothing of my time with the Liutkus family, only brief glimpses of life with the Levins. However, I can remember my mother's return with vivid clarity. It was in the middle of the night, and Erica switched on the light in the room where I was sleeping. I remember the bright light blinding my eyes, Erica lifting me while I was still half asleep, and carrying me to the corridor.

In the doorway stood a woman I did not recognize. When she saw me she began to laugh and cry at the same time; Erica put me in the woman's arms and I can still feel the strength with which she embraced me, so tightly I could hardly breathe. I still remember the fear that gripped me, and I was sure that I was being taken away again. I began lashing out at her with my arms and legs in a terrible fit of hysterics. Erica took me away and secured me back in my bed. I remember nothing of what happened the next day. I don't remember how I got used to my mother again, I don't remember when I started to call her Mama, I only know that I loved her very much.

In 1946, my father was appointed head engineer of the Lithuanian Construction Bank and we moved to Vilnius. Late one night in 1948, Brone Liutkiene, my former adoptive mother, appeared in our home with a 2-year-old child in her arms whom they had evidently adopted. Brone told my mother that they had been warned they were on the KGB lists for deportation. Her husband was hiding in a friend's house, and Brone was appealing to us for help. We were then living in a communal house that we shared with the family of a Russian officer whose wife did not work. Brone and the child had to stay in the bedroom at all times. Before leaving for work, my mother would leave food and a bucket for them in the room, but the most difficult thing was to keep a 2-year-old child occupied for hours on end without her crying. Evidently, they could not have been careful enough for one night loud knocks were heard at the door. Two KGB officers stormed in and went straight for the room where Brone was hiding. My father stood in front of the door of the room and swore on the honour of a Soviet officer that his wife and daughter alone were asleep in this room; the officers believed him and left. When Brone bade us goodbye the following morning she said to my mother, 'If we get caught and you want to help, do not on any account mention that during the war my husband and I had saved a Jewish child'. In the anti-Semitic atmosphere of late 1940s USSR, she feared this would have been regarded as treachery, not heroism.

Like many others who had lived through the ghetto and camps, my mother seldom spoke of her experiences. Every time she recollected something, she would end up in tears and then chain smoke. Yet those years had left their mark on us children as well. I was tormented by nightmares till I was 14 years old. I would wake in the middle of the night petrified and in tears. I would then be allowed to stay in my parents' bed. They were never cross with me, they always understood. Only with them did I feel safe. Until I was 17 I would not stay at home alone. My parents had to take me with them to their parties, to the cinema. The fear of losing them never left me. In those years, I was too young to understand that the trauma of the war years had not left my parents either, they had simply buried it deep.

I graduated from the Kaunas Polytechnic Institute as a civil engineer, and I married Pavel Ash who was from Moscow and we lived there for several years. I only came to understand the effect of the war years on my father when I became a mother myself. My son Aron (Arik) was born in Moscow. I took him to visit my father in Vilnius. My mother had already passed away. I noticed how much pleasure my father took in changing his grandson's nappies. Once he made a sad comment, 'I'd never had the chance to tend to my daughter when she was a baby; at least I get to do this for my grandson'.

In 1971 we moved back to Vilnius permanently because it was easier to obtain visas to Israel from Lithuania. We left for Israel in 1972 together with my father; my mother's grave is left behind in Lithuania. In our family it was she who had dreamt most of Israel. In Lithuania there are no other family graves apart from my mother's. The branches of my parents' families in Telshiai and Prenai had all been wiped out in those war years. I don't know the names of my grandparents. My parents never spoke of them.

We named our daughter Judith (Dita) after my mother. She was born in Israel and she feels privileged because of this. She is the only one of the family who was born in her own land. In 1982 my husband started working in the Russian Service of the BBC in London and we relocated to England.

In 1999, after reading *The Hidden History of the Kaunas Ghetto*,[2] I discovered that Dr Elkes, who had given me my name, had two children, Yoel and Sara Elkes, who were sent to study in England in the 1930s. I tracked them down and met with Sara, who now lives in Leicester and I spoke on the telephone with her brother Yoel, an American professor of psychiatry. In a sense I feel they are a strong link to my past. I told them that my mother would speak of their father with great awe. Through them at least I could express my gratitude to their father who had helped save my life.

London, 2004

NOTES

1. Ilana passed away on 24 March 2005 in London. She was buried in Israel.
2. United States Holocaust Memorial Museum, *Hidden History of the Kovno Ghetto* (Boston, MA: Bulfinch Press, Little Brown and Company, 1997).

3. Keep Your Eyes Shut

Rona Rozental-Zinger

Before the German occupation, my parents, Rone and Schmuel Rozental and my brother Leo, born in 1937, lived in Kaunas. My father was principal of the Yiddish primary Shalom Aleichem School. My mother studied in Strasbourg and in the university at Brussels. Since 1934 she had been the director of the kindergarten teachers' training college for early childhood. Some of my mother's students were nuns.

Figure 27. Rone Rozental, 1936. R. Rozental was a very active member of the anti-fascist underground, involved in rescuing many children. Perished in Stutthof in 1945.

My parents, like many other Jewish people, had foreseen the approaching catastrophe, and applied for visas to emigrate to other countries. But they were not successful. In August 1941 my parents together with my brother Leo, my mother's parents Oscher and Gitel Schmuilov and my 22-year-old Uncle Eli (Lusi) Schmuilov with his wife Chaja (née Glushakaite) were forced to move into the ghetto. My maternal grandparents were murdered during the 'Great Action'.

My parents and my uncle were active members of the ghetto underground resistance movement. Lusi Schmuilov was one of the leaders of the 'Young Underground' ghetto resistance fighters. He was denounced and arrested by the Gestapo during a joint committee meeting of the Anti-Fascist Organization in March 1942. He was tortured and murdered in the Ninth Fort in October 1942.

Father was forging identity documents and also teaching at the Yiddish underground ghetto school, which was located in a stable (see Figure 11). Education for Jewish children in the ghetto was banned in 1942. Mother's role in underground organization was to rescue Jewish children; she used her pre-war contacts with some of her student-nuns, and with their help she arranged hiding places for the children in a monastery, in Dr Baublys' orphanage and by placing children with Christian families. She had green eyes, and in order to look Aryan she dyed her hair blonde; she was able to enter and leave the ghetto without having to wear the yellow Star of David.

I was told that even the people who shared my parents' room in the ghetto did not know that my mother was pregnant until her ninth month; she was hiding it even from her friends. She did that by wearing a tight corset. Germans issued an order making pregnancy among Jewish women illegal. I was told that I was born on the coldest day, 31 January 1943.

Most of the time I was kept in a special hiding place *'malina'*, behind a wardrobe, that my father made for us. There were two babies that had to be hidden: myself and my cousin, Uncle Eli's daughter, Lusi Schmuilov, who was also born in the ghetto. My brother had to care for both of us, having to push the prams into the hiding place every time suspicious sounds were heard, and he had to keep us quiet. Father once remarked that babies in the ghetto never cried, as if they understood the dangers.

In August 1943 my father smuggled out my brother Leo in a sack of potatoes. He was hidden in a small village close to the Ninth Fort by the Macijauskas, a poor farming family. The family were later recognized as 'Righteous among the Nations' by Yad Vashem. They hid my brother and four other adults in a cellar dug under a farm oven until Kaunas was liberated. Later my brother was placed in the Jewish Orphanage.

In November 1943, I was smuggled out of Kaunas Ghetto and hidden by Mr and Mrs Stanionis, who lived in Nemuno Street in Kaunas. I was given a shot of Luminal that put me to sleep, wrapped up, and Pese Karnauskaite (today Musel), an active member of the 'Young Underground' fighters, carried me out of the ghetto, mingling with the departing night shift workers, and passed me to Mr Stanionis.

My cousin Lusia was smuggled out in similar way in December 1943. She was hidden by Brone Miliene until the liberation of Kaunas, and then was reunited with her mother. Her mother escaped from the ghetto in December 1943 and joined the partisan group called 'Death to the Occupants'.

Figure 28. Mrs Stanioniene with Rona Rozental-Zinger

The Stanionis couple had no children of their own. Mr Stanionis often used to get drunk and visit us with his drunken friends; Mrs Sofija (Zosia) Stanioniene was afraid that they could betray me, and she realized that it wasn't safe for me to stay in Kaunas, so she decided to take me to her mother in Zhemaitija, a western part of Lithuania.

They hid me right through the war and even for three more years after the liberation, until May 1949. They had me baptized and gave me a new name, Lily Stanionyte, and treated me like their own daughter. We went to church regularly and I was proudly wearing a cross. I still love organ liturgy and I visit churches, when I travel.

Zosia risked her life hiding a Jewish child and running from town to town and village to village to keep away from persecution and the front line. We were in constant danger of death; from outside as well as from inside the family. Even after the liberation a lot of persecutions took place, committed by the Nazi sympathizers who were hiding in the forests.

Zosia didn't tell her family that I was Jewish, but they suspected it. Her sister had a son with a Nazi collaborator, who left her and joined the German army. She wanted Zosia to adopt her son instead of me, which would clear her name. She denounced me to the 'forest brothers' and one night they came looking for me at her mother's place. Although I have very sketchy memories of those days, yet some events stand out very clearly. I remember that at my adoptive grandmother's place in the country, I slept on top of the farm stove because it stayed warm long after the fire had gone out. It was late in the evening when I was suddenly awakened by men in uniforms searching under the bed and in the cupboards, in the room I occupied. I had blonde hair but dark eyes, not like my foster parents who had blue eyes. It had been drummed into me to keep my eyes shut among strangers, which became a habit of mine in times of distress or during some danger.

I saw them searching when I opened my eyes and then quickly closed them. Because of my blonde hair, they assumed that the child sleeping on top of the farm stove was not Jewish. Soon after they left my room to search the rest of the house, Zosia grabbed me and ran to the other side, across the lake that was frozen and still covered with ice. It was early spring, the ice was breaking and we got very wet and cold as we were jumping from one piece of ice to the other. I became very sick but Zosia was afraid to take me to a hospital. Many years later she told me that we were hiding for three days in a cellar in the fields, and as result of that, she suffered from rheumatism. We were very close to the German border and Lithuanian 'partisans' were still searching for Jews.

My parents were among thousands of ghetto inmates deported to German concentration camps in July 1944. Mother perished in Stutthof just before the liberation in 1945. My father had been sent to Dachau where the American army liberated him. He was barely alive and spent months recovering.

On his return to Lithuania, the Soviet officials accused him of spying for America and interrogated him. But he was released and even gained a position in the Ministry of Education in Vilnius to supervise Yiddish schools. My father tried to reclaim me on his return, but the court ordered that in the absence of my biological mother, I should stay with the Stanionis family, who had brought me up until then.

I recall only a sensation of rejection that I felt towards my father when he was visiting me in Kaunas; he looked so old and frightening. I would accept the presents from him but called him '*Zyd*' (Bloody Jew) and run away. I remember that he gave me a beautiful German doll with big blue eyes that opened and shut. It was my first doll that could even cry; I never had one like that. All the kids in the neighbourhood wanted to play with this doll!

One day I decided to investigate how the doll could open her eyes. My dream then was to have blue eyes, just like my foster parents. I cut open the doll's head and removed the eyes and their attachments. Zosia would sometimes leave me alone at home while she went out to buy milk. That is when I proceeded to cut my forehead to replace my brown eyes with the doll's blue ones. On her return Zosia discover me bleeding a lot. Once my father took me to visit my brother in the Jewish Orphanage in Kaunas. I have never seen so many skinny, dark-haired children and I didn't believe that he was my brother. Life was tough. There were problems with housing, problems with food. Everything was a problem.

Finally in May 1949 my father managed to kidnap me with the help of his two friends. They came in police uniforms, while

Zosia was out shopping. I opened the door, one of them shut my mouth, carried me under his arm and ran quickly down the stairs and put me in a police car. Father and his friends managed to obtain the police car and the uniforms by getting two policemen drunk. They took me to my father's former student place in Kaunas and then to Vilnius where he settled.

Father renamed me Rona Rozental, so I was given my mother's name when I was 6 years old. He sent me to the Jewish kindergarten, which I attended till the end of August 1949. I couldn't speak a word of Yiddish. Children surrounded me, asking me what my name was. I began to cry and told them that I have a new name, which is very difficult to remember and I am not allowed to use my previous one. That didn't make sense to them; consequently nobody wanted to play with me. Father often had nightmares. His screams would wake me up in the middle of the night, and he would explain to me that he dreamt that the Nazis with dogs were chasing him.

In autumn 1949 all Jewish schools and organizations were closed. Father lost his job in the Education Department. He had to take other jobs, where the pay was lower. He was not able to focus on anything other than the loss of his wife and his profession. He was sick a lot and was often hospitalized. I was very sensitive to his war experiences and asked him very few questions about the past. At the young age of 7 I became his carer and his house-keeper; he never remarried. I was raised without a mother and I know how tough life is. I was reunited with my father and an older brother, but we all suffered from emotional traumas after the many losses that we experienced and we never could achieve any family closeness.

I was a very quiet, withdrawn and secretive child. I grew up with a guilt complex of being born during the war. I hardly had time to go out and have some fun. I too was sick a lot as a child, but I never complained, even when I should have, thinking that whatever the pain was that happened to me it would go away. I preferred to hide it from my father, I never asked for anything, never wanted to upset him. Following my reunion with my father in Vilnius, I had totally blocked out memories of my early childhood, and for many years they were locked away.

I re-established contact with Zosia only after 1967, and looked after her until she died in May 1974. She suffered badly from rheumatism and was bed ridden for many years. Mr Stanionis passed away in the early 1950s.

I graduated in 1964 from the University of Vilnius with honours in Mathematics and worked as an IT consultant. I married in 1971 and I have a daughter and a son. I had to reinvent parenting, as I never had any example or guidance about how to raise my children. In June 1978 we left Lithuania and arrived in Australia on 10 January 1979. Nowadays I am retired and work as a volunteer guide in the Melbourne Holocaust Centre. My brother and his wife, a child survivor from Kaunas, live in Vilnius, Lithuania. Their son, daughter and granddaughter live in Israel.

My father passed away in Vilnius in April 1984. The Lithuanian president honoured my mother with a 'Rescue Cross' in 1993. I grew up in Lithuania under the Communist regime, with almost no Jewish atmosphere at home and uninformed about the long history of the Jews in Lithuania; the Holocaust was ignored by Soviet historians. Survivors had their memories of the Holocaust silenced for many years and hid them inside themselves. They were deprived of the opportunity to openly acknowledge their losses and of honouring the memory of those who did not survive. People didn't expect the system to provide any kind of support for their emotional wounds. While we identified ourselves as Jews, due to prejudice and anti-Semitism, the younger ones did not have any clear idea of the Jewish tradition.

I remained unaware of my personal story until 1967, when *Ir be Ginklo Kariai*[1] (Unarmed Fighters), was published. This book is about the Lithuanian Gentiles who saved Jewish people during the Holocaust. There were two chapters in this book about my own and my brother's escape from the ghetto, written by my father. Until now I was never inclined to put down in writing what little I remember about my experiences as a child survivor, but I have been encouraged by Y. Zilberg into writing as much as I remember about those times. I should have asked more questions of my father and the people who knew my parents while they were alive. However, I accept that I am fortunate to have lived, that I worked, raised a family, and contributed to the community in spite of my fragile childhood.

Melbourne, Australia 2008

NOTE

1. S. Binkiene (ed.), *Ir be Ginklo kariai* (Unarmed Fighters) (Vilnius: Mintis, 1967).

4. My Chance of Survival

Yakov Zoreff (Goldshmidt)

My father, Meir-Lev (Leib) Goldshmidt was born in Nizhnij Novgorod in 1920 to Sara, née Poger and Haim-Shimon Goldshmidt. My grandfather served in the Tsar's army and, after the revolution, in the Red Army. After having been demobilized, he and his family settled in Jonava, where he owned a ceramics factory.

My mother Sonia was born in Vilnius to Gershon and Roza Burko. The Burko family moved to Jonava and Sonia attended the Yavne School, where my father studied. After his studies in the school my father went to *yeshiva*, but later turned to secular education. He had dreamt of becoming an actor and had enrolled to study acting in Kaunas. At the same time my mother studied music in the Kaunas Conservatorium. They were a young couple, working by day and studying by night; their whole future lay ahead of them. Father, a promising actor, was an active member of the Communist Youth organization. He was even accepted by the famous Moscow State Jewish Theatre, but declined the offer since Sonia was expecting a child.

Immediately after the German invasion, my parents together with the Luboshitzes and their two children, tried to escape to Russia. Near the Lithuanian-Belarusian border they encountered a German paratroops' unit. The young German officer treated them with respect, handed out some chocolates and warned them to avoid the SS soldiers; he said they could be very cruel to Jews. He added, 'Have mercy on the children'. They had no other choice but to turn back.

My parents parted ways from the Luboshitz family and went to Jonava where their parents were supposed to be; they never saw the Luboshitzes again. In Jonava, they met Justinas, a Lithuanian man they had known before the war. He invited them to his house and fed them. 'Do not enter Jonava', he said, 'My son and many others are killing Jews there'. My parents turned around and headed towards Kaunas.

About 4,000 Jews from Jonava were killed by the Lithuanians in the first days of the war. My paternal grandparents managed to escape from Jonava to Kaunas; there were nine children in their family. Besides my father, only 18-year-old Asia (Osnat) and 16-year-old Abraam survived the ghetto and concentration camps.

My grandfather Haim and my uncle Hirsh were captured in a synagogue and killed by Lithuanians in the first days of war. My grandmother Sara, and Icale, Bella and Gita Goldshmidt were executed among about 1,000 Jews in the Ninth Fort in retaliation for the alleged shooting of Kozlovsky, the commander of the German ghetto guards. At the time of this so-called 'Krishchiukaichio Street' round-up, Asia and Abraam visited my parents in the 'Small Ghetto'. They had heard about the 'action' and ran to find their mother and younger brothers, but the street was surrounded by policemen and nobody was let in. It is only by chance they both remained alive.

My aunt Malka Zinger-Goldshmidt, her husband Berl and their 3-year-old daughter Cilia were killed in the 'Small Ghetto Action'. My grandmother Rosa Burko, with her six children, were caught by Lithuanians in Jonava. A kind Lithuanian police-man, nicknamed Halabas, (a greeting in Lithuanian) led them by carriage to the Ninth Fort. He always sympathized with the Jews. Knowing what was in store for his prisoners there, he deliber-ately slowed down the horse carriage and so arrived much later than 4 p.m., the hour when shootings ceased until the next day. Halabas was ordered to take the Burkos to Slobodka.

Just before the war my grandfather Gershon was mobilized to the Soviet Army and his battalion fell into German hands. He was held in a POW camp in the Kaunas suburb of Zezmariai. Uncle Abraam was sent to do some work outside the ghetto. On his way he met Jewish prisoners of war and asked them if they had heard of Gershon; they told him he was amongst them. In search of help my father ran to Juda (Judke) Zupovich.

Juda, a young man from Yonava, had attended a military school when Lithuania was an independent country. Now he was appointed to the position of the Jewish police commander's deputy. Juda and my father had been opponents: Juda was a member of *Beitar* and my father was in charge of the Communist Youth cell. Yet Juda made great efforts for my family; he asked

Izia Rabinowich to help. Izia was the head of *Arbetzand*, responsible for the allocation of manpower in the ghetto. Fortunately Gershon was a baker by profession, and Izia convinced the Germans that there was an urgent need for a baker, so succeeded in transferring Gershon to the ghetto.

Both the Goldshmidt and the Burko families were quite poor and suffered terrible hunger in the ghetto. With the arrival of Gershon they built an oven and Gershon started to bake bread in secret. From Burko's family, only Yulia and Yocheved survived.

Meanwhile everything was arranged so that my mother would give birth to me outside the ghetto. Her singing-class teacher, Mrs Karnavichiene, agreed to hide my mother until my birth, and she would then transfer me to a childless couple who would keep me safe. But on their way to Mrs Karnavichiene, my parents saw a Gestapo checkpoint and were forced to return to the ghetto. I was born prematurely on 27 January 1942, attended by a nurse named Markovich. I was named Yakov after my great-grandfather Yakov, a scholar and a *Tzadik* (a righteous man). My parents decided to keep me with them for a couple of weeks.

When I was 8 days old, while my father was at work, Grandmother Rosa and her cousin Gita, after putting enormous pressure on my mother, invited a rabbi to have me circumcised. My father was very angry with the grandmother and aunt who stood by the decision they had made and claimed, 'He will survive, and if, God forbid, he will not, let him die as a Jew'. Even now after so many years, I feel they nearly destroyed my chance of survival. With no other choice, my parents kept me in the ghetto.

But how does one raise a child without food? A solution to the problem came unexpectedly. Mother's younger sister, 13-year-old Judith-Yulia, was a skinny, innocent girl. She asked, 'Why are we surrounded by a wire fence?' and 'Why are we so hungry, while we smell eggs and bacon cooking on the other side?' One day Judith approached the fence and discovered a narrow gap. When the guard was far enough away, she slipped her small frame through the narrow opening. She approached a house and, after explaining her situation, returned with food for herself and the family. The Polish family who lived there was deeply touched by her appearance and by her perfect command of the Polish language.

From then on Yulia became the family's provider. Thus they
raised me until the horrendous day, 28 March 1944.

When the rumour reached us that the Germans intended to
take children, the elderly and the disabled from their homes, my
parents sought a hiding place. Since the Nazis, abetted and
guided by the Ukrainians, would search every nook and cranny
of every house, my father dug a hole beneath a fireplace. He
formed an airway, camouflaging the opening with pipes and
junk strewn with '*Mahorka*', a Russian tobacco that dogs cannot
tolerate. Because they lived at the far end of the ghetto, they had
time to do this. A guard, most probably a Czech soldier, saw my
father digging but he did not give him away.

Father remembers the day of the 'Children's Action' as the
most horrible day of his life. On this particular day he was sick
and stayed at home. A few days earlier, a group of Jewish prisoners had been brought to Raudondvaris, a village near Kaunas,
where a young Nazi sadist had forced them into an icy lake for
hours. Then he ordered them to lie on the frozen ground. They all
got sick.

Why, father would wonder, did not the children cry or object
to being forced into a cramped hole in the ground? Clearly, I felt
the danger and so didn't object to the shot of Luminal that the
nurse gave to sedate me. I spent two days underground. My
parents took me out at night. I didn't cry; I ate whatever there
was. The next morning I extended my arm to get the injection
and crept back into the hole as if I understood everything.

Father could barely utter what he saw on that terrible day.
They awaited the arrival of the murderers with immense fear.
They saw a bus. From this bus blared loud music that could not
block out the children's cries, the mothers' pleas or the barking
dogs in their pursuit. Drunken, excited Ukrainians, brandishing
axes and iron rods, snatched children and the elderly from their
hideouts. All father's thoughts during those moments were of
the hole that concealed his wife and baby. The utter brutality
ended at sunset. Returning from their forced labour, parents
viewed the devastation.

My next-door neighbour, the nurse who administered the
shots of Luminal for me, hung up a bag of clothes from a shelf
on the wall. In it she hid her 3-year-old daughter. In search of
children a German officer had split the bag with the lash of his

whip, but revealed nothing. The lash caused a cloud of dust and the officer hurried to leave the room. When the mother removed the bag she found her tiny girl bent over, with an open gash on her back. The woman burst into tears but the little girl said, 'Don't cry, Mommy; it doesn't hurt'. The Germans knew that they had missed many children. They arrested Jewish policemen from the ghetto and tortured them in the Ninth Fort, demanding they reveal where children were hidden. One of them, Juda Zupovich, was severely beaten and his ears were slashed, but he said nothing. When the Nazis returned him bleeding to the group of other policemen, he told his friends to be strong and to say nothing. He died singing '*Hatikva*', the Zionist anthem meaning 'The Hope'. But not all of the Jewish policemen could withstand the torture; eventually some of them took part in disclosing the missing children.

My father had a friend, a teacher called Schmuel Rosental. His wife Rone was involved in the rescue of children from the ghetto. She offered to arrange to hide me in a monastery in the Green Mountain area Zhaliakalnis; my parents debated the offer. With no other choice, my mother placed me in a big sack and took me to the entrance of the monastery. A nun named Onute, who also worked as a nurse at the orphanage of Dr Baublys, took the 'parcel' and carried me to the orphanage. Since I was circumcised, they were afraid to keep me with other children and so they hid me in a cellar.

Mother was arrested on her way back to the ghetto. It was a terrible misfortune. On her way from the monastery she had met two friends, Sarale Katz and Alia Ranzuk, and together they made their way back to the ghetto. They were stopped by a Gestapo officer and searched. In Sara's pocket an old revolver was found; all three women were immediately arrested. Father was waiting for my mother near the fence. He saw her being led away by the German soldiers. All the efforts to save her were in vain, this was a lost cause: the three young women were executed.

Onute told my father after the war what I had gone through when I awoke alone in a strange place. I had been left in a basement with a woman who spoke no Yiddish. I did not cry but muttered constantly the words, '*Mama Sonia, Papa Leib*'. The woman told me that if I stopped saying these words she would let me out of the basement and allow me to play with the other children upstairs. I asked her if I could repeat Mama and Papa's names only in my heart, just to myself. This brought tears to her eyes and she agreed, saying, 'Yes, in your heart you can repeat these names so you'll never forget them'.

After the liberation my mother's younger sister, Yocheved, who had survived thanks to the righteous Catholic, Viktoria Krulickiene, went to look for me. With the assistance of the partisan Bella Ganelin, nicknamed Katiushka, Yocheved, recently married, found me and brought me to her and her husband's home.

Father and Uncle Abraam survived Dachau. Abraam went straight to Israel. Father, naturally, decided to go to Kaunas in order to find me. When I saw him, I jumped on him as if we had separated only yesterday, and not a year earlier. Mother's youngest sister, Yulia, had survived Stutthof and agreed to marry my father and with much patience, love and care she became my mother, though she herself needed mothering. Yet, many times I would wake up in the middle of the night sobbing, 'Where is Mama Sonia?'

After the war our family moved to Vilnius. Father and Yulia had another son and a daughter. I loved Yulia very much and never felt different from my brother and sister. I was never told I was not Yulia's son, but I knew she was not my biological mother, and my parents knew that I knew. Yet we never openly discussed this matter until Yulia's death in 2008.

Thanks to Yulia's Polish citizenship, we were able to repatriate to Poland and from there in 1957 we came to Israel. In Israel, after completing my military service, I worked as a technician in Israel's largest communications company until retirement. I am married, have three children and now I am a grandfather myself. My father worked as an actor in several theatres in Israel until his retirement. He is still in comparatively good health, clear-minded and he gave me much help in writing this memoir.

Holon Bat Yam, Israel, October 2008

5. Left on the Porch

Yakov Zilberg

My mother, Sonia Zilberg, née Elitzur, came from an established and educated family who originated in Panevezhys. There were eight siblings in her family. Mother graduated from the Russian Gymnasium in Panevezhys and from the Economics faculty in Liege. She worked in Brussels for a few years, and about five years before the war she returned to Lithuania.

My father, Abram (Abrasha) Zilberg, was the only son of Orthodox Jews who owned a small shop in a village called Vabalninkas. Father studied in the Jewish Gymnasium in Panevezhys and graduated from the Kaunas Medical School. My parents became acquainted when they were exchanging language tuition; he offered Hebrew tuition in return for her teaching him French.

Figure 29.
Abram Zilberg.

At the onset of the Spanish Civil War, my father and two of his friends, Micelmacher and Sheinberg, who were also doctors, volunteered to join the International Brigade. In Spain my father became a member of the Communist Party, and he was injured in one of the Brigade's campaigns. After the defeat of the Republicans he spent a couple of months in a special camp organized in France for the members of the International Brigade. Upon his return to Lithuania, he married my mother. They settled in Vabalninkas, where my father practised medicine; just before the war, they had a daughter called Mina.

After the occupation of Lithuania by the USSR, Communists were promoted to managerial positions. Father was appointed as a physician in charge of the Kalvaria psychiatric hospital. Although he had never been a psychiatrist, he quickly earned the respect of the patients and the senior college specialists in this field of medicine. According to my mother and father's friends, he was an exceptional man: happy, intelligent and courageous. He loved singing and was able to perform in all languages; Father could speak ten languages fluently. After the war, when I was introduced to people as the son of Abrasha, they would nod in recognition.

A few days before the war, my father went from Kalvaria to Kaunas to find out if it was advisable to depart immediately. He was assured that there was no danger and ordered 'not to panic'. On the night of 21 June the bombardment of Kalvaria woke my parents. They left absolutely everything and fled with Mina towards Kaunas from where they had intended to transfer to Russia. Exhausted after walking the whole night, they knocked at the door of a farmhouse. Mina cried; she was hungry. An old Lithuanian woman let them in and gave them some milk and food. Meanwhile her son came in with a rifle. They could see the cruelty and hatred in his eyes. Then he turned and gazed at Mina. She was a beautiful child with huge green eyes. My parents fled from the farm but this young man followed them: Mother was sure he was going to kill them. 'Walk on and don't look back', said my father. They heard the man behind them, 'If it was not for your daughter, I would kill you like mad dogs'.

When they arrived in Kaunas, the Germans were already there. In the early days of the occupation, my father's parents were killed by Lithuanians. My maternal grandfather Solomon, my aunt Aniuta, her husband and their two daughters (one of them 5-year-old Mirale) were murdered in Panevezhys. I regret I did not ask my mother more about events during the war, feeling that the memories were too painful for her. This is why I do not even know their surnames in order to commemorate them in the Yad Vashem Holocaust Museum. Mother's four other sisters had emigrated to Palestine several years before the war.

My parents and Mina found themselves crowded into the Kaunas Ghetto. Father immediately joined the anti-fascist underground organization in the ghetto. I learnt that my father had worked in the hospital in the ghetto and later in Aleksotas where he, together with Sh. Zaidelson and B. Preis, was a leader of the Aleksotas group of the resistance organization.[1]

When my mother discovered she was pregnant, she arranged to abort this unplanned pregnancy in the Jewish hospital in the ghetto. However, a day before the procedure, she changed her mind. The day she had been due in the hospital, the Germans burned it down with all the patients and a number of the staff inside.

I was born on 5 May 1942. Dr Pertzikovitz, who went on to become a prominent gynaecologist in Israel, attended at my birth. I was a premature and feeble baby with a huge swelling on my head. On top of that I developed a serious case of childhood asthma; I would almost suffocate at night, causing much anxiety to my mother who herself was suffering from mastitis and was not able to produce milk. Behind her back, people wished me dead so that my mother could finally have some rest. My parents, however, resolved to nurse me back to health. Mother used to go to the fence of the ghetto every day to exchange her food voucher for goat milk. To everyone's surprise I gained strength and grew up in the ghetto for over a year.

I was a year old when my parents decided to take desperate measures to save me. The plan was executed with the help of Yulia Yoffe, a friend of my parents. Yulia was a Jewish lady with Aryan looks who could walk more freely out of the ghetto. By then she had already managed to evacuate her own daughter Lyda and had placed her with a Lithuanian family. Yulia heard of a Polish family whose two sons were missing. They decided to send me there. I was sedated and put in a sack and in the morning among the crowds of people going to work, Yulia and my mother smuggled me out of the ghetto. During the day, they hid somewhere, and when night fell they arrived at the home of the Polish family and left me at the steps of the house. They knocked at the door and fled at the sound of vicious guard dogs. My mother and Yulia spent the following night and day in ravines, hiding in shrubs. Towards the evening, they attached themselves to crowds of returning labourers and re-entered the ghetto.

Figure 30. Yulia Yoffe with her daughter Lyda, 1939. (See Chapter 32.) After Yulia smuggled her daughter Lyda, this brave woman, risking her own life, organized Yakov Zilberg's rescue operation. Later Yulia escaped from the ghetto and was in a hide with Lyda in countryside.

Following a number of anxious days my father embarked on another dangerous mission. He gathered some of my belongings, and left the ghetto with the intention of selling these to the people with whom I had been left. The mistress of the house purchased these objects, all the time suspiciously eyeing the Jewish-looking gentleman before her. Father returned to the ghetto alive. He told my mother that my belongings had been bought, which meant that I must be safely in the home; Mother could now be assured that I had been taken in and not abandoned.

Fortunately I was not circumcised. Although I already spoke some Yiddish, I didn't say a word and I did not cry. I was christened and renamed Richard; I became a Polish child. My parents continued to live in the ghetto. Mother told me several times that my father was already very much disillusioned with the communist ideology. They decided that if they survived they would head for Palestine at the end of the war.

I do not know and will now never know how my 5-year-old sister Mina was taken away. She disappeared, most probably in the 'Children's Action', as did countless other Jewish children.

During the liquidation of the ghetto, my parents and some others hid in a bunker ('*malina*') that had been dug under the house during several months. All the houses were systematically blown up and burnt by the Germans. When, because of the heavy smoke, the people in the bunker could not breathe and clambered out, the Germans had already left the ghetto. A priest led them to a hiding place in the town; I believe they were hidden in the cellars of the War Museum. He led part of the people from this group, including my mother, first; the rest of the group, who were more Jewish in appearance, were supposed to come later under cover of darkness. Father stayed with the second group; he was supposed to lead them to the hiding place. Mother felt uneasy about my father staying behind, and tried to persuade him to go with her, but it was in vain: the second group never reached the shelter. The Red Army was already approaching and the defeat of the Germans was near. Despite this, on the evening of my father's disappearance, Lithuanians were still picking up Jews. Some of these captured Jews were killed on the spot, others at the Ninth Fort.

After the liberation my mother went to collect me from the Polish family. She was aware of hostile looks and could hear people whispering behind her back, 'This is Richard's Mother'. I was playing in the yard but I immediately approached her, took hold of her and would not let her go. My foster-parents greeted my mother coldly and demanded that she leave. Mother left to the sound of my tears only to return the following day with a militiaman after Yulia had testified as to my identity. I was reunited with my mother for good. I am entirely unable to remember my foster-father, and barely remember my foster-mother. She visited us several times and I still called her 'Mama' while for some time

I called my real mother '*Tiotia Mama*', which means 'Mrs Mama'. After the war my foster-mother sold ice-cream on Laisves Avenue and would always give me a treat when I passed by alone. They never forgave my mother for having survived, but their resentment subsided when their sons returned. Eventually, our contact with them was completely severed.

After the war, my mother moved in with Naum Shafransky, without ever having officially married him. It was the union of two survivors who helped each other to overcome the nightmare they had both endured. He had been a neighbour of ours in the ghetto. Naum and my father had then made an agreement: if one of them was killed, the other would take care of both families. He was a good, simple and warm man. He had lost his entire family in the ghetto, including his wife Genia and his only son Rouven (Ruvik). Naum had been a member of the resistance as well; he knew many Lithuanians in the countryside and moved in and out of the ghetto on missions for the underground. He helped several ghetto inhabitants to escape and was sure he would be able to save his family. Naum never spoke about the ghetto and his family.

In 1946 my sister Salomea (Saly) was born and we moved to Vilnius. Yet another shock awaited my mother. Naum was arrested in 1948 and sentenced to ten years in a labour camp in Siberia. He returned after five years and was by then in poor health. He had been an active Zionist since youth and always dreamt of Israel. He died in Vilnius in 1971, six months before our departure to Israel. In 1972 my mother, Saly with her son and myself with my wife and our eldest daughter Dina, landed in Israel.

Despite all she had endured, my mother remained an optimist. She didn't lose her love of life and knew how to derive joy from the simplest pleasures: from a drive in the countryside, from good food, from wine and even a cigarette. She prided herself on my achievements and adored her grandchildren. My mother died suddenly in my arms at the age of 80 from a heart attack; she had been lucid till her last day. Despite her first husband and son having been physicians, she did not like to visit doctors or take medication, claiming both 'gave her headaches'. Even though she rarely spoke of the past, she carried much pain with her.

Several years after my mother's death, Yulia Yoffe who had helped my parents rescue me all those years ago, also suddenly passed away aged 80. Recently, Yulia's daughter, Lyda Yoffe told me that after the war she'd asked her father why the skin on my mother Sonia's face was patchy in places. Her father explained that during the war, when the Germans (or Ukrainians) were trying to snatch her daughter Mina away from her, Sonia struggled and refused to let her go. Dogs were set on her and ravaged her.

Mother had never shared this with us but I remember her telling me how strong is the human instinct to survive. She said she had known a woman in the ghetto whose daughter had been brutally torn from her arms and killed. The woman, though hysterical, had then mingled with the crowd and fled. Perhaps this was her own story.

We managed very well in Israel and from our first steps there we felt at home. My wife worked as an engineer and later as a maths teacher. For more than seventeen years we lived in kibbutz Sde Nachum in the Beit Shean Valley where I practised medicine. From 1976 I held several high managerial positions in the Israeli health care system. Now we are both retired and enjoy our life and family, three daughters (two, Dalia and Yael, born in Israel) and five grandchildren.

Kfar Sava, Israel, 2009

NOTE

1. B. Bliutz, *The Fate of the Jewish Doctors in Lithuania* [Yiddish] (Tel Aviv: The Association of Lithuanian Jews in Israel and 'SELA', 1974); The Association of Lithuanian Jews in Israel, *Lithuanian Jewry. Vol 4. The Holocaust 1941–1944* [Hebrew] (Tel Aviv: Reshafim, 1984), p.102.

6. If the Child Is Circumcised, He Will Be Saved

Benya Chaitas

In September 1939 my mother, Genia Saitovich, at the age of 18 set off from her native town of Rokishkis to Kaunas in search of employment. She began to work in one of the local kindergartens. In Kaunas she met Leibe Chaitas, who was a carpenter by profession; they married in 1940. When the war started my parents decided to flee to Russia. My mother was seven months pregnant at the time. They had not covered a large distance from Kaunas, when the Germans caught up with them at the small town of Jonava.

The Germans and their Lithuanian collaborators drove everyone into the Market Square in Jonava to sort them out. At the time there were Soviet planes above the square and they started bombing. The Germans fled to seek safety and everyone else naturally started running off in all directions too. My parents ran back to the direction of Kaunas.

When my parents finally managed to reach Kaunas it was already occupied by the Germans. They returned to their flat under cover of night; they were too frightened by then to set foot outside. Only occasionally my father would go out looking for food.

Vilijampole, the district where my parents lived, had been chosen as the site for the ghetto, so some relatives moved into my parents' room. The time for my mother to give birth was approaching, and my parents were getting very worried. I was born in 1941. A midwife by the name of Markovich attended my mother in secret; she survived the war and emigrated to Israel.

One of our relatives was a very religious woman. Naturally, the next question to be decided was whether or not I should be circumcised. The religious relative demanded that the circumcision should go ahead, saying, 'If the child is circumcised, he will be saved'. So they did. The other problem arose immediately after I was born. Mother had no milk. The religious cousin took on the task. Every day she managed to get hold of 50 grammes of milk, which was very little, but better than nothing.

The Germans began to register all the inmates of the ghetto. They checked out everybody who was in the flat and removed everything that took their fancy. Mother told me about the 'Great Action':

On 27 October 1941, Germans left the first shift of workers at Aleksotas airport and did not let the night shift to go to work. This is why Leibe had not been at home at night between the 27th and 28th. On the evening of the 27th members of the Jewish police went round all the houses explaining that the next day, at six o'clock in the morning, all the inhabitants of the ghetto had to assemble in Democracy Square. In the morning I was shivering with fright. It was raining and freezing cold, so I grabbed you, wrapped in as many pieces of cloth as I could find, turning you into a big bundle, and went out into the street. I went to the square with my cousin and her family. I could not hear you breathing and I was worried that I had suffocated you. Only when it was time for feeding did you start to give any signs of life. I sat down in some inconspicuous corner, the family stood round me and I fed. Meanwhile the Germans were lining everyone up in rows. I passed you to my cousin and ran to look for my husband. Once I had found Leibe, I felt calmer.

The men from the SS were drawing nearer and nearer to us to start sending people to the right or the left. The old and ill were being moved to the right, while the young and healthy were sent to the left. Our religious cousin was sent to the right and we went the left. Those sent to the right were then led away to the Ninth Fort.

On our return home, I found you were wet from head to foot.

In place of our cousin and her family, the ghetto police sent two more families to move into our quarters. Leibe's brother Zalman and his wife Sara Chaitas also moved into our flat. So we lived, all crammed together until October 1943, when Zalman and Sara were sent to the Klooga Camp in Estonia. Zalman died there, Sara his wife was transferred to Stutthof and survived.

Initially I had hoped we would be transferred to Klooga as well. Zalman advised us to stay in Kaunas promising that if the conditions there were good they would let us know and, if it proved possible, we would join them later. The conditions in Klooga were perfectly dreadful...

When their area of the ghetto was reduced, my parents were ordered to leave their flat. Father found a small storehouse, cleaned it and we moved in there. We were joined by another of my mother's cousins, Sara, her husband, Berl Shpak, and their son Boris. All three survived. Boris came to Israel and lives in Bat Yam. We lived in that storehouse, until the 'Children's Action' took place.

Figure 31. Beny Chaitas with his mother Genia Chaitas in the Ghetto, 1943.

That morning my father had gone off to work, leaving Mother to sleep on. Suddenly my mother's cousin appeared, shouting, 'Why are you still asleep? Get up, there's a round-up! You can't imagine what's going on!' Mother dressed in a hurry and was sitting there totally bewildered.

From Mother's memoirs:

> There was chaos outside in the streets. Lorries were driving to and fro. Warnings were coming through loudspeakers: the Germans were insisting that everyone stay inside. I grabbed you and opened the door. Our neighbour suggested to me, 'Come over to us: we'll be together'. This remarkable German woman had come into the ghetto to stay with her Jewish husband Burstein. I was about to go over to join her, but at that moment a German appeared and insisted that I should go back into my own quarters. When he left, I ran to the neighbour's house. My cousin ran after me. In the house we saw Gutner, a Jewish policeman. He led Germans into the room where he himself lived. They did not come out of it for a long time. Out of curiosity I peeped in through the keyhole. I saw Gutner lift up the sofa, take something out and hand it to the Germans. The Germans walked out and left a mark on the door to show that the house had been checked. Gutner saw us and demanded, 'Leave immediately! There are too many children here.' I couldn't help myself and said, 'I saw what you did in your room. I know that it must have cost you dear. I am ready to pay you as much as I can, but please let us stay. This house is less dangerous than the others.' 'No, no!' Gutner shouted at me, 'Get out of here!' 'All right', I said, 'We will leave, but if I lose my son, you will lose your two children'. After a short silence Gutner said, 'Hide in the upper storeroom'. Gutner brought along his children, his girl friend and his parents and we lay there, while the Germans went from house to house carrying out their search.
>
> The screaming outside was terrible. The crying of the children and their parents was enough to break one's heart. Children and old people were being loaded into lorries. Suddenly you began to cry as well. In that larder there was a clock and you demanded that it should strike 'Ding-dong'.

I tried to make you keep your mouth shut, but I failed. A German heard a child crying and threw a hand grenade into the house. It went off, but luckily no one was hurt. We sat there the whole day. When darkness fell, the Germans left the ghetto.

At the end of the day columns of men and women started coming back from work. The terrible suffering of that day was a blow for everyone. You had been saved, but this had to be kept secret from everybody. We were afraid that the resentment of those who had lost their children could lead to tragedy.

Kazys Tamashauskas, who worked with my father, told him that if I was still alive on his return to the ghetto he was prepared to help to save me. However, he seemed to be in no hurry. Mother decided to go out to work with my father, leaving me behind with her cousin. She met the Lithuanian, fell to her knees, kissed his feet and started to weep. She begged him to take me as soon as possible. Kazys promised that he would take me within a few days. When my parents met him after the war, he said to my mother, 'You fell to your knees and kissed my feet: I couldn't refuse.'

One evening my mother had gone to see the members of the Jewish ghetto police who were due to be on watch at the gate and told them what she was planning. She asked them to help at the gate, when she and my father would be searched. One of them was called Jankele (probably Lipavsky) and the other Matskin. Next morning I was given a Luminal injection. Father put on his work overalls, stuck one of my legs into the inner pockets and tied me tightly up against him with a towel. Finally, he put on a large coat and set out.

He was standing between tall men in his roomy coat. One of the team leaders turned to him and asked whether he had started dealing in illegal trade. Jankele shouted at the leader, 'Be quiet and stop asking questions'. Suddenly I started coughing and everyone froze. Jankele, who had also heard the coughing, gave an order to the whole work brigade to start coughing forthwith. Jankele stopped another man, who was also wearing a coat too large for him, and began to search him. He found he had a duvet wrapped round him. The man was punished by being sent to Aleksotas. A lorry took my father and mother to their work place. By this time I had woken up, poked my head out of father's coat and began talking. The German who was accompanying the team said, 'I can hear a child's voice'. One of the men distracted the German's attention saying, 'If you want to hear a child's voice, just listen!' He then proceeded to imitate a child. 'If you want to hear a cock crow, I can lay that on too'.

My father had warned the German in charge of them that he would be bringing along his baby and asked him to allow us to spend the day in the attic of the work premises. The German made no reply: his silence was assumed to imply his agreement. I finally woke up in that attic, began to cry and wet myself. My urine began to drip down on the heads of the men working below. 'What's dripping over there?' asked one of the Germans. Fortunately he had to leave soon after that.

At the end of the working day the Lithuanian team leader, whose wife was meant to be coming to fetch me, delayed the whole team until she finally appeared. His wife took me, loaded me into a cart and carried us off to the village of Panemune. On the way back to the ghetto my parents saw that celebrations of some kind were going on in Kaunas. It was 20 April, Hitler's birthday. My mother was weeping. Someone said to her, 'You shouldn't be crying, you've handed your child over to save him'.

Now that I was safe with Jadzia and Kazys Tamashauskas, my parents decided to escape from the ghetto, but did not succeed. Mother was sent to Stutthof. From Stutthof they transferred her to Tranza, where my mother survived until the camp was liberated by the Red Army on 22 January 1945. The Russians sent my mother to work as a nurse in a military hospital. She wrote a letter to Kaunas asking the authorities to contact the Tamashauskas family and find out what had become of me; she did not receive any answer.

I was not allowed to leave the Tamashauskas house, but I was growing and so was my curiosity about the outside world. Somehow I managed to get out of the house. I saw a horse and a German standing near it. I called, 'horse, horse' in Yiddish. Jadzia, on discovering that I had left the house, came running to fetch me. The German asked her, 'How come the child knows German?' Jadzia quickly recovered her calm and said, 'My sister married a German, who was killed in battle and this is her child. It's difficult for her to bring him up and so he lives here with me.' The German treated me to a biscuit. The Tamashauskas family had a 12-year-old son called Vitas. Jadzja and Kazys taught Vitas to play hide-and-seek with me, telling me that I should hide in an enormous wooden box they had, if any stranger should come into the flat unexpectedly. Two months later Jadzia, without telling anyone took me to another village, to stay with a woman and her daughter.

She wrapped me up in a blanket and laid me down near the door of that woman's house. It was raining hard at the time. I soon got wet and began to cry. The woman I was to stay with heard a noise outside the door and thought it was a cat meowing. She opened the door and carried a 'parcel' into her house. I was already 3 years old by that time. The Gestapo, however, came for me. I was a thin, fair-haired boy with blue eyes; nobody had ever imagined that I was Jewish. They had not even bothered, or maybe did not want, to take my trousers down to check whether I was circumcised. One of the neighbours, who came to the woman's house, looked at me and pulled down my trousers, confirming that I was Jewish. By now the Russian troops were not far from Kaunas and she said to the woman looking after me, 'Keep the child. If the parents turn up they'll give you good money for your pains.'

After liberation, a young man, Shmuel Peipert, who was released from the Red Army, took upon himself the task of looking for Jewish children living with Lithuanian families. He would travel around the local villages, talking to people and asking questions, which is how he came across me. He immediately told the woman that she should hand over her Jewish child to him. She refused: 'Not for anything. I promised to give the child back only to his parents.' When the woman went out of the house, Peipert grabbed hold of me and made off. He went with me to Panevezhys, where Mother's sister Sara, with her husband, Gershon Oshri, lived after they had returned from Siberia. Peipert turned to Sara, whom he already knew, and told her that he had found a Jewish child who was not well and needed looking after. However, Sara refused to take care of me, saying that she wanted first and foremost to find her sister's child.

My father survived the Dachau camp. He learnt that Sara and Gershon were in Panevezhys and informed Sara that his son had been living with the Tamashauskas family. Sara and her husband went to Kaunas, found the Tamashauskas family and asked where the child was. Jadzia said that she handed me over to a good family in a village, but then a Jew in army uniform came to their house and kidnapped the child. When asked to describe the child, Kazis brought out a tiny photograph and showed it to them. They looked at it and Sara realized who I was.

Figure 32. Shmuel Peipert with Beny Chaitas, 1944. Peipert sold the horse and cattle farm that had belonged to his family and dedicated the money to find Jewish children who had been hidden by Gentiles and brought them to orphanages in Kaunas and Vilna. He was murdered by Lithuanian bandits.

Gershon and Sara went to see Peipert in Panevezhys, who, by this time, had placed me in an orphanage. Sara and Gershon rushed to the orphanage, where the director turned out to be a native of Rokishkes and had even been Sara's classmate. He agreed to hand me over to Sara.

I began to grow used to Sara. I started understanding and speaking Yiddish again. I began calling Sara 'Mama' and Gershon 'Papa'. It was not until 12 December 1945 that Mother eventually came back to Lithuania. Her cousin, Sara Shpak, who had been in hiding with a Lithuanian family, informed my mother that I was safe in Panevezhys, and that my father had survived.

Mother then went to Panevezhys. She arrived there late in the evening; it was dark and cold. She did not know where her sister lived. She just walked into a house chosen at random and asked, 'Perhaps you know where Sara Oshri lives in this town'. The man, who was Jewish, led my mother to Sara's house. When Sara, who was pregnant at the time, saw her sister, she fainted. In the flat Mother saw two children sitting at the table. She immediately recognized me and came running over to me. She took my hands and started kissing them. I began to cry and tried to pull my hands out of hers. 'You're not my Mama, make her go away, Mama', I shouted. Next morning my mother began talking to me, giving me sweets and toys, which she had brought from Germany. I began to get used to her and gradually came to understand that she was my real 'Mama'. I went on calling Sara 'Mama' and my mother 'my real Mama'. Mother took me to Kaunas, told me about my father Leibe, and showed me his photographs. Almost every day we would go down to the station to meet my father. Yet, in August 1946, my father happened to turn up on one of the few days we were not at the station.

Normal life could begin once more. In Kaunas my brother was born. We all left for Israel in 1967. I married Sara Zaczepinksi, we have two sons. For thirty years until retirement in 1998 I worked in the Haifa Oil Refinery. After retirement I volunteered for the Israeli Police force.

Haifa, Israel, April 2009

7. Father Hoped for a Good Outcome

Irena Aronovsky-Voschina-Savir

My mother, Gabriella (Ela) née Sobovska, and father, Leon (Liolia) Aronovsky, were married just before the war. In the ghetto, my parents shared a flat with the Zupovichs. My mother became pregnant, but courageously, she refused to comply with Gestapo orders to have an abortion. I was delivered on 31 August 1942 by Dr Natan Nabrisky in very difficult circumstances. Later, Dr Nabrisky was to become the director of the maternity hospital in Kfar-Saba, Israel.

I remember my mother telling many stories about these terrible times: there was no food, no bread and certainly no food for babies. I was fortunate to feed on my mother's breast milk for a few months. When the Germans entered our house, she would hide me under the bed. Thankfully, I did not cry.

Figure 33. Liolia Aronovsky, father of Irena Aronovsky-Voshchina, a member of the Jewish Police in the ghetto. He was killed in 1944 for refusing to search for survived children after the 'Children's action'.

At the end of 1943, my father, who was in the Jewish police, heard about a planned 'Children's Action'. He decided that it was time for my mother to escape with me. One day, he arranged that the Jewish policemen would create a commotion; the Germans went to investigate what had happened. At that moment my mother ran out through the ghetto gates with me hidden in her coat. A Lithuanian family hid us in their village. I still have letters that my father wrote to my mother, about his hope for a good outcome, but it was not to be: Father was murdered at the Ninth Fort for refusing to disclose the location of hiding places in the ghetto.

My mother survived the war. She married Dr Baruch (Boria) Voshchin, who had escaped from the ghetto and was hidden by Lithuanians together with Dr Nabrisky. My grandparents and my uncle and aunt were burnt alive in their hiding places, when the Germans liquidated the ghetto. From all our extended family only two of my uncles survived, having left Kaunas before the war.

In 1969 I came to visit my uncle Abrasha Aronovsky in England. I did not return to Lithuania, but left for Israel. My mother came to Israel with Boria in 1972. He died in a car accident in 1976. My mother passed away in 1984 at the age of 75, when my twins were 11 years old. Until retirement I worked as an anaesthesiologist and was director of the obstetric anaesthesiology unit in Kaplan hospital in Rehovot, Israel.

Rehovot, Israel, 2008

8. A Red Dress with White Polka Dots

Sara Gillman-Plamm

My parents, Moshe Gillman and Sheina, née Codikovaite, a young couple, lived happily in Kaunas. Father worked as a leather lathe operator and my mother was working in a shop called *Rosemarin*. Mother was pregnant when the war began. I was born in the ghetto on 3 September 1941. Mother does not recall who delivered her, but she was able to tell me that I was born in a secret place where Jewish women were taken to give birth.

Mother's family lived in Petrashunai, a Kaunas suburb; many members of her family were killed there during the first days of the war. My grandmother, Nessia Gillman, was living in the region designated for the ghetto, and when Jews were forced out of their homes and sent to the ghetto, many of our relatives came to live at my grandma's home. The house eventually became full of people and was very crowded; there I spent the first few years of my life. My grandfather, Berl Gillman, was shot by the Germans during the very first days of the occupation.

One day my parents heard a rumour that the Germans would soon take all children from their parents. Father's youngest brother, Lebale Gillman, was only 18 at the time. He was my hero and a hero to many others as well. He was a courageous and resourceful young man who knew many people outside the ghetto, and he would help fellow Jews in the ghetto. He arranged for my rescue by finding a Polish family who would be willing to hide me.

I was nearly two and a half years old at the time. My parents gave me a sleeping pill, and somehow succeeded in bringing me to the gate of the ghetto where the Polish man was waiting with his horse and carriage to take me away. Suddenly I found myself in a family of strangers; I do remember crying a lot.

I called the man 'Papa Leivus' and the woman 'Mama Genia'; they named me Christina and spoke to me in Polish. They were good to me; 'Papa Leivus' would bring me candies and play with me. I also remember three visits while I was there. The first was from a woman. I remember being locked in a room with a frosted glass door; through it I saw a white shawl. My instincts told me that the woman had come to see me. Later my mother told me that I was crying hysterically and banging on the door and begging to be let out to see the woman, who was in fact my grandmother. I was very close to her because she was the one who mostly looked after me when we all lived together in her house in the ghetto.

The second visit was from someone else. Again I was crying and banging on the door to be let out. The door was finally opened; I don't remember the person's face but I do remember grabbing him around the neck and holding very tightly, so much so that I tore his collar. This was a visit from my Lebale, whom I loved very much.

The third visit was from my mother. One day she felt compelled to see whether I was alive or not, and she didn't care what might happen to her. She took off the Star of David and made the long trip on foot from Slobodka to the centre of Kaunas where I was being hidden. I remember very few, yet very dramatic details. I was lying with her in a bed in a dark room with all the blinds shut and the lights off, where we both cried incessantly. Finally I fell asleep and when I woke up she was gone; I became hysterical, and Leivus and Genia could not calm me down for a couple of days. So they brought me back to the ghetto where I was fortunate to be picked up by the Jewish police; they knew my uncle Lebale and took me back to my family. But I could not remain there for long and Lebale once more found another refuge for me.

Lebale knew a Lithuanian man who shared his interest in motorcycles; his name was Jonas Vaicekauskas. He had a wife and a young son roughly my own age. He also had an older daughter from a previous marriage. I was given the name Kristina Vaicekauskaite. I do remember that life there was a terrible horror. I remember crying so much that I would shake and eventually fall asleep. I started bedwetting and Jonas would threaten to beat me with a big belt for doing so. I would wake up terrified in the morning and would check my bed to see if I had wet it. His wife Ona, however, was a good woman, and would protect me. I don't remember if he did ever beat me or if he just threatened to.

Figure 34. Sara Gillman with Ona and Jonas Vaicekauskas, 1944.

Sometimes they would hide me in a dark cellar or closet with their daughter when the Germans were nearby. One morning, when I was ill with chicken pox, I was sitting on the bed with Ona. She was cleaning my hair, which was full of lice, when a couple appeared. The man looked terrible, he was barefoot and his legs were bruised and bleeding. The woman was the stronger one of the two and she supported him. They both leaned against the wall and looked at me. The man fainted. I did not know who they were and did not go to them. The woman called to me to come to her, 'Sarale come here'. I understood that they were Jewish. I had probably heard that Jews were bad and should be hated so I started to yell, 'You're Jews, I hate you. Go away, I don't want to know you.'

The woman was wearing a red dress with white polka dots. I don't know why, but it suddenly struck me that I had seen that dress somewhere before. It appeared later that mother had worn that dress when she had come to visit me at my first hiding place: the dress made me feel drawn to the woman. It was a happy ending for me, the couple were my parents. Since then I have never left them and they have never left me.

Lebale was killed, but before that he told my parents the name of the man who was hiding me, and that he was going to move to a village along the River Neiman near Kulautuva, where people would not know him. When the war was over, my parents left their hiding place and went along the Neiman by boat and stopped in each village along the way to ask if Jewish children were being hidden there. Eventually, they reached our village and found me.

The three of us walked to Kaunas. The journey took us two days and we spent the night in a stranger's barn where we slept in the hay. I wouldn't leave my mother; I would even follow her to the washroom. I used to sleep with her and hold on to her hair so that she would not leave me. In my early years at school Frida Glazman and Yulia Meltz were among my friends, both survivors of the Kaunas Ghetto; we were all in first grade in the Jewish school, which the Soviets permitted for only two years.

I grew up in a very loving family with my sister Liuba and my brother David, both born after the war. My parents were very busy people, so when one kind Lithuanian woman offered her service to look after children, they accepted her. Onute Pechkyte was our nanny for year, and when I became a mother myself she took care of my eldest son. Onute became a member of our family. It appeared later that during the war Onute had helped to save the life of Shalom Eilati. We kept in close touch with this wonderful woman, supporting her in life and death by putting a stone on her grave.

I studied medicine in the same class with P. Tkatsch and Y. Zilberg at the Kaunas Medical School. I was married, and have two children who are already doctors, daughter Naomi and son Lev, who is named after Lebale, my hero. In 1972 we emigrated to Israel, and after several years moved to Canada, where I am a family physician.

Toronto, Canada, 2008

9. Driven by Longing

Michael (Misha) Langevich

My father, Misha Langevich, was born in the small town of Vilkavishkis, and he moved to Kaunas in the hope of making his fortune. There he met Haviva (Hinda), daughter of Fivel Korabelnik, and they married shortly before the war began. I know close to nothing about their work and life before the war.

Figure 35. Misha Langevich's parents and relatives, 1940 or 1941, just before the war. Upper row left to right: Moshe Langevich, the father; Shijus Langevich, Misha's adoptive father after the war and uncle Juda Langevich (perished). Lower row left to right: aunt Sara Langevich and Haviva, Misha's mother. Moshe Langevich was killed by Lithuanians in the first days of the war. Haviva survived the ghetto and Stuthof, but was killed on her way to Kaunas.

In A. Faitelson's book *Not Defeated*, there is an account by Faitelson's wife Sima, which mentions my father's death. She says,

> Before the war, in a building on Laisves Avenue, the central street in Kaunas, Lithuanian and Jewish families lived in relative harmony. Their children played together, speaking a mixture of Yiddish and Lithuanian between them. A lame Lithuanian caretaker lived in a flat on the lower floor. On Jewish holy days he always received money and gifts from the other tenants.
>
> On the morning of 25 June somebody knocked on our door. It was the caretaker accompanied by several armed Lithuanians. They dragged my father and brother out of our apartment. At that moment, a German officer appeared and ordered the Lithuanians to release them. Later from another apartment the same Lithuanians led a man with his teenaged son and another young man, Moishe Langevich, to the cellar and shot them.[1]

When my widowed mother entered the ghetto, she was four months pregnant. Shmuel and Hava Shilkiner gave her shelter; my mother spent all the terrible years of the ghetto with this kind family. I was born in November 1941 and named Moshe in memory of my father.

The situation in the ghetto was becoming highly dangerous, and many families were looking to find an escape, at least for their children. Mother succeeded through Dr Kudrika in finding a Lithuanian woman who agreed to take care of me. I was given sleeping pills, or a shot of Luminal, nobody can now tell me which, and was smuggled by Shilkiner's daughter Keile out of the ghetto. Keile brought me to Viktoria and Petras Lemberis. On the liquidation of the ghetto, my mother was sent to Stutthof.

In January 1945, when the Russian Army was approaching the concentration camp, all the surviving women were led away on foot to another camp. Hungry, cold and ill, they were close to death when the Soviet Army liberated them from Germans. Although terribly weak, my mother refused to wait to get stronger. She wanted to reach Kaunas as soon as possible to find out what had happened to me, and she went straight to Lithuania alone. She never reached Kaunas. One day she stopped a cart carrying Russian soldiers. The following day the upturned cart was found with my mother lying dead beside it.

My uncle, Shijus Langevich, served in the 16th Division of the Red Army during the war as the guard for A. Snechkus, the future Lithuanian Communist Party leader. After he was demobilized he came to Kaunas and collected me from the Lemberis family. He and his wife Sarra adopted me.

My adoptive parents never told me that I was not their biological son. I called Shijus and Sarra 'Daddy' and 'Mama'. I do not remember exactly when I was told the truth by our housekeeper, but I never raised this issue and played along.

Naturally, I knew nothing about the people who saved me; there was no contact between our and the Lemberis family. Many years later my close friend Alik Abramovich introduced me to a girl named Dana, who was approximately my own age. It appeared that Dana either lived with the Lemberis family or had been their neighbour, and she remembered that we had played together when we were kids. We became quite good friends. Dana organized a meeting between myself and Victoria Lemberiene, the lady who had looked after me. On another occasion she took me to a hotel on Laisves Avenue, where a man welcomed me and introduced himself as Petras Lemberis. He was a receptionist or guard in this hotel and had seen me many times passing through but for some reason had never talked to me. We chatted a little bit, about nothing special; we never met again.

I graduated from Kaunas Polytechnic Institute in 1965 as a mechanical engineer and married Polina, a student in Kaunas Medical School. In 1972 we emigrated to Israel with our daughter. In Israel Polina and I immediately found work in our professions, and in time we made quite good progress. In 1976 our son Arnon was born. In 2008 I retired; my wife, a professor in rheumatology, continues her clinical and scientific activities.

Kiriat Ono, Israel, 2008

NOTE

1. A. Faitelson. *Nepokorivshiesia* (Not Defeated) [Russian] (Tel Aviv: DFUS Ofset Israeli Ltd, 2001), pp.24–6.

10. Living Proof of Defiance

Yulia Meltz-Beilinson

The Germans in the ghetto used to say, 'You'll soon only see a Jew in a museum.' My mother remembered that phrase and it imprinted itself clearly on my mind as well. I was born in April 1942 in the Kaunas Ghetto, to Meir Meltz and Henya Meltz, née Krubelnik, when pregnancy was a crime punishable by death. During my mother's pregnancy and labour, she was in the care of Dr Pertzikovitz and Dr Nabriski who risked their lives simply by carrying out that routine medical duty. Living defiance of the Germans, we children of the war and the ghetto miraculously survived and did not merely become 'museum exhibits'.

Every morning my parents were taken to work outside the town: my mother to the airfield and my father to work for the German firm 'Grün und Bilfinger', which was building a bridge. Despite the fact that Jews were thoroughly searched by the Jewish Polizei, when they went back through the gate leading into the ghetto in the evening, they nevertheless succeeded every now and then in exchanging some valuables for food. If such an 'offender' was discovered, however, if he was lucky he would be given a cruel beating, but more often than not such 'offenders' were simply shot.

At the time when the Germans burnt down the hospital with all the patients and medical staff still inside my mother was ill. Fortunately my father had not sent her to the hospital, but treated her at home with medicines, which he managed to get hold of from a pharmacist. Before this happened, my mother had allowed the pharmacist to share our accommodation.

I spent eighteen difficult, dangerous months in the ghetto, because the whole of that time my very existence had to be kept secret. At dangerous moments we used to hide in a dug-out, known as '*malina*', for which the entrance and exit were by way of the toilet. Naturally I had to be given sedatives every now and then to make sure that the people hiding me would not be discovered because of a child's cries.

When rumours started spreading about the 'Children's Action', my father managed to find a place for me at the farmstead of Maryte and Pranas Kurpauskas in the Jurbarkas district. The first attempt to take me out of the ghetto covered by crockery in a large bag had failed. On that occasion there had been a Jewish policeman named Tanchum Arnstam at the gate. His reputation was far from flattering, so my parents decided not to risk it. The second time my father and my grandmother managed to smuggle me out when they left the ghetto on their way to work. I was asleep after having been given a sedative and once again I had been tucked into a bag under a pile of crockery. Yankel Lipavski was at the gate that day; he was one of those who always tried to help the people inside as much as he possibly could.

I had been taken out in the morning, because at the other end of the day the checks were more thorough and carried out by Germans with dogs, which would have been able to detect me. Father handed the 'precious' bag to a peasant woman by the name of Butkiene, who was waiting in the agreed place with a cart. She, in her turn, handed me over to Orchik Keltz, who knew the area well. Sara Libmanaite, a 17-year-old blonde, who did not bear the slightest resemblance to a Jew, was helping Orchik. She explained to the peasants who had come to meet her and to the people she had spent the night with on her way to the Jurbarkas district, that I was her daughter, the result of a 'night on the town', who would be a shameful disgrace for her family and her own undoing. We had had many adventures on the way there and had been obliged to hide from both Germans and Lithuanians. It was especially dangerous when I had woken up and started to cry. Orchik told us that at the time he had felt sorely tempted to suffocate me there and then. At the end of the journey Orchik had taken me out of the cart and walked a long way away from the road. It was not until several days later that he had eventually reached our destination with me, the farmstead of Maryte and Pranas Kurpauskas. Their family was poor and they just had one daughter, who was mentally retarded.

Maryte explained to the Germans and her neighbours that I was the illegitimate daughter of her unmarried sister. Maryte used to wash my hair with 'daisy juice' to make sure that my hair – Heaven forbid! – did not turn dark. After some time I began to call Maryte 'Mama' and Lithuanian became my 'native' language.

In 1944, with help from remarkable peasants by the name of Cheslavas Rakiavichius and Mrs Butkiene, my parents managed to escape from the ghetto themselves. They were brought to the Erzvilkas district, where many Jews were hiding. Among them was a couple by the name of Brik, whose son, Aaron Barak, became president of Israel's Supreme Court many years later.

It was impossible to stay in one location on a permanent basis and my parents had to keep moving from place to place. Most of the time they went deep into the forest to hide during the day and at night they would knock at doors, each time managing to find a roof over their heads and at least something to eat in the house of kind, trustworthy peasants. My father knew the area well and that made all the difference.

It was not until several months later that my parents were able to visit me and the Kurpauskas family. When my mother saw me for the first time she started to sob, because I did not recognize her and called her *'Pone'* ('Missis'). I was dirty and wearing torn clothes. When my mother saw me dip my hand into a bucket of leftovers for the pigs, pull out a mushy piece of potato peel and stuff it cheerfully into my mouth, she realized that I too was hungry. Despite all that, my parents were very grateful to that simple Lithuanian family, who risked their lives to take me in and protect me. We shall remember what they did for the rest of our lives.

The neighbours, who were starting to realize that the Kurpauskas family had taken in a Jewish child and that their house was being visited at night, began letting their guard dogs off their chains. This meant that my parents had to make the return journey at night, falling into snowdrifts and shivering with cold and fear, without managing to see me, as planned.

On one occasion one of the neighbours came into the house and noticed that, after falling over, I had run off to wash my hands. That put her on her guard, and she began to suspect that I was not a village child; Mother was sure that Maryte and Pranas would have been reported to the Gestapo. It was very dangerous for me to stay in that house, where I had spent nearly a year.

The Kurpauskas were very frightened of their neighbours, they felt they had to find another refuge for me as quickly as possible. Later on, after the war, I saw that neighbour again. She was standing with her husband by the fence and even warned me that it was dangerous to walk in the woods, because there were so many snakes. My mother then commented that there was no worse a snake than she was.

My parents fetched me from the Kurpauskas household and began to look for another refuge. Mother used to tell me how frightened she had been in one farmstead, where we had been taken in temporarily by another peasant family, when suddenly some Germans appeared. The adults of the family had been out somewhere in the woods at the time and my mother had stayed behind with me and their two small children, and the Germans. Mother pretended to be dumb so that her accent should not give her away and, without saying anything, she saw to the needs of the uninvited guests. I was perched there in the arms of one of the Germans, while my mother went down into their cellar to fetch milk, pork fat and cabbage. Her hands were trembling with fright as she laid the table. The Germans sat me down on the table and played with me. When they had eaten their fill they left. When the owners of the house came rushing back from the woods, they were very surprised to find us safe and sound. That was probably when my mother's hair turned white, since for as long as I can remember she has always had white hair.

So I had to move on and our father's friend Rakiavichius once more found another place for me, this time in the family of a bookkeeper by the name of Jakubauskas, who had three daughters of his own. At the very beginning when I was brought to his house, he became anxious and was afraid to let me stay; after all there were cases when whole Lithuanian families had been shot for hiding Jews. My mother burst into tears and started pleading with him; she had nowhere else to go. In the end Jakubauskas took pity on my desperate parents, who were at the end of their tether, and agreed.

When the German occupation came to an end, my parents came to fetch me, but I was not very keen to leave that Lithuanian family. I shouted for a long time that I was not Jewish but Lithuanian.

In Kaunas we lived first of all with the family of Dr Gurvichiene. She helped me regain my strength after I arrived there, run down, lice-ridden and covered in septic cuts. Later a Jewish kindergarten was set up and even a Jewish school, which I attended for two years (see Figure 15: Julia Meltz is in the fourth row, third from the left). I shall never forget our Jewish teachers, Mr London and Mr and Mrs Gertner. My Jewish education did not last for very long though because the Soviet authorities closed down Jewish institutions. I was given a place at Russian school No. 11. At that time the only words I knew in Russian were '*Do svidaniya*', and so I used to play truant often.

During the first years after the war my father, with other men from the Jewish community, used to go round the nearby villages looking for children who had been rescued in local families. I remember very clearly how every now and then dark-haired little boys and girls would appear in our house and then disappear again somewhere. At that time I did not show very much interest in such things and now, sadly, there is nobody left to whom I can put those questions.

I married a Jew from Estonia and then began my medical studies in Kaunas, completing them in Tartu. In 1966 my parents together with my two post-war sisters left for Israel. In 1974 after one refusal, we were given an exit permit and set off to join the rest of the family.

All these years we have kept in touch with the Lithuanians who came to our rescue. Cheslavas Rakiavichius lived in Kaunas, regularly attended the synagogue and was an active member of the Jewish community. He came to Israel for a solemn ceremony at Yad Vashem, where he was given the medal of one of the 'Righteous' in the presence of several Jews who had been rescued, including Aaron Barak, who had been aged 6 or 7 in the ghetto. The Kurpauskas family was entered in the list of the 'Righteous' as well. In 2000 in the Vilna Gaon Jewish State Museum I unexpectedly came across a letter from Pranas Kurpauskas, in which he described how his family had taken in and rescued a little Jewish girl called Yulyte Melzkaite. That letter really touched me and I sobbed over it for a long time.

I hope that my children and grandchildren will never have to experience anything like what happened to us.

Tel Aviv, Israel, February 2009

11. A Precious Plaid Blanket

Aviva Tkatsch (Thatch)-Sandler

My father was one of the five children of Leib and Rhoda Tkatsch. Isaac, the oldest, had emigrated to Mexico at the age of 17, and Pesach, the youngest, had been killed in Palestine while guarding a Jewish settlement. Moshe, Sarah, and my father Benesh remained in Kaunas. My maternal grandmother, Emma Efron, was originally from Vilnius. She had a brother who had moved to Shanghai and a sister living in Sweden; I believe that she moved to Kaunas and was waiting to hear from her sister about emigrating to Sweden. In Kaunas, she met and married my grandfather, Isaac Markielevich. They had two children, my mother Riva and my uncle Shmuel. Mother was 4 years old when my grandfather died and my grandmother went to work in a textile store to support the family. There were no other family members in Kaunas, and it was a very difficult and isolated life for the three of them.

Father, who was ten years older than my mother, had been educated as an attorney, but went into business as a textile importer. He met my mother when she was 14; she lied about her age, and by the time he found out that she was so much younger, they had developed an attachment. He took her under his wing, introduced her to the Maccabi sports group, helped her with her homework, and became her mentor and eventually her husband. My parents were married at the end of May 1941. Grandmother Emma had remarried just before my mother and father were married; her second husband Yolk and his four sons did not survive the war.

Mother said that she and Father were on their honeymoon at a cottage in the country and heard that the Germans were about to occupy Lithuania. They quickly returned to Kaunas to be with the rest of the family. In the ghetto they moved in with father's family. Many people were living at close quarters; I think it was very difficult for my mother to live with so many people.

When she discovered she was pregnant with me, it was a

mixed blessing. I was born on 4 March 1942. It was spring and my Zionists parents gave me the hopeful name of Aviva (*'Aviv'* means 'Spring' in Hebrew).

There were many 'actions' when children were taken. My aunt Sarah and her child were taken during one of these 'actions' and never heard from again. My parents told me that there was a hiding place made under a sofa, big enough for my mother and me, and when there were rumours of 'actions', we were hidden there. I have no idea how my mother kept me quiet for hours, but I know that now I panic if I have a blanket over my face. We lived like this for two years.

As time went by, it became increasingly clear that over time all the Jews were going to be killed; it was imperative for my parents to get me out. I remember my parents telling me that they had a discussion about what would happen if they did not return for me. Wouldn't it be ironic if I were raised to be an anti-Semite? Of course, the desire to save me won out, and they began to look for someone who could be trusted to save a Jewish child. They found a woman who was willing to take me. She ran a boarding house for college girls in a nearby town. I was sedated, placed in a sack and loaded into a wagon under a pile of hay. When I found myself in a strange place, with people speaking a foreign language, I was very upset and cried and raged. Since there was a lot of coming and going in the house, the woman, Letuliene, became frightened. Assisting Jews was punishable by death and she felt she had to find another place for me to stay because everyone in the house was in danger.

She gathered some of the girls together and told them that she would take me to a field at a certain time and leave me there. She pleaded that one of them should take me and find a safe place for me; she did it in this manner because she did not want to know who took me and where I went. That way, if she were interrogated, she would have nothing to tell the Germans. One of the girls (or maybe more than one) came to the field, and she took me home to her family's farm. When she appeared with a child, her parents said to her, 'Do you know what you have done to us? You have put all our lives in jeopardy.'

However, they were kind people and took me in. I came with very few things: an unusual plaid blanket that my father had brought back from one of his trips to England, a few clothes, a hairclip that my mother had created out of different coloured electric wires, and a picture of my parents. Having been given away twice, I was traumatized and very meek for a while. At that time I only spoke Yiddish, but learned to speak Lithuanian very soon. I was fortunate in those circumstances to have blondish hair, small features, and green eyes. I was introduced to the community as some distant relative, christened Vitute, and connected to these very loving and brave people. I called the woman '*Mamyte*'.

As it became clear that the war was ending, a Jewish Soviet soldier appeared at the farm and said that he heard that a Jewish child lived there; he wanted to take me to his family after the war ended. My foster-parents told him that they would only give me back to my parents, the people in the picture I brought to them. If my parents did not return, they would continue to raise me.

After the liberation, my mother and grandmother, who had escaped from Stutthof together and were in hiding for several months, split up. Grandmother was to go to Kaunas and find me, and my mother went to Lodz, where she heard that my father had been seen. When my grandmother and my uncle, Moshe, went to Letuliene's house, no one knew where I was or if I was even alive. In despair, my grandmother went to the farmers' market in that town to look for something to eat. As she was wandering around, she suddenly was struck by the sight of a woman who was wearing a jacket that was the same unusual plaid wool as my blanket. She rushed up to the woman and demanded to know where the child, who came with that blanket, was living. The woman brought them to the farm and my grandmother became hysterical when she saw me.

I was in no rush to go with her, and the family was reluctant to let me go with her. Only after she asked about the picture of my parents, and if they had ever seen the wire hairclip, did they believe she was my grandmother and let me go with her. Grandmother returned with me and reunited with uncle's Moshe family, Peshele, aunt Dvora, and whoever else was living there.

I was told that soon after Grandmother came for me, I became very ill. They thought that I had meningitis and might die. Suddenly there was a knock on the door, and it was *Mamyte*. She had a dream that I was very sick and she walked for miles to find me and bring me some medicine that had helped me in the past;

I recovered with remarkable speed. In my analysis, it was thought that what I actually experienced was *'marasmus'*, a deep childhood depression. The sight and sound and kisses of *Mamyte* brought me out of the depression and I began to thrive again.

Once I was well and papers were obtained, my grandmother took me by train to meet my parents. I do not remember the reunion. I know I was given a big doll and told that everything was fine now that we were all together. In rural Europe at that time many crossroads had crosses and a pile of stones, and I insisted that we stop at each one so that I could pray. It drove my mother crazy. They found a priest who sat with me and explained that I was now with my real family, I was Jewish, and didn't need to pray at every crossroad.

Our family went to a Displaced Persons camp, St Ottilion, a former monastery, to recover. Father had a terrible skin condition. My mother was and remained very nervous and suspicious. I played with the few other children, and learned to be Jewish again. I remember that a lot of people there would look at me and cry. It took years before I understood they were mourning their own dead children, sisters, brothers. I did not realize it at the time, but my parents, at my mother's urging, cut off any communication with my Lithuanian foster-family. They were not to be mentioned; that part of my life was over. It was more subtle than that, but the message was very clear.

After Father's health had improved, he chose to stay in Munich, Germany for several years. He felt a need to help run an ORT programme that helped young men who had been robbed of their education to learn trades and have a means of support. During the time in Munich my sister Rhoda was born. Also, during that time my father visited Palestine and his brother's grave.

He came back with the realization that he could not live in that climate with his skin condition and Mother also refused to go to a place where there was a very good chance of another war. While my father was directing the ORT School, several Americans, who were collecting money to fund this type of endeavour and help European Jewry, came to see how their money was used. Some gave my father their business cards and told him that they would have employment for him if he chose to come to Detroit, Michigan or Phoenix, Arizona.

My parents had never intended to stay in Germany forever. They looked at a map of the USA and saw that the climate in Detroit was similar to that of Kaunas. They saw the great lakes surrounding the state and felt that this would be the place they could settle and raise a family.

We emigrated to the USA in 1949, and after a short stay in New York and Philadelphia, we came to Detroit. The Holtzman and Silverman Co., true to their word, gave my father work. He stayed with them for his whole working life, starting as a field construction management trainee and ending his career as a highly respected vice-president of the company. He appeared to adjust to our new life. He was very charming to everyone, and all the people he dealt with on a routine basis became his friends.

Mother had a much harder time. She was a nervous, bordering on paranoid, individual. There was always tension in our home. I think she lost all trust in the basic goodness of people as a result of her war experience. 'Neighbours could turn you in, don't talk to people about anything personal. Don't trust anyone,' she would say. My brother Leonard (Leib) was born in 1956. Right around that time, my mother began teaching 'after school' Hebrew classes and going to college to finish her degree. Teaching was her area of competence. When a Hebrew day school opened, she was recruited to teach at our synagogue. People stop me on the street almost weekly, to tell me that my mother was the best teacher they ever had. She retired at age 80. Most of the community had been her students at one time or another. We rapidly moved from one neighbourhood in the Detroit area to another until we ended up in a lovely area.

I married Robert Sandler in 1962 and we lived in Cambridge, Mass., while he attended Law School at Harvard. We returned to Detroit to settle and raise our family of three children. I returned to college for an advanced degree in Clinical Social Work. I have often worked with children of survivors.

My mother now lives in a Alzheimer's Disease care facility. She is completely incoherent, but recognizes her children.

About sixteen years ago my parents asked me to come over. They showed me a letter in Lithuanian that had been received by my cousin Peshele (Polina-Tkach-Davidson). She had sent it on to them and they had sat with it for several months; Father finally convinced my mother to give it to me. It was from the college girl

Konstancija Povilaikaite-Babinskiene, at the time of the letter in her 60s. She had gone to the Jewish agency that had opened in Lithuania after the break up of the USSR, looking for the little girl that her family Petras and Ona Povilaikas had taken in during the war.

Mother had written her a very short letter in reply; I have no idea what it said. She was hysterical when she read me the letter. She thought I had always wanted to go back to Lithuania to live with these people. It was useless reassuring her. She attributed some sort of evil intent to that letter. I took this letter to a friend who could read Lithuanian and dictated a return letter, explaining my mother's nervous condition and that I was thrilled to hear from them. We corresponded for a few rounds, but my house burned down in 1996, and the address was inside.

I suppose I could have researched and recovered the information, but I was almost paralyzed by the conflict I felt. In my few communications with them I expressed my gratitude for my life and offered to help them in any way. They replied that they were in need of nothing, but had always wondered what had happened to 'Vitute' when she left them. There are no words that can possibly express the gratitude I feel for the love and safety that this family offered a strange child at the risk of their own lives.

When Moshe and his family came to Israel from Russia, my father and brother went to see them; Father was so excited to see his brother and the family after so many years. I went to Israel twenty-six years ago and we reunited with Peshele and her children. Peshele also came to visit Detroit. In 2008 Peshele called me to tell about this project, and I am pleased to add my story to this sadly thin pile of stories from children who survived the Kaunas Ghetto.

Detroit, USA, 2008

NB: While writing this story, I was able to re-establish contact with Konstancija Babinskiene and her daughters. We exchanged letters, emails and pictures. She died last year. One of her daughters, Virginija, was called Vytute by her family.

12. My Patriotic Song Did Not Help

Ruth Bass-Glikman

My father, Leiba Bass, worked in the family's fur business owned by my grandfather, Chaim Bass. He travelled a lot in Europe. On one of his business trips to Liepaja, in Latvia, he met Tirca Galperin; she was only 22 years old, much younger than my father when they married. In 1938 my brother, Eliezer Bass, was born. Our grandmother, Miriam Galperin-Borovsky, moved in with my parents in Kaunas after she was widowed. I was born in the Kaunas Ghetto on 26 January 1942.

Figure 36. Ruth Bass, certificate of identity, Ausweis No 16313, issued in 1942.

My parents' friendship with a young gynaecologist, Natan Nabrisky, turned out to be lucky for me. A Lithuanian woman, Jadvyga Babarskiene, felt indebted to Nabrisky. She used to secretly provide food for him and once asked if there was any other way she could help him. Dr Nabrisky pointed to my mother and explained to Jadvyga that this beautiful young woman had two children. He asked her to save them.

Figure 37. Ruth Bass with Jadvyga Babarskiene, her son and daughter Danute. Ruth is on the left without flowers, 1946?

By then my brother already spoke Yiddish, which posed a threat and would make it difficult to shelter him, but Jadvyga promised that she would do everything to rescue me. Although I was about 9 months old, my mother still took this desperate measure and agreed to give me away alone. She carried me out of the ghetto in a sack on her way to work and handed me over to Jadvyga who was waiting for her at the appointed place.

I found myself living with a Catholic Lithuanian family in Marjiampole. My adoptive parents were educated, intelligent people: Jadvyga was a pharmacologist and her husband, Alfonsas Babarskis, graduated from a commercial school in Switzerland. Their own daughter Danute was one year older than me. Jadvyga dyed my hair blonde and told neighbours that I was the daughter of a Russian officer.

At some point Babarskis were ordered by the Germans to leave Kaunas within forty-eight hours; I do not know the reason behind it. We fled Kaunas and went to live in the house occupied during the summer. Alfonsas Babarskis was a wealthy man and we should have lived well. However, when the Germans retreated from Lithuania, they set all the houses alight and our summer house was burnt down. We were left owning nothing when we went back to live in the Babarskis' residence in Marijampole.

Babarskis told me that he had seen my father several times but then all trace of him was lost. I learnt later that my parents were burned to death during the liquidation when the Germans set the entire ghetto on fire. My father's younger sister Judith and my grandparents also perished. Another of father's sisters, Sonia, was killed in Latvia. My brother Eliezer was either killed during the 'Children's Action' or died later with my parents; I searched through archives in Europe trying to trace him, but to no avail.

Around 1947, in the early hours of the morning, there was a knock at the door. The Soviet militia searched our house and my adoptive mother was intimidated; they were looking for her husband. I was nearby singing a song about Stalin our 'father and saviour'. My patriotic song did not help. Having been educated in the West, and being the son of wealthy parents with a three-storey property in the centre of Marijampole and a summer house outside of town, Babarskis posed a very real 'threat' to the Soviet regime; he was arrested and taken to Karaganda concentration camp. From that time onwards the awful years began. We had nothing to eat and very little to wear. My neighbours would give me food. Babarskis was rehabilitated and released only in 1956. During all that time, Dr Voshchin's family kept close contact with us and supported the Babarskis family.

When I was 13 years old my Lithuanian parents agreed that I should go to live with a Jewish family. Dr Voshchin introduced me to Grisha Mendelbraut from Vilnius and I went to the Mendelbraut family, where I lived for two years. Mendelbraut's neighbours were Eta and Mitia Ginkas; they both cared about me very much. Eta suggested that David and Chaya Markauskas (Markovsky) would adopt me. The Markovsky's own daughter, Rosa Markovsky, had been hidden with a Lithuanian family during the war. She had been betrayed by the Lithuanians who had fostered her, while David and Chaya were in the partisan detachment. Chaya Markauskiene did have another daughter, Dalia, born after the war, but after so many years she was still desperately mourning her lost daughter Rosa. Chaya was deeply touched by my story and when I was 14, the Markovskys offered to adopt me. I was happy to be the daughter of such wonderful people and agreed immediately.

I graduated from the Economics Faculty of Vilnius University, married Leon Glikman and in 1971 we emigrated to Israel with our 2-year-old child and my husband's elderly parents. My adoptive parents emigrated to Israel as well. I was head of the Cost, Budget and Control Division of the Dead Sea Bromide Group and my husband was a senior urologist in the Beer Sheva Hospital. We have two children and three grandchildren.

Over the years I remained in close contact with my Lithuanian family. For all those years they had safeguarded my birth certificate from Vilijampole/ Ausweis N 10313, issued by the Germans! Jadvyga and Alfonsas Babarskis were recognized by Yad Vashem as 'Righteous among the Nations'.

Tel Aviv, Israel, 2009

13. Trustworthy Neighbours

Sarra Levin-Burmenko

My mother Sonia, born in 1916, was one of five daughters in the poor family of Shmuel and Sarah Kriger in Zhaisliai, a small village near Kaunas. Grandmother Sarah died at an early age and my grandfather Schmuel went to South Africa before the war, looking for a better life. Only Aunt Lena stayed in Kaunas.

My grandparents, Isaac and Fruma Levin, lived in Odessa before the war; they had ten children. Grandfather Isaac was a captain in the Russian Navy and later a captain in the commercial shipping industry. In 1917, when the Revolution started, my grandfather took the family and fled to Turkey on his ship. Nobody knows why, but not all the children were aboard: two of his sons did not go with the family. One of them was my father, Leibl Levin, who somehow made his way to Lithuania, where he met my mother.

When my parents were placed in the Kaunas Ghetto my mother was pregnant. She had to tighten herself to keep her pregnancy secret from the Germans. I was born in November 1941. At some point, my parents decided to give me away to my aunt Lena; her husband, Kolia Stonys, was a Lithuanian. Lena had blonde hair and blue eyes and passed for a Lithuanian during the war. They had three children of their own, Ruta, Saulius and Meta.

Someone gave me a shot of Luminal so I would not cry, and arrangements were made for my aunt to pick me up. My parents put me in a basket and took me to the wire fence where I was passed to my aunt. Later, my aunt told me that when she picked me up, she saw German soldiers not too far away. She got very scared and ran into a house nearby to hide and waited for a while till it was safe to go home.

I was kept inside the apartment all the time, because my aunt and uncle were afraid of the Germans and neighbours. Once, when I was outside with my aunt and my cousins, a German soldier passed by and, pointing to me, he asked my aunt, 'Why

does this child have black hair when all the others are blonde?'
Fortunately, the neighbours were very good people, because they
knew I was a Jewish child and did not pass this on.

My father died in the ghetto. He was an accountant and it was
difficult for him to work at a construction site. Later one of his
friends told me that because there were no washing facilities in
the ghetto, the cement became embedded in the pores of his face.

My mother was transferred to Stutthof, which she survived.
After Mother returned from the concentration camp, she stayed
at my aunt's place, so that I could get used to her. In the beginning I used to say that she was not my mother. I would say that
my mother was the '*mazha*' mama, which means small, short in
Lithuanian; it took me a while to get used to my mother.

In 1946 my mother remarried and all three of us moved to our
own apartment. My stepfather, Saul Burstein, was a good father
to me. He had been in the ghetto as well. Saul came back to
Lithuania from a concentration camp hoping to find his wife and
son. Unfortunately they had died in the gas chambers.

My first language at my aunt's place was Lithuanian. At home
with my parents I learned to speak Yiddish, and I went to a
Yiddish school for two years. I liked going to this school very
much; my grades were very good and I felt very comfortable
being among only Jewish children. In 1950, when the Yiddish
school was closed, my parents put me in a Russian school. I did
not like it, because I did not know a word of Russian and I had
no friends. My grades went down. Because of the anti-Semitism
of the Lithuanians, my parents felt very strongly that they did not
want to send me to a Lithuanian school. I do not know how I
would have felt in the Lithuanian school, but in the Russian
school I did not experience any anti-Semitism. In the town I felt
it much more. Once, I was returning home from an ice-skating
ring. It was very cold and I was wearing a hat, which was
attached to my hair with a pin. Four Lithuanian boys came
towards me and without knowing my name they started to
shout, 'Sara, Sara', because they knew I was Jewish; they would
call a Jewish boy 'Abraham'. One of the boys pulled the hat off
my head. It was painful, because a pin attached it. Of course, they
did not return the hat to me; I got very scared.

Later on, when I was already married and lived in a dormitory
among Lithuanians, it was one of the hardest times in our lives.

My daughter was only 9 months old then. Many times I heard the word *'zhydialka'*, which means Jewish in Lithuanian, but in a derogatory way. My daughter also experienced that; many times she would come home crying, because the children called her *'zhydialka'*.

I graduated from Kaunas Polytechnic Institute having studied civil engineering. I met my husband, Mark Burmenko, who came to Kaunas from Kiev to study electrical engineering. The anti-Semitism in Ukraine was even worse than in Lithuania and although Mark had very high grades in school, he was afraid he would not be accepted into a university in Kiev. Mark had lost his father, who volunteered to go to the war and was killed.

After graduating from college, Mark applied for work in Kiev. A very famous scientist who interviewed Mark wanted to hire him, but the Human Resources Department would not allow it. It sounds anecdotal, but Mark got an answer that his 'profile' did not fit. And the scientist told my husband, 'Mark, I am really ashamed and disappointed in our system. I thought this discrimination did not exist at our facility. I am very sorry.'

My parents had been thinking about leaving Lithuania since I was a child. They had to wait for the opportunity for a very long time. My parents and my brother, Moshe Burstein, born in 1947, left for Israel in May 1972, and in late November 1976 we came to the USA: we were free to do what we wanted in this country.

New York, USA, 2008

PART TWO

MEMOIRS OF THE ACTIONS

14. The Horror of the 'Big Action'

Rieta Volpert-Lesokhin

I was born on 6 December 1934. My father, David Volpert, was a well-known lawyer. My mother, Ida Gurvich-Volpert, was a famous pianist; they were both very busy people. Father spent most of his time in the courts or in his prosperous private practice and my mother in the conservatorium or at concerts. I remember my father used to eat his lunch hastily, causing my mother much discontent. On the rare occasions when he was free, he would take me for a walk, which I liked very much. Mother was a lovely woman: warm, happy and intelligent, always surrounded by many friends.

Figure 38. Rieta Volpert with parents, David Volpert and Ida Gurvich-Volpert and her rescuer, Elena Chlopina, 1939. Both parents perished.

I spent most of my time with my nanny, Elena Grigorievna Chlopina (Chlopinaite). She had graduated from the 'Institute for Respectable Young Ladies' in St Petersburg, where highly qualified governesses were trained. She came when I was 2 months old and stayed with me for years.

When I grew up, a French lady from Paris was invited to live with us. Since then I speak French fluently. In our family my parents usually spoke in German; Father's brothers and sisters lived in Germany and my mother graduated from the Berlin Conservatorium. We all spoke Russian and Lithuanian fluently as well. At the age of 5 I started to take piano classes and was very successful in them.

I did not attend regular school, I was educated at home. I was quite a pampered child, and got everything one can imagine. We lived on Laisves Avenue in a large beautiful apartment. We were a secular Jewish family, but we did celebrate Passover, and we also marked Yom Kippur.

I remember playing in the garden and suddenly there was a lot of noise from Laisves Avenue. We ran to look. There was an enormous commotion. Tanks rolled into the avenue with Russian soldiers smiling atop of them. People in the crowd, among them numerous Lithuanians, on both sides of the avenue were cheering, applauding and throwing flowers.

Soon supplies were running out in the shops and the Soviets started the deportation of the 'bourgeois' to Siberia. I remember one evening a van stopped outside the entrance to our building and all our neighbour's family were led away one by one. My parents were very much afraid that we would be sent to exile as well.

I remember how the war started and the first sounds of bombardment, and how anxious my parents were when the telephone connection was cut. Our good friend, Dr Dugovsky, tried to reach us in order to take our family and run away, but he could not get in touch. So we stayed in occupied Kaunas.

The first days of the war, when the Russians had left and the Germans had not yet come, were the most terrifying. The Lithuanians robbed, raped and pillaged the Jews in great numbers. Father's friend, Professor Tumenas, took our family to his house in order to save us from the rage of these wild mobs; we spent a couple of weeks there. Later when the Germans had restored some order, we returned for a short stay in our apartment.

I remember how we went to the ghetto. My parents put a few things on a carriage and we moved to a nice house in Slobodka in the area called the 'Large Ghetto'. At the beginning we lived alone, three of us in a very big room. I liked this house and the room and thought we had moved, as we usually did during the summer time, to a *dacha*. Moreover, this time we were all together, not as in previous years when it had only been my nanny and me. Later my uncle Misha Volpert with his wife Mira and their 6-year-old twins, Lionia and Zhenia, came to live in our room.

Life in the ghetto was really quite a shock for my parents, who had lived in luxury just several months before. My parents joined the work brigades and used to bring back some food. I stayed at home alone and was happy to play freely with lots of other children on the streets of the ghetto; I even used to smuggle some food from our family and share it with other poor children.

One night my father was arrested by a Lithuanian policeman. He disappeared for a few days; when he returned he was dirty, skinny and unshaven. He had been caught up in the so-called 'Intellectuals' Action', when about 500 educated men were rounded up to perform 'professional work'. In fact they were taken to the Ninth Fort and ordered to dig a huge pit. They all understood they were digging their own grave. While they were digging, a Lithuanian man approached my father, it seems he had been his client, and ordered him to run away. And my father took this chance. Apparently only my father and Dr Voshchin escaped this round-up alive.

The ghetto orchestra was organized, and my uncle Izya Rosenblum who was a most talented violinist, joined it; he used to take me to concerts. Later Izya and his 14-year-old son Liolik Rosenblum died in Dachau concentration camp.

And then I remember the horror of the 'Great Action'. We were woken up at five in the morning. The Germans were driving on the streets announcing by megaphones, 'Attention, attention! Everybody stay at home. Anybody who will appear on the streets will be shot!' The Germans and the Lithuanian policemen started systematically taking people out of their homes and leading them to Democracy Square. It was so cold and so horrifying to stand there in the square. I was so afraid of the big dogs barking at us. We stood there from the early morning till evening, and eventually during the 'selection', we were sent to the right-hand line. Misha Kopelman, who was Mother's former classmate, was now head of the Jewish police. When he saw us, he led our family to the left side in exchange for another family, which he moved to the right.

The people in the right-hand line spent the night in the location where the so-called 'Small Ghetto' had been before its liquidation. The next day they were led to the Ninth Fort and shot. Most of our relatives from Mother's side perished in the 'Great Action'. I remember the sorrow of my parents when they returned from Democracy Square; many people from our circle had disappeared.

My parents invited the Finkelshtein family, who did not have a place to live, to move into our flat. We now numbered eleven people in our room. A garden was allocated to all the tenants of our building; in our small plot my father grew tomatoes. This was the only source of vitamins in our meals. Since then I hate tomatoes. I noticed that the adult men surrounding me, including my father, would disappear in the evenings. I learnt later that they were digging a refuge ('*malina*') where we would hide at the next 'action'.

Father's old clients would come to see him to take legal advice. They tried to persuade my father to escape from the ghetto, but he refused to leave us. Gradually we had less and less food. I still remember how much I liked dishes made from potato peelings.

My pre-war governess Elena started to bring us food to the ghetto fence. Once she was caught by the German guards and warned that the next time she would be imprisoned. But she went on helping our family. At that time she worked as a housekeeper for two German officers; she lived in a small room in their apartment. It was agreed she would take me to live with her. The German guard was bribed. I clearly remember him turning his back on us while I slipped under the fence. A Lithuanian woman, who lived near the fence, used to lead smuggled children to their destination. It was she who took me to Elena.

I was 8 when I was separated from my parents. Elena told the officers I was her niece. The German officers' names were Hantz

Hart and Shtekman; I remember Hitler's portrait hanging in their guest room. The Germans treated me very well, especially Hart who was a very intelligent and pleasant person. I played the piano and spoke fluent French with him so he very early suspected I was Jewish. He persistently asked Elena if I was a Jewish girl. Yes, was her reply. After that Hart treated me even better. At some point he suggested taking me to Hanover in Germany to his family.

Soon after, Hart was transferred to serve in Latvia. We stayed with Shtekman. When he found out who I was, he gave Elena two weeks to find another shelter for me. She found a woman who agreed to keep me for payment, but not until certain arrangements were made.

In the meantime, Elena took me back to the ghetto, until false papers in the name of Danute Kazlauskaite were prepared. That was when the 'Children's Action' took place. We went to the cellar, where behind the cupboard door was a secret room. Now I understood why my father had so often disappeared in the evenings: he and other men were digging a shelter for us. During those two terrible days we stayed in this room: my parents were with me, and Dr Pertzikovitz's family with their son Alik.

At one point a woman came in. Without saying a word she left us a crying baby and ran away. The baby cried all the time and in order to quiet him, Dr Pertzikovitz had to inject him with morphine. The baby fell asleep, but not for long, so the injections were administered several times. At one point, we heard a Ukrainian policeman outside the door saying 'There is somebody hiding there', the cries of the baby may have attracted his attention. Yet somehow we were not discovered. The baby eventually died in the hideout. His mother never came to fetch him.

After the 'Children's Action' it was impossible for children under 12 to appear on the streets of the ghetto; the policemen would capture them and take them away. I was coached to say I was 12, and my birth certificate was changed accordingly.

My aunt Anna (Niuta) Beilinson worked in the ghetto *Workshtater*, where they made wigs. She took me to work there and organized a certificate proving that I was working there. I made hair for dolls and even earned some food for my work. I remember once a German soldier caught me by my coat collar and shouted, 'How old are you!?' 'Twelve and a half,' I replied and showed him this certificate. Later Niuta was hidden by Lithuanians. For some reason she decided to change the hiding place and was killed during attempt to move there.

After the war, Niuta's sons, Yakov and Pavel Beilinson, who had served in the Soviet Army, were among a group of Jews who tried to escape from the USSR. It appeared there was a provocateur who led the group into the trap of KGB. Some were shot, and most, including Pavel, were arrested and spent ten years in Siberia. Yakov somehow succeeded in crossing the border to Poland and later he emigrated to the USA.

I was quickly transferred back to my nanny. Shtekman saw me and asked why I was still there. Elena promised to take me straightaway to the small town of Mazheikiai, if Shtekman would help her get permission to move from Kaunas to the province; he provided her with a permit and we left Kaunas. Our journey lasted a few days. We waited for our train in Shauliai where I saw a lot of wounded soldiers being transported, and this made a strong impression on me.

In Mazheikiai we lived with a teacher, a very brave, friendly woman called Evgenia Musteikiene. She had two daughters of her own, Laima and Tamara; everybody treated me very well. While we lived there Elena's brother was arrested, taken to a jail in Shauliai and shot for rescuing POWs.

Hart visited us several times in Mazheikiai, always bringing food and presents. He still asked Elena to let him take me to Germany. When the front was nearing Mazheikiai and the Russians started bombardment and shelling, we all moved to a village called Krumaichiai. Elena returned to Kaunas. It appeared that Elena also saved the life of my cousin Lionia. However his twin sister, Zhenia Volpert, was taken during the 'Children's Action' and their parents perished in the concentration camps.

The German soldiers helped us to dig a shelter, and we hid there during the bombardments. One of the Germans was wounded and somebody in the shelter bandaged him. Suddenly armed Russians appeared and shouted to all of us, 'Come out with your hands up.' The children there, including me, started to cry. We were all so frightened, especially after the Russians saw the German soldier among us. At first, they were very angry, believing we were collaborators, but eventually they calmed down, arrested the German and released the rest of us.

In 1945 Elena appeared in Krumaichiai and took me to Kaunas. I asked her about my parents and she told me they had been sent to the camps. Elena had witnessed the deportation as my parents were led away from the ghetto. As they left, they managed to point out to Elena the place where they had hidden their money and jewels. Most of the hidden valuables disappeared, but some of it Elena found and used to support us.

When mother's best friend, Masha Gocaite, returned from Russia she found me and for some time we lived with her in Vilnius. Later my relatives, Sasha and Vera Rosenblum, collected me and I grew up in their house together with my cousin Ela, whom I regard as my sister. Elena became a governess at the house of Antanas Snechkus, the head of the Lithuanian Communist Party.

It was Alik Peretz's mother who told me that my parents had not survived. Mother was shot in Stutthof and my father, although he was released from Dachau, died on his journey home. A group of released prisoners had found boxes of food. They had been starved and now devoured this food, but their bodies could not take it after such a long period of starvation.

Since I did not go to school before and during the war, there was a huge gap in my education. Although I spoke several languages, I did not know how to read or write. When my cousin, Aleksander (Vava) Rosenblum, a lawyer, came from Russia and began to correspond with me, I could not read his letters. Masha would help me with my schoolwork. Unfortunately Masha became sick and died at a young age. Vava supported me and helped me a lot in my future life.

Eventually I finished high school and the conservatorium in Vilnius and took a Masters degree in the Moscow Conservatorium. After completing my education I was sent to teach in Shauliai. Elena came to live with me.

When I applied for permission to emigrate to Israel, I was called to the KGB and asked, how can I leave Elena, who had devoted her life to me? My answer was, 'We are going to Israel together'. After several threats and refusals we both received visas and came to Israel. We settled very well here, I started to work as a teacher in the Haifa Conservatorium and I still give piano lessons. In 1980 I married Yuri Lesokhin. Elena lived with me till she passed away at age of about 85. While still alive she had the great honour to be awarded the title of 'Righteous Among the Nations'.

Haifa, Israel, 2009

15. The Ominous Sound of Cheerful Music

Rivka Feller-Milner

Today I am telling the story of my rescue for the first time. I have always avoided talking about this subject. I was born in 1935 in Kaunas to Aaron Feller, a well-known paediatrician, and Berta, née Neiman, Feller.

During the occupation my father had not wanted to work as a doctor and he was a general labourer in the factory. One evening, when my parents thought I was asleep, I heard my father saying that my sister Aviva and I had to be taken out of the ghetto. Mother was against any such move. 'What will happen to the children, if we are killed?' she asked. Father replied, 'My brother Noah will be coming and he will take them to Palestine.' Noah Feller had left for Palestine before the war and had since become a leading figure in the healthcare system there. I remember how I lay in bed and started thinking about that unknown country, Palestine.

In the first days of the ghetto, Jews were ordered to hand over all jewels and gold to the authorities. The Nazis found out that our neighbour Meck had concealed his money and jewels. They hung him near our house. It was the first time I saw a hanged body. This horrific sight I will never forget.

I remember when I saw my father crying for the first and last time in my life. That was after he had gone to visit his parents Leib and Sara, and his sister Dvora Kaufman with her husband Yehuda and little daughter Altale, who lived in the 'Small Ghetto', and found that they were all killed. We were told that little Altale had been buried alive.

We lived in a house where you could see people being led away to the Ninth Fort. I remember the 'Great Action' clearly. We were dressed in our winter coats; 16-month-old Aviva was ill with measles and had a temperature of nearly 40C. Father was carrying her. We were lined up along four sides of the square. I saw one of the Germans cross the square carrying a child's potty-chair (with a hole in the middle of the seat); he went over to Father and said, 'Sit the little girl down, it'll be easier.' Nor will I ever forget the scene when an old man fell over and one of the SS planted his foot on the old man's chest and started pulling him along by his beard.

During the 'selection' my father and we children were sent off to the 'good' side, while my mother and Reiza, my grandparents' housekeeper, were dispatched to join the other column. My father grabbed Mama by her sleeve and literally dragged her back over to us saying, 'This is my Frau.' Reiza perished.

In 1943, not long before the 'Children's Action', I was sent to live with a Lithuanian family in Vilijampole. I was dressed in a grown-up woman's frock and put on high-heeled shoes before leaving the ghetto with a group of women workers. Andrius and Katrina Vasiliauskas, who already had a son of their own, took me in without asking for anything in return. They remembered that my father used to treat children from poor families for free.

Unlike my sister Aviva, who did not look Jewish, my features were 'typically Jewish'. My rescuers were very scared of their neighbours. Even after the war they would ask us not to say anything about their having saved a Jewish girl, because they did not know what the next regime would be like and what its attitude to such questions would be. They managed to get hold of false documents for me, first of all papers where my name was down as Viktoria, and later more plausible ones where my name was Danute. I was taught to pray and taken to church wearing a scarf tied round my head, as was the custom; to reduce the suspicions of their neighbours, it was always me who would put money in the collection bag brought round the congregation by the servers. Just before the round-up of children, the Germans came looking for Jewish children in the town. The Vasiliauskas family took fright and brought me back to my parents in the ghetto.

I saw that our flat had been 'compressed': there was another family in it by the name of Bloch. My father told me that I had to hide, because my parents did not have any papers acknowledging my existence. It emerged that while I had been 'outside', all the ghetto population had been registered, and so I was now 'non-existent'. One day near the Krishchiukaichio Gate, jolly music was being played very loudly. It was a bad sign: the Germans always used to play cheerful tunes and songs over the loudspeakers when people were being rounded up. My father, who had already passed the gate, came back to warn my mother about it. I was hidden in an attic containing a double partition. I was there with Henale Kuchinka, who had whooping cough and was coughing away all the time. I could see through a gap in the partition how the Germans and the Ukrainians dragged my friend Fira Gurfinkel out of the house. Her mother ran after the SS men in tears, begging them to give her daughter back. A police dog was set on Fira's mother. Fira was hurled into the back of a lorry, while her mother was shot on the spot. The old people in the Bloch family were taken off as well. When the first section of the attic was searched they found Henale's eldest sister, Mirka. The Polizei brutally raped her, and after that killed her there. They did not bother to search further, so did not find Henale and myself; I remember a soldier looked around and murmured in German, 'Nobody is here'.

It was impossible for me to stay on in the ghetto. I was dressed so as to make me look as grown up as possible, complete with lipstick, and my parents arranged with a Lithuanian woman that she would be waiting for me at the other side of the ghetto fence. When we had managed a smooth exit from the ghetto, it was only to find that the woman was not there at the agreed place. Mother and I set off in the direction of Vilijampole. Mother was very frightened, but I, in my childish naivety did not feel any fear at all. We wandered through the town for a long time until we reached the Sixth Fort. From there I already knew the way to the Vasiliauskas' house. My mother spent the night under their roof, and the next day she returned to the ghetto.

My parents also succeeded in escaping from the ghetto, thanks to help given them by the grateful parents of my father's previous patients. Until the liberation they were hiding in Shanchiai, in the bunker of the '*Metalas*' (steel) factory.

After the war I studied in a Jewish school and, when it was closed down, in a Russian high school. I went to study in the teachers' training college in Vilnius, and after that I taught English in Kaunas. I married and in 1972 we left for Israel, where I worked for more than twenty years as a teacher. My father died in 1988 at the age of 86; he even managed to work for a time in his chosen profession in Israel. Mother lived until she was 96, and for most of her life she was able to live independently.

Netanya, Israel, September, 2008

16. We Would Even Have Given You to Gypsies

Polina Tkatsch-Davidson

I was born in Kaunas on 27 February 1940 to Moshe Tkatsch and Dvora, née Levinsky. My name is Polina though I am registered as Pesia, in memory of my father's brother Pesach. Before the Second World War my mother was a Hebrew language teacher. During the Soviet regime, it was prohibited to speak and, naturally, to teach Hebrew; the communists regarded it as a nationalistic language. Later, in Israel, my mother would give free private Hebrew lessons to children in the neighbourhood. My father went to work when he was very young, enabling his four brothers and sisters to receive an education.

In 1935, my uncle Pesach and my father, who was the captain of a football team, participated in the Second Maccabia games in Palestine. After the games, my father returned to Lithuania but my uncle remained in Palestine where he became a '*Shomer*', a guard, in a military organization that guarded Jewish settlements. In 1938 he was killed by Arabs. My grandmother continued to receive letters written by others in his name. Only when I was born and named after him was she informed of his death.

I know all this from my father's stories; Mother never spoke of these things, she never laughed, she never cried, the Germans robbed her of her laughter and tears. When my old friend from our student years, Yakov (Yashka) Zilberg, contacted me to discuss the project about the hidden children of Kaunas, I begged my mother to tell me what had happened to us during the Holocaust. I finally convinced her to share everything she remembers and in 2002, for the first time, I recorded her story. About half a year later, my mother passed away at the age of 84. I am so grateful to Yashka, that thanks to his persistence, I have my mother's voice recorded.

Yashka and I spent six years in the same group of the Kaunas Medical School. Though we were close friends, we knew nothing about our common past as hidden children of the Kaunas Ghetto.

FROM MY MOTHER'S MEMOIRS

During the so-called 'Intellectuals' Action' the Germans invited the educated members of the community to volunteer for more 'professional' work. My father persuaded his youngest brother Benesh not to volunteer. With this he saved his life. All 500 intellectuals were shot. By doing this, the Germans straightaway eliminated people of the highest calibre from the community and thus weakened it.

On 28 October 1941, the darkest day of the ghetto, during the 'selection' we were sent to the left side and survived. I can still hear the bitter weeping that sounded from homes of the ghetto.

During so-called 'Children's Action' I was fortunate to conceal you in my friend's kitchen. She put up wallpaper and camouflaged the door that led to the kitchen. She covered that wall with pots and pans and the Germans overlooked it. There were other mothers and children in this hideout. They put pressure on me to take you out from the hiding place since you were suffering from whooping cough. I would stuff a towel in your mouth whenever we heard the Germans approaching. It was a *'Nes'*, a miracle, that we were not discovered.

After this event I feared letting you out of the house. I was even afraid of the neighbours whose children had already been taken away. When they asked me where my daughter was, I'd say 'same place as yours'. You were a bright girl and knew to crawl under the table when someone knocked at the door. I laid a long tablecloth over this table to conceal you. We knew that we had not yet seen the last of these 'actions' and we started considering ways of getting you out of danger. We understood that if there was at least a small chance that you would survive it was in a caring Lithuanian home. We opted therefore to give you to virtually whoever would accept. We would even have given you to gypsies.

Occasionally we managed to smuggle things out of the ghetto and exchange them for food. One day, your father managed to bring home butter. Usually, butter obtained in this way would be filled with sawdust, but on this occasion the butter was genuine. On the basis of her evident honesty, your father decided to find the woman who had supplied us this butter and ask if she might help us.

We lived in one room with four other families and, when they had all fallen asleep, your father told me that he had found this woman and that she was willing to take you. I was horrified at the thought of separation but he urged me to meet her. Her name was Anele Janavichiene. She looked like a simple woman; she brought bread rolls with her that she had baked especially for you. She took me into her home which was a small room in a very modest house. Anele subsisted by trading goods. I asked her how we could pay her for her assistance, others had wanted only gold. She looked at me with surprise, saying for this one does not charge. She warned me that she would not be able to keep you for long, that she would teach you to speak Lithuanian and then send you to her friend in a different village.

Your father and I had to figure out how we would manage to get you out of the ghetto. We bribed the guard. Moshe pretended that he had to deliver bread to the ghetto and to do this he required a carriage and a sack. The sack was filled with hay, you were sedated and we covered your face with muslin. You fell asleep but awoke not far from the gate and started asking us in Yiddish where you were being taken to. We had to turn back.

The following day, I dressed in my best outfit, removed the yellow star and begged you to stay quiet as we left the ghetto. We crossed the river in a boat and arrived at Anele's home. As soon as we entered, my heart stopped: a Gestapo's army uniform hung on her wall. Upon seeing my expression, Anele tried to assure me that the uniform belonged to her lover, that there was no cause for concern and that I must calm down. I stayed with you the first night and the next day returned to the ghetto alone. Though a bond was struck instantly between you and Anele and I could see that you loved her, the sight of the Gestapo uniform continued to disturb me.

Anele's neighbours very quickly began to suspect that you were a Jewish child and Anele, having changed your name to Maryte Jonavichiute, transferred you to the friend who lived in a different village. I corresponded with him through Anele, I asked him not to beat my daughter. His wife was expecting a child. He himself was a Communist and the Germans soon had him killed.

The ghetto was liquidated. I was taken to Stutthof, your father was sent to Dachau. I found out only after the war that he did not even make it to Dachau. He had jumped off the train.

POLINA

There was nothing to eat in the house and I was sent out to beg. I went outside; it was a day when Germans were snatching Lithuanian women at random. They were abducted from the streets and sent to Germany to work. I was standing with my hand outstretched when the abductions began. A young Lithuanian woman saw me, took me in her arms and feigned to be my mother so she would be left alone. She later fed me and let me go. I know I lived in several other places, I think I remember only the last. There was a young childless couple and an old lady. I was loved there and they hoped I would remain with them.

My father found me. There was only one house still standing in the village and I was in this house. The old lady understood immediately that it was my father. She did not want to let me go when she learnt from my father's accounts that my mother's whereabouts were unknown and that it was not clear if she was dead or alive. I was wary of acknowledging that this was my father. Only when he revealed a blue bonnet, which I recognized to be my mother's, I could identify him as my real father.

When my mother was released from the camp, she decided to write to Professor Mazhylis, a famous gynaecologist in Kaunas. The envelope did not have an address. Mother did not know him personally but trusted that it would reach him. In the letter she requested that he pass this note to the first Jew he encountered. This letter eventually found its way to my father and thus he came to know that my mother was alive. By then I had been living with my father and my cousin Aviva, whom my father had also located.

I remember the day I was reunited with my mother. Father was suffering from a headache and with a wet towel on his head he opened the door. A woman was standing there, crying and crying. It took a long time for me to register that this was my mother.

In lectures at the Kaunas Medical School, I would look into the eyes of Professor Mazhylis, always intending to thank him for having delivered my mother's letter to the right hands. When finally I resolved to do this, I saw the announcements that Professor Mazhylis had passed away. Nothing important in life should be delayed.

I graduated from Kaunas Medical School in 1965. I married a fellow student. Our first son Erik was born in 1964 and the second son Simon in 1970. We all emigrated to Israel in 1972.

We always remained in contact with Anele, she had no family. We wanted to take her to Israel with us but she was not prepared to leave Lithuania. A photograph of her hangs in my bedroom, I am eternally grateful to her. She had been a special lady. There had not been many of them. Anele was awarded the title of 'Righteous Among the Nations' after her death.

I worked as a paediatrician in Netanya. For the last twelve years before retirement I was in charge of a large clinic in the Israeli Health Maintenance Organization. Whenever I walk along the streets of Netanya, the children who were my former patients (most of them are parents today), or their parents greet me warmly. It is touching to know they still remember me.

Netanya, Israel, 2008

17. We Grew Up Fast

Rachel (Lialia) Blumenthal

I was the only daughter of Theodor (Teddy) Blumenthal, a civil water engineer and a businessman, and Ester (Esia) Sandler. My parents were divorced before the war. I attended the private Shwabe School in Kaunas. When the Russians occupied Lithuania in 1940 it was closed down and I attended a Russian school.

The Soviet authorities started to deport to Siberia anyone whom they considered a potential threat to the Soviet regime. There were many Jews in the list of deportees on the 14 June 1941. My grandmother, Cerne-Beile, and grandfather, Rafoel Sandler, with their youngest daughter Lyka (Lea), were among them. Ironically, in this way, they were saved.

Just before war broke out there was already something in the air. Suddenly sirens would wail and we would flee from the streets looking for refuge. We were taught that this was 'manoeuvres'.

I will never forget 22 June 1941. In my childhood I was forbidden to take my cat into my bed, a rule that I always disobeyed. The cat gave birth to three kittens. That night all four slept under my blanket. At 4 a.m. I felt my mother shaking my shoulder and telling me to get up because there was a war. As I emerged from sleep, my first thought was that the cats would be discovered and that I would be scolded. I did not want to get up and said, 'Mama is it manoeuvres?' She replied, 'No, this time it is real.' Mother drew my blankets aside and the cats emerged. There was no reaction. Now completely awake, I realized that the situation was grave.

The airfield in Aleksotas had already been bombed. Mother called my father, who came to our home immediately and for the time being remained with us. We then all moved to the apartment of Anna Karnovsky, the mother of my Aunt Gita's husband. We slept there for several days.

Eventually we decided that it was safe to return home. I remember us walking along Laisves Avenue. I was instructed not to look around, preferably to look only ahead and better still to look down. However, from the corner of my eye I glimpsed that before the bridge ahead of us, a group of people were being led away by the Germans. Later I discovered that my father's cousin was among this group. Where they were taken and what became of her, we were never to know.

We returned to our apartment where our housekeeper Yadzia, a sympathetic and loyal woman, had remained. We were scared to go outside, we feared opening the door. Yadzia would go out, returning with food. Later, we Jews were to suffer terrible restrictions. We were forbidden from walking on the pavement. Then, wearing the yellow stars became obligatory. Later, food tokens were introduced and we were restricted to purchasing food only in selected places.

The first pogroms began. My uncle, Boris Blumenthal, was killed by Lithuanians at the Ninth Fort. Later his elder brother Adolph was taken away together with his 16-year-old son, Kolya. It was then announced that by 15 August all Jews had to decamp to the ghetto. All Jews had their phone lines cut off. My mother and I moved to the ghetto on 5 August; I was 10 years old. My father was invited to join the committee of the Jewish Council. He was able to arrange for us to have a two-bedroom apartment where ten people, the whole Blumenthal family, sheltered. Uncle Adolph returned to this apartment, now without his son Kolya, who had been shot dead. My uncle sank into depression. He would sit motionless and silent for hours, staring at one spot. Later he too perished, in Dachau.

The atmosphere in the ghetto was always tense. The water supply and heating had been cut off and I remember the first winter was particularly harsh and all the pipes burst. During the day, Father would be taken to the town to work in a steel plant, and there he obtained a metallic cylindrical bin. With a plank from a wooden stool he made a toilet seat. On returning from work it was father's duty to empty this bin.

There were half-built warehouses on the outskirts of the ghetto. In order to remove Jewish children from the streets so they would not draw too much attention from the Germans, the Jewish Council founded a makeshift school consisting of different faculties. I was first allocated to the Agricultural Faculty. They built allotments and took us there to clear out weeds and plant tomato seeds. Later I studied in the Tailoring Faculty where there was just one sewing machine for the whole group. I was also taken to my uncle, Samuel Kapit, a celebrated maths teacher, for classes a few times a week. In the adjacent apartment lived two sisters with exotic, unusual names: Carmela (today Carmela Heibron) and Renata. In these conditions, one's childhood somehow dissipated. We grew up fast.

Before an 'action', the official line would always be that we were simply being transferred elsewhere. We were instructed to prepare and warned to take only hand luggage. Since a handbag will not hold much, we would dress in layers, carrying our clothes on our back. I remember one appalling 'action'. We were made to assemble in Democracy Square; it was a cold day and my toes froze. We stood there all day until we were approached. Rauca, the head of the Gestapo, an enormous, pale, broad-faced man, would point with his whip either to the left or to the right. We had already passed to the 'good' side but instead of moving on, my mother remained where she was, anxious as to the whereabouts of her sister Gita with her daughter Mika (Mitchka) Karnovsky. It was only in the evening that she saw Gita with her pram, and was so relieved that they had been fortunate to escape 'selection'.

We lived on the third floor; from the window we could see the road that led uphill to the Ninth Fort. We saw how the deportees were marched the following day. By now we already knew where the route led and what the Ninth Fort signified. In one way or another, information would infiltrate the ghetto; we knew what went on in other ghettos. We knew about an upcoming 'Children's Action'.

Before the war, my mother and father had a very close Lithuanian friend called Valchunas. He was acquainted with one of the Baublys brothers; there were six brothers in all. I was entrusted to the younger brother, Sergey, who lived on the outskirts of Kaunas. Before I was sent away, Mother put a huge enamel bowl on a stool, placed me in it, and scrubbed me from head to toe, saying that from tomorrow I would have to look after myself.

I parted from my parents on the morning of 4 January 1944.

The Baublys family had a son called Petriukas; Yadzia Baubliene was expecting their second child. Yadzia's younger sister, Maryte, was also living with them, as well as Baublys' parents. I was ascribed with three different biographies: only Baublys and his parents would know my real identity; to the rest of the family I would be Lena Vorobyova, a Russian girl. I would explain that I spoke Lithuanian because my mother, Lithuanian by birth, married a Russian and had left for Russia.

Trains carrying people who were taken to work in Germany would sometimes stop in Kaunas. Many women would push their children out of the wagons in the hope that someone might foster them. In our case, I was to claim to the authorities that I was such a child. To the neighbours I was a distant relative of Yadzia's from the countryside, brought there to help Yadzia with the birth.

People had long known of the planned liquidation of the ghetto, and the inhabitants began organizing themselves and preparing hiding places, which were called '*malina*'. There was no sewage system in the ghetto; people would use toilets in their yard. There were hiding places where people had to plunge into faeces to scramble to a place where they thought the Germans would not find them.

After the 'Children's Action' the Germans arrested the Jewish policemen and attempted to extract information about the location of these hiding places. Some cracked under interrogation, but most kept quiet. In all, thirty-four policemen and representatives of other Jewish authorities of the ghetto were shot. Among the murdered, I remember well our neighbour, Liolia Aronovsky.

Since the home of the Baublys family was situated on the outskirts and the front was approaching, Mr Baublys' wife, Yadzia, decided that it was time to leave. She had some relatives who were millers in a village called Bruzhe, and we were offered a room there. Before the war we would go there to our *dacha* for vacations. The family of the millers was relatively poor and to feed us was no small task. From the millers' house we could see smoke from the direction of Kaunas. No one could understand what this meant. One of the villagers had been to the town and reported back that the ghetto was on fire.

Of all the numerous Blumenthal family, only my father survived. My mother died from typhus in Stutthof on 18 January 1945, held in the arms of the nurse Judith (Judica) Kamber.

The front was getting nearer still; at night we heard an endless rumble. Only later we discovered this was the sound of the German tanks retreating from Lithuania. We spent the last days sleeping under the concrete staircase of the miller's house, fearing we might be hit.

In a week or two, when we were assured that there was no more danger, we headed back to Kaunas. Half way there, a Russian army truck picked us up. From there I saw that the ghetto was essentially gone. All the wooden houses had been burnt down; all that remained were the brick chimneys. In the ghetto we had lived in a brick house, my mother had even hung a flowerpot where she planted onions to provide us with at least some vitamins. I saw this suspended pot crumbling apart on the sill of what had once been our home.

Those Jews who had managed to hide and survive were now returning to the town. Mr Baublys would inquire as to the whereabouts of my family. Relatives of Gita's husband, the Gudinky family, were known to have survived and I was sent to live with them.

I remember the day Gita's husband, Grisha Karnovsky, returned from Dachau. There was a loud knock on the door early one morning and since I slept on the floor in the kitchen, I got up to answer it. After two months Gita returned, still bloated from hunger. I lived with my Aunt Gita and Grisha; Mitchka and I grew up as sisters.

I remember Victory Day. We heard about the surrender on the BBC; 9 May was considered Victory Day in the Soviet Union. I remember Grisha's friend, Marcus (Mendke) Kamber, appearing in the house. He was still in his army uniform and waving a revolver. He burst on the balcony and started firing bullets in the air.

By then I already knew that my father had survived and was somewhere in Bavaria. He remained in Germany after his concentration camp was liberated. Just before the Germans had entered Kaunas, a list of individuals whom the Russians had not yet managed to exile to Siberia was found. Certain Blumenthals featured in these lists. For this reason Father chose not to return. I remember feeling so low sometimes that I would write him a letter for which I had no address. I did however occasionally receive letters from him, signed not 'Papa' but Teddy. Various people sent them from different parts of the world.

I graduated from the Physics and Maths Faculty of Vilnius

University in 1955. When Gomulka came to power in Poland, it was permitted for former Polish citizens to travel home to Poland. I arranged to marry a Polish man in order to obtain Polish papers and I left for Warsaw on 17 March 1957. From Warsaw I called my father; we couldn't speak, we just sobbed. After six and a half months I received a foreign passport and I set off for Geneva to be reunited with my father.

I recognized him immediately, though he was shorter than I had remembered. In Switzerland, my father was working for ORT. I had spoken German from childhood and so I quickly found work as an analyst and as a translator. My workplace sent me to Russia for three years, and I took the opportunity because it meant I would see my cousin Mitchka there. I retired in 1993. I am still in regular contact with Mitchka, who lives in Israel.

Winterthur, Switzerland, 2008

18. A History Never Discussed

Bluma Alkanovich (Tolochkiene), Alik Abramovich and Frida Glazman-Abramovich

BLUMA

After so many years I still cannot help but cry when I speak about my family. I was born in 1934, the eldest daughter of Mendel Alkanovich, and Rise Alkanovich-Melamed. The vast Melamed family was well known in my mother's small provincial home-town of Vievis. All of them perished during the Nazi occupation.

My younger sister Frida was born at some time between 1937 and 1939. My father worked as a clerk in a big Jewish firm and my mother was a housekeeper. When the Germans invaded Lithuania my mother urged my father to escape, but he hesitated. He did not believe that any harm would come to us at the hands of such a civilized nation as the Germans. So they stayed: my father was arrested immediately by the Lithuanians and sent to dig trenches in Kaunas. Mother used to bring him meals everyday. One day she came as usual, but no one was there. She learnt later that all the Jewish workers from this group had been shot by the Lithuanians at the Seventh Fort.

Once in the ghetto, my mother found herself alone, with two daughters to care for. At the beginning we lived with a couple with two children in the 'Small Ghetto'. After this was closed, we went to live in a wooden house with the Beiders and their three sons, Chaim, Olef (Alek) and David.

I can clearly remember the horrific 'Great Action'. It was cold, tiring and so frightening! Our family and our neighbours were all sent to the right side. That, as it appeared later, meant that we were sentenced to death. Cvania Beider, the husband of my mother's sister Mina, held a position in the *Judenrat*. He noticed that we were included in this 'selection' and managed to transfer us to the left side.

I know that we did not starve. Our resourceful mother worked outside the ghetto and always managed to obtain enough food for us.

During the 'Children's Action' my mother, Frida and I, together with Mina and Olef, hid in the wooden attic. At first we were not discovered by the Germans, although they did search in the attics. We kept very silent behind a load of garbage. But at the second round-up they came with vicious dogs, which discovered us immediately. We were all dragged from our hiding place and led by armed policemen to the van that picked up children and the elderly. For some reason – perhaps the policemen thought that Olef and I were big enough to work – they let all us go back to our home. But not so my sister Frida, who was taken away for ever.

As far as I know, all the Beiders perished in the ghetto or in the concentration camps. I searched intensively to find a trace of them among survivors, but to no avail.

Having lost Frida, my mother would not leave me alone in the ghetto, and took me with her to the factory called '*Incaras*', where I started to work as well. Without telling me, my mother found a Lithuanian woman who agreed to look for a hiding place for me. People told me later that she was actually a Jewish woman who had converted to Catholicism. This woman led many Jews across the river to hide in a bunker in the woods near Kaunas.

I was hidden in a sack among empty baskets on a cart that was bound for Kaunas to fetch bread for the ghetto. I was smuggled through the fence, transferred to another cart carrying straw and brought to a woman who, I am almost sure, was called Steffa. She took me by steam boat to Kulautuva or Birshtonas.

I was blonde, and with my looks, no one would suspect that I was Jewish. I was placed on the second floor of a country holiday home, a *dacha*. On the first floor, a Lithuanian woman and her son were on holiday. I spoke with this boy and although I could speak Lithuanian well, his mother probably suspected something, and hastily left for Kaunas with her boy the very next day. My hostess immediately sent me in the opposite direction to a remote farm. I remember a pretty place on a hill on the bank of the river. It was totally isolated, no one came there. The owners were nice to me. I remember some old women taught me to work on the spinning machine.

I stayed in this farm till autumn, when Steffa appeared. She told me, 'We are going back to Kaunas'. I was happy. I thought we were going to see my mother, but in Kaunas Steffa told me that my mother had been killed.

I learnt that after my rescue operation, the woman who had found where to hide me had organized my mother's escape to the same bunker I mentioned above. Close to the end of the war she was asked by two Latvian men to help them to hide from the Germans. She agreed and led them to the bunker. These Latvians turned out to be provocateurs. The bunker was blown up, together with all its Jewish occupants, including my mother.

For a short time I lived with Steffa. Then I was passed on to the Taft family, who at that time had three children: their son Yakov, and Matias and Riva Taft, a nephew and niece whom they adopted after the war.

From the Tafts I went to live with the Rachkovsky family, and eventually I was taken in by Naum Meriesh, my father's cousin, and Feiga Abramovich. There I grew up together with their son and daughter who had been born after the war, and Feiga's son Alik. We were one happy family.

With Naum Meriesh we went to look for Steffa. I remembered exactly where she lived. However, when we knocked at the door, a strange woman greeted us with hostility and said there was no one by the name of Steffa living there.

I graduated from Kaunas Medical School in 1959, and married a young physician, Tolochka. We have a son and two grand-children. Until my retirement I worked as a neonatal paediatrician and intensive paediatric care specialist in Lithuania.

Vilnius, September 2008

FRIDA

Alik was born on 9 May 1941 in Kaunas. His father Shlomo Abramovich moved to Kaunas from Klaipeda in a search for a work. His mother Feiga, née Kulbak, was an active member of the Lithuanian Communist Party. After the infamous Ribbentrop–Molotov Pact and the occupation of Lithuania by the USSR, she was appointed to be in charge of the big factory '*Jega*', which means 'Strength' in Lithuanian.

When the Germans invaded Lithuania, the Abramoviches and their newborn son tried to escape by foot to Russia. They were captured by Lithuanians and forced to return to Kaunas. Shlomo was arrested, but the very brave Feiga went to the Gestapo, and by some miracle succeeded in releasing him.

Shlomo and Feiga decided immediately to join the anti-fascist detachment, but first they needed to find a safe place to hide their child. While they were looking for somebody they could trust, Brone Rosenbergiene, a Lithuanian worker in the factory and her husband Jonas, a shoemaker, managed to locate their old friends the Abramovichs in the ghetto, and together they started to plan Alik's rescue.

Although Alik was not circumcised, it wasn't an option to transfer him to the Rosenberg family because their neighbours were serving in the SS. Their close friend Marcele Galvonaite was afraid to keep Alik with her for the same reason.

After an intensive search, the Rosenbergs and Marcele Galvonaite found a safe place for Alik with Jonas and Stase Statauskas in the countryside. Marcele and Jonas Statauskas came to take Alik from the ghetto gates. Alik's father (or, according to another version, a German soldier) smuggled Alik, wrapped in tatters, and gave him to the rescuers. When Alik was in safe hands, his parents joined the detachment. Shlomo was the first to escape from the ghetto. Feiga told me that she asked Chaim Elin's help to reach the detachment. Elin said, 'With your brains and energy you need nobody's assistance.' He was right, and very soon Feiga found her way to the forest.

Shortly before the liberation, Shlomo Abramovich was killed in battle, together with Yankale Levy.

The Statauskas couple paid the heaviest price for Alik's rescue. When, after the liberation, Alik's mother came to take him back, it became evident to all the villagers that Statauskas had harboured a Jewish boy. Feiga was sure it was very dangerous for the Statauskas family to stay in the village; she suggested that they should move with her to Kaunas. Sadly they refused and were killed by Lithuanian bandits, the '*Zhaliukai*' in 1946.

After the war, Feiga married Naum Meriesh, who returned from Siberia, where he had been deported with his family before the war. After finishing school, Alik went on to study at the Kaunas Polytechnic Institute, but he did not complete his studies and returned to work in the factory.

I knew Alik from the Jewish kindergarten. We became close friends during our school days and in 1964 I married him. Our son was born in 1966 and was named Solomon (Shlomo) in memory of Alik's father. It turned out that both of us were among the 'hidden children'.

Figure 39. Alik Abramovich with Stase and Jonas Statauskas, 1945. Both were killed by Lithuanian bandits for rescuing Alik. Alik died aged 50.

Before the war my parents lived in a small town, Semelishki. When the Germans entered Semelishki, where the majority of the population was Jewish, they and their Lithuanian collaborates killed every Jew they could find. My father, Shlomo Glazman, saw his parents and eldest brother Meir being shot. Later on, the whole town was set alight by the Lithuanians.

My parents, together with my maternal grandparents, fled to the forest. My mother, Katia (Kune) Glazman, née Kranik, was pregnant. I was born in a bunker in the winter of 1941/42; I actually don't know the exact data of my birth.

A childless Polish-Lithuanian couple, Urshulya and Juozas Abukauskas, agreed to take care of me. Abukauskas baptized me and I received a false birth certificate in the name of Lalia

Abukauskaite. After my grandparents died in hiding, my parents joined the detachment and fought from February 1942 till the liberation.

In 1945 my parents collected me from my adoptive mother and father, whom I loved deeply. I was scared in my biological parents' house. These 'strangers' had separated me from my beloved Urshulya and Juozas and forced me to live in a house where people talked a strange language. I could not eat and cried all the time, until Urshulya came to spend some time with our family, and eventually I became used to my biological parents. (See Figure 15: Frida Glazman is in the second row, first from right.)

In 1959 I entered the Kaunas Polytechnic Institute; I studied in the civil engineering faculty together with Ilana Kamber, Mika Karnovsky, Sarra Levin, Lyusya Borstaite and Aaron Frank. Only now do I know that all of them were also hidden children of the Kaunas Ghetto; we have never discussed this issue, neither with my schoolmates nor with my husband.

In 1972 after a long struggle against the Soviet authorities, which involved Alik's travelling to Moscow to demand visas, we emigrated to Israel. I maintained contact with Urshulya's family until our emigration in 1972; I always felt Urshulya was my mother and called her '*Mochute*' – Mummy.

In Israel I worked as a civil engineer in the Ministry of Transport. I was actively involved in almost all the bridge and road construction projects in Israel for the last three decades. Alik was an extraordinary person: talented, with an excellent memory and broad knowledge – really a walking encyclopaedia. He was a natural leader, always surrounded by a lot of friends. But some self-destructive power caused difficulties and led him to failures in his professional and family life. In 1976 we divorced.

Our son served in the Israeli Air Force. Now he works in Israel in a high-tech firm. Alik married for a second time, but died from cancer when he was only 50 years old. Mariesh's family supports his wife and twin children.

Ramat Gan, Israel, 2009

19. 8,000 Rubels for Yehuda

Pesah (Petya) Joselevich

My father Shimon was a printer by profession and owned a printing house until the Soviet regime began; my mother Lea, née Shames, helped him in the business. My sister Chana was born in 1932 and myself on 29 April 1940.

Although I remember very little of our life in the ghetto, the constant feeling of hunger and fear stayed with me for a long time. My father used to go out of the ghetto under escort to work in the printing house. My mother worked in vegetable gardens and from time to time, risking her life as she did so, she used to bring in some vegetables. Usually she came back with little frozen beetroots, which I used to call '*mamalada*', as they reminded me of the sweets known as 'marmalade'. On one occasion, Mother brought a cucumber from the vegetable garden and fed it to me. I fell ill with dysentery afterwards and she had to carry me over the bridge to the 'Small Ghetto' to see the doctor. By the time we reached him, I had already turned blue and was virtually dying. The doctor had no medicines but he gave me a direct blood transfusion using Mother's blood, and so saved me from certain death.

After miraculously surviving all the previous 'actions', during the 'Children's Action' we all hid in a tunnel which my father had already prepared beneath the cellar. On that day I can vaguely remember looking out of the window and seeing buses drive past with windows painted white.

On 27 March 1944 my father did not go out to work, but instead we all clambered into that tunnel. As a 4-year-old child I remember shouting out, because there was so little air to breathe and it was so dark and frightening. My mouth was being held shut, I think by my sister. Father stayed behind a heap of rubbish outside our hiding place. On that occasion they did not find us, but by then my parents realized that it was only a question of time before we would be taken off to our deaths.

Figure 40. Petya Joselevich with mother Lea, Yehuda and his
sister Rivka, 1945. Rivka survived the ghetto, but died after
liberation from meningitis in 1946. Yehuda lost both parents and
was adopted by Lea Joselevich.

My parents were looking for a safe shelter for us for a long
time. Eventually my father made contact with one of his pre-war
colleagues, Yulia Vitkauskiene. She got in touch with another of
father's colleagues, Pranas Vocelka, who had a Jewish wife called
Feiga in the ghetto. Mr Vocelka had already helped many people
find refuge and agreed to keep me for a while. Yulia then made
contact with Elena and Mikas Lukauskas, also printers by
profession. They lived on Green Hill and had no children of their
own. Elena was a well-known chess player, the women's
champion of Lithuania.

I was frightened of Germans and knew that we had to hide
from them. One day Father came home with an Austrian soldier,
who agreed to help carry me out of the ghetto. When I saw the
soldier in uniform I scampered away under the bed and no
amount of persuading was enough to drag me back out again. So

his first attempt to get me out of the ghetto failed. Mother decided that I should be given a sleeping pill, and after that I was hidden in a sack of hay, loaded on a cart and it was agreed that the woman driving the cart would take me out through the gate. Just as we were going past the guards, a piece of straw tickled my nose and I sneezed: the cart driver turned back and threw the sack down near our house. On the next occasion I was given a double dose of sleeping pills and I was dead to the world as I slept. All I remember next is being on the sofa in Vocelka's home.

From there I was sent on to join the Lukauskas family. All those who helped rescue me did so, risking their lives, out of kindness, not for payment. How they managed to get my sister Chana out of the ghetto I do not know. Finally, she turned up too at the house of the Lukauskas family.

I still have a letter our mother wrote to my future rescuers, whom she did not know at the time. Elena Lukauskiene eventually returned it to me after the war. My mother had written:

> To strangers, who are now close dear friends!
>
> I do not have enough words to express my gratitude to you for your humane deed. We are wretched, but at the same time happy in the knowledge that at this time, when the human race is behaving in a bestial way, good and warm-hearted people have come forward to save our children... We are not religious ourselves and it is not important to us in which religion our children are brought up...Death is no longer frightening for us, because we know and shall remember that our children are in safe hands. One last request: if we do not survive, please tell our children, when they grow up, that their parents were killed by beasts in human form and that they were honest, hard-working people, who lived only for their children...May fate be more merciful to all of you than to us. Our gratitude to you knows no end...

At that time I only spoke Yiddish and it was not easy for the Lukauskas family to cope with me. Towards the end of the war the Germans started taking Lithuanians to make them serve in their army, and one day they turned up at the Lukauskas home.

Mikas Lukauskas ran to the attic to avoid mobilization. At the time the family had a large bulldog. Elena threw me on to the bed and told me to say nothing or just to call out 'Mama, Mama!' She put my sister on the couch and said that she was ill. The Germans were terrified of illness and gave her a wide berth. The Germans were about to go into the kitchen, when the dog threw itself at them. They wanted to shoot it but Elena Lukauskiene stood between them and the dog and said, 'Shoot me!' The Germans went off after that, saying, 'Don't get involved with this crazy woman.' Apart from my sister and myself, Lukauskas was also sheltering a Ukrainian POW, whom we called Opanas, in their attic. The entrance to the attic was via the kitchen. If they had found the prisoner and Mikas, we would all have perished.

On the first day after the liberation, Mikas Lukauskas smacked me and said, 'Cry as much as you want, but I'm now going to teach you to speak Lithuanian come what may!' Before that all I had ever come out with in response to his requests to speak Lithuanian was three words of Yiddish, '*Ich vil nicht!*' ('I don't want to!'). His insistence helped, and I instantly started talking Lithuanian.

Immediately after Kaunas had been liberated, father's brother, David Joselevich, went seeking for surviving relatives. He had been hidden during the occupation by a Lithuanian woman. When David came to fetch us, Elena Lukauskiene cried because she considered us part of her family and was sad to part with us.

My uncle David was also looking for the children of his sister, my aunt Masha. Masha Joselevich-Garunas and Bentsel Garunas had two sons: Hirsh born in 1932, and Meir (Meika) in 1936. Before the war their family had been on the NKVD list for deportation to Siberia. When preparing for their departure they had stamped all the items of clothing which they were planning to take with them. Eventually the Soviets failed to deport them.

Meika was taken out of the ghetto twice in a sack of potatoes. The first time he started crying near the gate and had to be brought back in again; the second time he was given sleeping pills and the escape went according to plan. He had been entrusted to a Lithuanian family for payment, but the very same day they turned the little boy out into the street and Germans picked him up. The people who saw him being arrested tried to convince the Germans that the little boy was Polish (he spoke Polish fluently), but the

Germans checked, and took him away. After the war David managed to find the Lithuanian who had abandoned Meir to his fate. He also found Meir's garments which the parents had stamped with his name. The Lithuanian confessed that he had turned in the small boy and he was eventually convicted.

The eldest brother Hirsh was taken to Auschwitz with 130 other Jewish children from the Kaunas Ghetto; only twenty of them survived. He was liberated by the Americans at the end of the war.

My aunt Masha had been killed by a Soviet bomb in Poland after the Stutthof concentration camp had already been liberated. Bentsel Garunas survived Dachau but died a year later, and Hirsh was taken in by another uncle, Moshe Joselevich, who had also returned from concentration camps. Hirsh died in Vilnius in 1987, aged 55. His wife Lyuba and daughter Masha Brener (Garun) live in Israel.

After my uncle found us, I was sent to a Jewish kindergarten and my sister started attending school. I remember that we, the children at the kindergarten, were all fearful. On one occasion there was a fire near the kindergarten and some firemen turned up in helmets, which were trophies captured from the Germans. The children were terrified at the sight and it took a long time to calm us down.

A few days before the ghetto was disbanded our father was taken out to work with the rest of his team; no one ever saw any member of that team again. Mother was transferred to Stutthof and took part in the 'death march'. In the end she fell ill there with typhus and was abandoned in a hut to die. Thankfully she had not fallen ill on the way, because the sick had been shot on the spot during the march. Soviet soldiers found her in that hut and delivered her to an army hospital, where she took a long time to recover. Mother returned to Kaunas a good deal later and took us back from my uncle's flat.

For a long time after the war, in nightmares I saw different pictures from our life in the ghetto. Whenever I described the nightmare to my mother she would say to me, 'This is how it was and how it really happened.'

Apart from my sister and myself, Mother also took in an orphan boy, Yehuda Edelman. My mother had met a distant relative of hers in the Stutthof camp and they had promised each other that whoever survived would take care of the other's children. Yehuda, born in 1939, had been taken in by a shoemaker, who had a cobbler's shop in a basement on Laisves Avenue, where he and his family and little Yehuda, renamed Algis, lived. My mother found Yehuda and brought him back home after paying Liuda Kibartiene, the shoemaker's wife, 8,000 rubles, an enormous sum of money in those days, in return for the cost of looking after him during the occupation. To be able to do that, Mother had sold our house in Viekshniai.

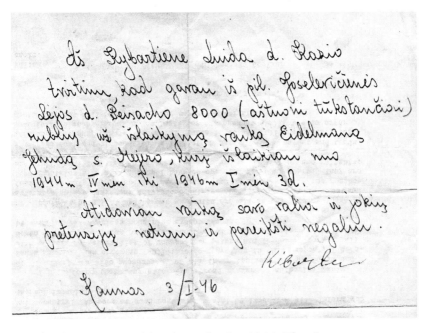

Figure 41. 8,000 rubles for Yehuda, 1946. The document says that Mrs Kibartiene Liuda received from Mrs Lea Joselevich 8,000 rubles for caring for Jehuda Eidelman, son of Meir from April 1944 till January 1946 and has no more demands.

Mother now had to look after three children on her own. She moved to Vilnius and worked there as a proof-reader in the publishing house, from which she had been dismissed as an 'unreliable' element. Next she found a job in the printing house. The four of us were living in one room attached to the printing works. We children slept in one bed and sat on wooden boxes instead of chairs, we had no furniture.

Mother was a very strong woman. Despite all that she had suffered and lost, she kept her spirits up and never lost her will to live. She earned her livelihood and looked after us as well as she could; we had clothes on our backs and did not go hungry. Yehuda and I were going to kindergarten, while my sister Chana went to school, where she did well at her studies.

Mother knew that Yehuda had relatives in the United States. She managed to find his uncle, the well-known Rabbi Soloveichik. In 1946 Mother paid a Polish woman, who undertook to take Yehuda to Poland and send him on from there to the United States. I remember how we went to see Yehuda off at the station and how he left with this woman sitting in a goods truck. He just disappeared, there was not a squeak out of him until Mother received a letter from a children's home in Prague, where Yehuda had ended up for some reason. She managed to contact some people in Israel, and via them Rabbi Soloveichik. Eventually, Yehuda reached his uncle that same year; it turned out that when she had sent him off to Poland, Mother had sewn her address and the address of the uncle into the lining of Yehuda's coat. Mother learnt that Yehuda had arrived safely when she received an encoded telegram from the Rabbi. She gave a sigh of relief after that, knowing that the promise given to Yehuda's mother had been kept.

Unfortunately our tragedies did not end; in 1946 my sister Chana died from meningitis.

After finishing school I naively tried to gain a place at the Leningrad Polytechnic, but naturally I did not get past the admissions committee, I was after all an 'unreliable element'. I graduated from the Vilnius Polytechnic Institute as a mechanical engineer. In 1966 I married a young physician, Vita Israelyte. My mother died in 1987. In 1990 I went with my wife and two daughters to Israel. Both of us are working here in our professions.

Yehuda Edelman studied to become a rabbi, like his uncle. He has nine children; one of them lives in Kiryat Sefer in Israel. Whenever he comes to visit his son, we meet up with him and remember old times. Yehuda says that he no longer remembers anything connected with the war. He considers that my mother saved his life and there is a good deal of truth in that.

Hulon, Israel, 2008

PART THREE

PLACES OF REFUGE

20. Scalded by Borscht

Yaakov Taft

My father Leib was a paediatrician in Kaunas, and most of his patients were Lithuanian children. My mother, Hanna Taft, was originally from the small town of Shakiai. She was a dentist. I was born in 1940. The family, although not religious, observed some Jewish traditions. The spoken language in our family was Yiddish, and my parents strongly supported the Zionist movement. I was the only child in this happy family and we lived in a very comfortable, spacious apartment. Many years later I found out that my parents owned a supermarket and a bakery, as well as my father's big private clinic.

My father had many brothers and sisters, who all perished during the occupation. Some were killed by the Germans but most of them were murdered by the Lithuanian collaborators. My mother's relatives were exiled to Siberia just before the war, so the Soviets, ironically, had saved them from the fascists.

In the ghetto our family found itself in a small flat which we shared with more than thirty other people. There was one advantage to this situation: together it was easier to ensure there was a food supply. My very first memory is of a huge pot, where borscht, a soup made from beetroot, was being cooked. I liked it so much that once I fell down into this pot full of hot soup: I suffered burns over 50 per cent of my body. I remember this vividly; I was treated with bandages soaked in fish oil, but my general condition was very poor, and I very nearly died. I can remember the painful procedure of changing my dressing and how my parents pleaded with me, 'Please do not cry, Yakov. If you cry, Germans will come and kill you.' And I would not cry, suffering in a silence.

My grandparents were burned alive before the 'Great Action', while my parents watched their death helplessly. During this 'action' our family was sent to the 'bad' line: my parents knew this meant they were going to be killed. In despair my mother pleaded with the SS officer in her fluent German, 'My son is

dying, let me take care of him and let him die in my arms.'
Probably something in my mother's voice touched the officer
who shouted, '*Raus!* Get out of my sight!' and pushed her to the
other line. Mother pointed out my father, 'This is my husband, he
is a children's doctor and he treats the child. We cannot manage
without him.' It is beyond belief, but this officer let my father
pass to the 'good' line as well. How fate plays with people: my
condition saved our family from being killed. A scar from these
burns will remind me forever of what had happened to me.

Every morning my father with a team of others was led to
Aleksotas. On his way to work and back he took every opportunity to barter food in exchange for clothes and other utilities. My
parents realized that miracles could not be counted on forever, so
they began to look for a place to hide me. One day my father
slipped away from the work brigade and went to see a priest
named Bronius Paukshtys whom he had met before the war.

Figure 42. Bronius
Paukshtys, the
Catholic priest, who
was active in the
rescue of many Jews.
Photo courtesy of
Y. Taft.

'Kind Sir', he appealed to Paukshtys, 'all my life I treated and saved Lithuanian children, please help me this time to save my own son.' The priest, who was a very tall man, looked down at my father and warned, 'But your son would become a Christian'. 'He can become anything, even a Chinaman, as long as he remains alive', was Father's reaction.

I remember my arrival at the priest's house because, strangely enough, there was a fox tied to his porch. The priest's servant took me and later I stayed at the monastery located in Kaunas until the liberation under the name of Juozas Timoshaitis. There I was kept in a barn together with pigs, hens and other animals. I spent most of the time eating and sleeping with my new 'neighbours'. There was not enough food, I felt constant hunger and I remember taking some food from the animals. Ever since then I have been fond of pets, especially dogs. I later bred them in my house and was even awarded some prizes.

I do not remember if I was fed, washed and cleaned by somebody. I never cried and would stretch my arm and beg for food when adult people occasionally appeared in the barn. Since that time I cannot throw away food, especially bread, and we never waste it.

I learned to pray and sometimes helped the priest during mass. I had no contact with my parents at all throughout the time I spent in the monastery. Later on, the German authorities recognized that I was forced at the age of 3 or 4 to perform labour (a Jew serving in the church!). However, by German law only persons who were engaged in labour from the age of 5 and upwards were entitled to receive compensation, so I got nothing.

During my stay in the monastery I also learned to be afraid of people. Some came to the monastery, probably looking for their children; I remember when one Jew appeared, I ran away, I did not know if I was allowed to speak or even to be seen at all. I did not know, or I had forgotten, that I was a Jewish child. I was like a small animal, some kind of Mowgli.

My parents managed to escape from the ghetto and found shelter with a Lithuanian family in a village, where they carried out all kinds of agricultural work and survived. When they came, I did not run away but was hiding behind a corner, peeking at what was going on. Mother saw me immediately and started to cry, but I refused to approach her. My father took out a pocketknife and with this trick he succeeded to persuade me to come. Since this episode I am very fond of all kinds of pocketknives: maybe I even chose my profession as a physician in the field of surgery because of scalpels.

After the war my parents started to work and our life settled down. In 1946 my younger brother was born. Paukshtys, the priest who saved me, was involved in the rescue of many other Jews, five of whom I know personally; among them are my two cousins, Matias (Matetiahu) and Riva Tafts. They were actually my cousins twice over: our fathers were brothers and our mothers were sisters.

Figure 43. 'Hidden' Jewish boys after the war. From left to right: Moshe Parasonis (with a ball; Rina Joels' husband), Matetiahu Taft, Gidon Sheftel and Yakov Taft (all three were hidden children), Gudzinsky and Solomon (Saly) Taft, 1947 or 1948.

Matias was born in 1938 and Riva in 1934. Father Paukshtys organized a hiding place for them with a Lithuanian family, but the neighbours of this family betrayed them. The children were caught and transported to the Ninth Fort. They told us how Lithuanian policemen were mocking and teasing them, singing a song about how the poor children would be killed. By some miracle, I do not know the details, Matias and Riva survived. Their parents were killed and they came to live with us as our brother and sister.

Paukshtys was arrested by the Soviets and sent to Siberia. It appeared that besides the Jews, after the war he had hidden Lithuanian partisans known as *'Zaliukai'* ('forest brothers'). My parents sent money and parcels to Paukshtys till 1956. Before the war my mother had studied in high school with Justinas Paleckis, Chairman of the Presidium of the Supreme Soviet of the Lithuanian SSR. She went to see him, and asked that Paukshtys should be allowed to return to Lithuania. She succeeded in her mission and Paukshtys was released and came home. Paukshtys was a very talented and educated person and, according to the 'Voice of America', he could have become archbishop of Lithuania, but he returned from Siberia in very poor health.

After the war I attended the Jewish kindergarten, the Jewish school and later a Lithuanian school. It was not customary to talk about the occupation and the ghetto in our family, although a sense of the Holocaust was always in the air.

In 1967 I graduated from Vilnius University Medical School, where I often heard, 'It is a pity to spend state money on your education. You all (Jews) will eventually go to Palestine.' Matias became an electrical technician and Riva graduated from the Faculty of Chemistry in Vilnius University. Matias came to Israel and was successful there; Riva with her family went to Canada. Unfortunately both of them died comparatively young from cancer.

I married in 1961 and my wife Shulamith is a physician as well. During one of the priest Paukshtys' spells in hospital he was in a state of clinical death and my wife resuscitated him successfully. So the circle was closed in some way: Paukshtys organized my rescue, and my wife saved his life. Unfortunately very soon after this event, Paukshtys passed away.

Our family had always thought about moving to Israel and as soon as it became possible we applied for permission. In 1972 we landed in Tel Aviv with our two sons. Almost immediately we started to work as doctors. I served in the Yom Kippur war as a physician and my division reached the Suez Canal. Our youngest daughter was born in Israel. All our children fulfilled their regular service in the Army and are officers; our daughter Orit served as a paramedic. In 1996 during the terrorist action in Kfar Darom she was wounded, but did not leave the battlefield and went on helping other wounded soldiers. She was awarded the Medal of Bravery for her actions.

Here in Israel we, a group of people who were saved by Paukshtys, applied to Yad Vashem and consequently Paukshtys was honoured with the title 'Righteous Among the Nations', and a tree in his memory was planted in the garden in Jerusalem.

The cause of the Holocaust is very emotive for me. I will never go to Germany and do not spend my small German pension, leaving the money for my grandchildren's education.

Jerusalem, Israel, 2008

21. Many Rescuers of One Little Girl

Rosian Bagriansky-Zerner

I often wonder how it would have been had the Second World War never touched my life. My father, Paul Bagriansky, was partner in Ratner and Bagriansky, an international wool import-export business. He had a law degree, was a Lithuanian officer, and a good soccer player. His father, Solomon, owned the first electric flower mill in Lithuania, in Prienai, and a three-storey multi-apartment building at 3 Kestuchio Street in the centre of Kaunas. Dad's Latvian mother, Amalia, was the one who taught him German, in addition to the Lithuanian, Russian and Yiddish, which he spoke fluently. That is how he could communicate with my mother, Gerta Chason, born in Königsberg; she spoke only German and French when he married her. She had studied piano in Paris, and she met her future husband during a stopover to see a friend in Lithuania. It was love at first sight. Mother celebrated her hundredth birthday on 8 August 2008 in the USA, where we have lived since 1951.

Figure 44. Paul Bagriansky and Rosian Bagriansky-Zerner, c. 1938.

My maternal grandparents, Julius (Judel) and Anna Chason, as well as my aunts Bella, Henia, and Uncle Fredy, emigrated to Palestine the day after I was born; they had hoped that we would all live there together. However, my father was not a Zionist, and hoped that all the rumours about the Germans were false. In Kaunas we lived a privileged life: servants, a 1935 Ford, vacations at the seashore and in the countryside. When the danger of the reality ahead struck it was too late to leave, even though Father had purchased land in Canada.

My grandfather Solomon was tortured and murdered within the first weeks of the occupation, as was my grandmother Amalia, who forgot to wear the required yellow star. A neighbour denounced her as she was standing in a line to purchase bread.

We were herded into the Kaunas Ghetto with whatever possessions we could arrange to take. I remember that Mother did not know just what would be useful, and took a huge ficus plant that shortly thereafter died in the freezing ghetto quarters. Our home there was a room that contained four beds; Rivka Shmukler (later Oshorovich) lived with us. There was also a table and that ficus, for a while. And one of the coldest winters on record and no heat! I recall that a glass of water would freeze before I could drink it, and Mother would peel potatoes that seemed always frozen.

The placard declaring we were workers and the *Lebenschein* (the official paper that proved it) that our family obtained through Mother's tireless efforts saved our lives in the 'Great Action'. However, my parents did not wait for the upcoming 'Children's Action' and decided they had to take a chance and escape. I would be the first since I was in most danger. I was 6 years old and children were dispensable. Painstakingly, at great risk to their own lives, my parents dug a hole under the barbed wire, and timed the guards and lights so that they could safely push me through that hole.

Almost miraculously I found myself on the other side of the barbed wire where Brone Budreikaite waited for me. Brone was my father's secretary and the sister-in-law of Jacob Gens, the head of the Vilnius Ghetto. She kept me with her only a short time since I was crying so much, but she did visit me at the farm of Lyda Goluboviene, where I was hiding, and had me call her 'Mummy'. Apparently, the story was that I was her illegitimate child and that she was keeping me in the countryside because of her shame. Margarete Holzman, who with her mother Helene were also my rescuers, joined Brone in some of the rare visits. My wartime name was Irena Budreikaite.

As with most other Jewish children who were hidden, my places of refuge needed to be changed whenever the situation became dangerous. I hid in barns, woods, on top of old Lithuanian stone stoves, and pretended to be who I was not. My other rescuers were Natasha (Natalija) Fugalevichiute, Natasha (Natalija) Melioranska whom we called Pavlasha, Vitautas (Pavel) Kaunetskas and Stefania Andriuniene, who did not know that I was Jewish when I was hiding at the orphanage which she headed. In that orphanage there were nuns who betrayed me and a priest who saved my life.

There were people who hid me for a night, who baptized me when they knew I was Jewish, who pretended not to know when they knew. The main rescuers are now listed as 'Righteous among the Nations' at Yad Vashem; they all risked their lives and through this act of moral courage became transformed from ordinary to extraordinary individuals.

After the war my parents sent packages and I returned to Lithuania to thank them, but I do not know if one can ever thank rescuers the right way or enough. How does one thank for giving life? I know I will always feel deficient, that my gratitude, although boundless, was never expressed as it should be.

The miracle was that my father, my mother and I survived as an intact family. Few children were reunited with both parents after the war. My father was able to escape the Kaunas Ghetto from his work brigade and went to the Vilnius Ghetto where Jacob Gens put him in charge of food distribution before my father became a partisan. My mother escaped the Kaunas Ghetto and joined my father and then went into hiding after Dad left. She actually visited me once in Kulautuva at Lyda's farm where I learned how to churn butter, picked apples, milked cows and was as helpful with the farm as a child could be. She brought me the only real toy I remember from those years: a doll she made from rags with clothes knitted from yarn remnants. I treasured that doll for many years.

After the war my parents intended to go to Palestine. With false papers we crossed into Poland, continued through Czechoslovakia and Hungary, to Austria, which was then divided, to a holding camp for displaced persons from which we had hoped to find a bus that would take us to the ships that left for Palestine. But it was not to happen, as the buses were no longer going. So my parents decided to leave for Italy.

We arrived in Milan in 1945, just after Mussolini and his mistress were hung in Piazza Loreto; the scaffolding was still on display. We slept on stone floors at the Jewish Community Centre at 5 Via Unione. Meals were whatever was available and we had no possessions, but we did have our lives.

Soon enough, my father was providing for us once more. Again we had a housekeeper and a chauffeur for Dad's Mercedes. My brother Joachim was born in Italy. I enrolled in the first grade at the Jewish Community School at the age of 10, my first formal schooling, without knowing the language. But I was not alone. So many displaced children of all ages were there together, beginning a new life.

I also entered an accelerated school at the *Brera* where I managed to squeeze three years of schooling into one. Mother then had me accepted as one of the first foreigners ever to join the Ballet School of La Scala. Somewhere in between, I lived in the village of Avigliano in a *Hachschara*-style environment that prepared us for Israel and fighting with the *Haganah*. I remember vividly the Israeli songs, dances and the pea patch that I tended in our vegetable farm. I almost died there of scarlet fever just before the group went to Israel; my father's chauffeur picked me up in the Mercedes to drive me back to Milan. The *chalutzim* just gawked!

When the Korean War broke out, my parents decided to emigrate to the United States. The USA has been good to me and has given me the choices in life I may not have had elsewhere. I managed to graduate from Barnard College, married and divorced, had two sons and now have four grandchildren. I did not look back. I was told to forget the past and live life to the fullest. I followed this advice until the year 2000 when I was compelled to reconcile myself to my past and reconnect with my childhood. I travelled to Lithuania to retrace my past. I have lived the last eight years rediscovering myself within the history of the Holocaust and giving back to the survivor community in the spirit of gratitude. I am one of the fortunate ones. I am alive!

Newton MA, USA, 2008

22. A Childhood of Orphanages

Liuba (Lyusya) Borstaite

In 1924 my father, Friedrich Borst, a German by birth, adopted the Jewish faith and married Lea Nemanuncaite, born in the small town of Seshkiai. In 1930 my parents built a big house in the Shanchiai neighbourhood, Kaunas, where they owned a bakery. There were four children in our family: Ida (1925), Leon (1927) now known as Arie Borst, Frida (1931) and myself, Lyusya, born on 1 June 1941.

In 1940 the Germans had ordered all their citizens to return to Germany. Knowing what Jews might expect there, my parents applied for and received their Lithuanian citizenship. None of my mother's relatives survived the war. In one of the first round-ups, my aunt Chaya Rachoviciene and her two daughters, Rachel and Riva, were shot in the Ninth Fort. Mother's two nephews, sons of her brother, who had died before the war, served in the Soviet Army and were killed in battles.

After Kaunas had been occupied by the Germans, my parents were forced to move to the ghetto. My uncles on Father's side heard about it, arrived from Germany and obtained permission for the whole family to live outside the ghetto, on condition that there would be no complaints from the neighbours. First of all my father was allowed to leave, and then the whole family.

When rumours started spreading through Kaunas that families with even one Jewish parent were beginning to disappear, my parents decided to send us, the children, into hiding. Ida was a blonde, so she was hidden in Kaunas. Frida, given the name Grazina Baniavichiute, was entrusted to a Karaim family in Shauliai. The real Grazina's mother, Ona Baniavichiene, had provided my mother with her daughter's papers.

Leon was sent to an acquaintance of our parents, Mr Kavaliauskas, a peasant, where he worked as a shepherd. I was transferred to a family in Panemune. No one visited me there until the liberation came. Unfortunately, I never met my rescuers after the war, and I do not know their names.

Father died in 1943 from a stroke, according to Leon, or after an operation to remove a brain tumour, according to Ida. Mother was taken back to the ghetto, probably because someone had informed on her. She met her end there. In 1944 Ida was somehow issued a document to the effect that she was a Lithuanian, and she left for Austria since it was too dangerous to stay in Lithuania with false papers.

Figure 45. Lea Borst, Lyusya Borstaite's mother, probably close to her death, winter 1943–44.

After the war we all were returned to our family house in Kaunas. However, the house was requisitioned by the Soviets, so we lived on our own in one room on the second floor of the house. Leon was only 16, Frida was 13 and I was three and a half. When an orphanage for Jewish children was set up, Leon sent me to live there, while he and Frida, with the help of the Irgun, left for Palestine. It was a long and difficult journey: Poland, orphanage in Italy, Cyprus and an unsuccessful attempt to reach Palestine in 1947 – their ship was turned back by the British authorities. They reached Israel only in 1948.

Our parents had previously bought land in Haifa, as they had been planning to move there from Lithuania, but were unable to set off in time. Leon had managed to preserve papers regarding the land purchase, which he took with him to Palestine, and was thus able to establish his right of ownership to the land in question.

Leon travelled from Israel to Lithuania with all his extended family in 2006. We visited our parents' abandoned house and a manor where Leon was hidden. The owner of the manor had emigrated from Lithuania before it was released by the Russians. The house burned down several years ago, and nobody came to claim ownership of the manor, consequently Leon knows nothing about his rescuers' fate. Frida died in Israel when she was only 34 years old; her children and grandchildren live in Israel.

Ida returned to Kaunas in 1945, but with her husband, Benya Zhemaitis, emigrated to Israel in 1969. I lived in the Jewish Orphanage until it was closed down. I was sent to the Lithuanian orphanage in Marijampole, and then to the Russian orphanage near Vilnius. After completing my school studies in 1958, I was offered the chance to go and live on a Soviet collective farm, a *kolhoz*, but I turned it down.

I was then given a travel voucher to a small town to earn my living as an ordinary construction worker. I did various kinds of manual work there, before gaining a place to study in the Polytechnic Institute in Kaunas. I did not enter the Institute immediately after I graduated from the high school. My teacher told me after graduation exams that there was no sense in my continuing to study: 'The government had spent enough money on your education', she said. 'It is time now to pay your debts to the country by productive work.' I am sure now this decision was made on account of my ethnicity.

Figure 46. Jewish School in Kaunas 1947–48. First line: first from left: Lyusya Borstaite (white dress); third: Izya Brainin?; third from right: Dora Frumanaite? Second line: teachers: Yehuda and Sheinale Gertner and Elena Hackelis and next to her Rina Zupovich-Kaplan. Third line: first from left: Leiba Aronovich?; second: Simon Kaplan (hidden child); third: Meir Rabinovich; first from right: J. Gitlin (Hasia Aronaite's future husband). Top line: second from left: Zvika Melemedovich (hidden child); third: Josef Parasonis; fifth: Misha Langevich (white shirt); seventh: Boris Dvogovsky; ninth: Cilia Segal (hidden child).

Yakov Zilberg once asked me if I had experienced any anti-Semitism: certainly I did. This is why I had forgotten Yiddish, although I spent three years in the Yiddish school; now I could probably only recall this language under hypnosis. I learned to pronounce my 'R's 'properly', and not in a Jewish way. I deliberately did not make friends, since I was always expecting someone to shout 'Bloody Jew!' during any argument, and tell me what cowards we Jews are, and how we add babies' blood to *matza*. Only in the Institute, where lots of my classmates appeared to be Jewish, did I make friends, hear positive things about Jews and stopped feeling ashamed of being Jewish.

After graduating, I did quite well working in the Institute for Town Planning in Vilnius, and was put in charge of a team of construction engineers. I retired a couple of years ago. I now live alone in a small apartment; I set great store by this place of my own, after all those years spent living in orphanages and hostels. This is probably why I did not emigrate to Israel, where my friends and close relatives live.

Vilnius, Lithuania, 2008

23. Will You Be My Mama?

Estera Elinaite

My grandfather, Benjaminas Kormanas, was a well-known lawyer in Lithuania. My paternal grandfather, Leiseris Elinas, was an outstanding figure in the Kaunas cultural scene. He established the Jewish Public Library, and 'Elin's library' became an integral part of the cultural life of Lithuania's Jews.

My father, Mejeris Elinas (1910–2000), after completing his education at the Kaunas Hebrew Gymnasium, went on to Germany, where he trained in the Civil Engineering Faculty of the Polytechnic Institute in Darmstadt. After he returned to Kaunas in 1935, he continued to work actively as both an engineer and writer. His stories and articles were published in literary collections and in the Jewish periodical press, and his anti-fascist publications and speeches were greeted with an enthusiastic response in Palestine. In 1939 he was sent a certificate entitling him to enter Palestine, but he was not prepared to leave his family in Lithuania behind.

An attractive and musically talented former classmate of Mejeris Elinas, Busia Kormanaite (1910–2006), was to become his wife in 1935. (See Figure 15: Busia Elin is in the 4th line, 1st from right.) She had graduated from the Prague Academy of Music and after returning to Lithuania had devoted herself to performing and teaching music. I, Esther Yellin (Estera Elinaite), was born on 9 September 1940 in Kaunas.

The attempt by the Elinas-Kormanas family to escape from Lithuania after the German invasion to the USSR failed: the refugees were surrounded by German troops, and locked up in a district prison, where they expected that they would soon face the firing squad. But because of his work as a lawyer, Benjaminas Kormanas knew the men in charge of that particular prison. He managed to get his family released on condition that they went back to Kaunas.

On 15 August 1941 my family and I found ourselves behind the barbed wire of the ghetto. For any person with common sense it was obvious by this time what fate awaited all the inmates of the ghetto, without exception. It was not, however, in keeping with the spirit of the Elinas-Kormanas family to reconcile itself to the situation in which it found itself and passively wait for the end.

On 31 December 1941, the AKO (*Antifaschistische Kampforganisation*, 'Anti-fascist underground organization') was founded, led by my uncle, Chaim Elinas, who was to become a legendary hero. One of the important tasks of this organization was to establish contacts with people on the other side of the barbed wire. A duty taken on by my mother was to seek out people who were not indifferent to the fate of the Jews and possessed sufficient courage to hide children, who were secretly taken out of the ghetto.

Figure 47. Chaim Yellin, a commander of the Kaunas Ghetto anti-fascist resistance, 1943. Reproduced here courtesy of M. Musel.

Mother herself crawled through the barbed-wire fence of the ghetto on more than one occasion. Her Aryan appearance helped her to conceal her Jewish origin. Once on the other side of the fence, my mother would remove her yellow stars and boldly walk through the streets of occupied Kaunas and its suburbs. This was a considerable feat in itself, because in the town where she had spent her youth and started out on her teaching career, there was a real danger that my mother might become the victim of some Lithuanian collaborator and end up in the hands of the Gestapo.

One frosty morning in December 1941, Chaim came hurrying into the house, as always in order to further some new conspiratorial plan. He was dressed on that occasion as the peasant Vladas, one of the roles he used to assume in those grim days. He reported that the atmosphere in the ghetto was full of anxiety and that people were expecting the Germans to embark on some new, as yet unspecified activity that very day. 'Busia, are you ready?' he asked. 'Of course I am', she replied.

Mother quickly dressed, threw a warm coat round me, her 12-month-old daughter, and carried me as she accompanied Chaim, while he cautiously made his way towards the ghetto fence. They could hear warning shots in the distance, but what frightened them most of all was the deep snow on both sides of the fence: the footprints they would leave behind them could give away their escape attempt. There was no time, however, for any long deliberation. Choosing his moment carefully, Chaim lifted up the barbed wire so that mother and child could make their way through to the other side of the fence.

After waiting till dawn in a small church not far from the ghetto, Mother set off with me to the address she had been given by Chaim. The house in the attic of which Mother was to go into hiding was opposite the German commandant's office. Chaim was convinced that this hideout would be safe, since nobody would imagine anyone would seek shelter right opposite the HQ of the occupying forces. It was in that flat that I took my first steps.

It was extremely difficult to remain in the same place for a long time; we kept on having to change our refuge. We were taken in by the Pranavichius family, and later by that of the shoemaker Apuokas. At the same time, Mother, on instructions from

Chaim, was continuing to establish contacts with prominent representatives of the Lithuanian intelligentsia. After a relatively short time, it was clear that it would not be possible to find a safe hiding place for me in the long term. Mother returned with me to the ghetto. On 9 September 1943 our family celebrated my third birthday. It was a charming occasion, lovingly organized by Mother for children in the ghetto, possibly the last such party in their short lives.

After the deportation of about 2,700 Jews to the labour camps in Estonia on 26 October 1943, Mother made a last attempt to take me out of the ghetto. After hesitating for a long time, she decided to turn to the family of the outstanding Lithuanian painter and composer, Mikalojus Konstantinas Chiurlionis. It was becoming increasingly dangerous by then to leave the ghetto and move about the town. After reaching her destination, on this occasion without mishap, Mother knocked at the door of the house of the Chiurlionis-Zubovas family, in one of the beautiful central districts of Kaunas.

The widow of Mikalojus Chiurlionis, Sofija Chiurlioniene-Kimantaite, the Lithuanian writer and a major public figure, lived in that house along with the family of her daughter, the writer Danute Chiurlionyte-Zuboviene, her husband, the architect and architectural historian Vladimiras Zubovas, and their young children Dalyte (1939) and Kastytis (1940). The family proved very understanding and sympathetic. Danute even apologized for giving us such a modest room! Many representatives of Lithuania's Jewry are grateful to the Chiurlionis-Zubovas family for their gift of life. Their fearless behaviour was to set an example for the service of all that is good and of justice, which they have also extolled in their creative work.

Vladimiras Zubovas constantly rode through rural settlements and villages in the Kaunas region, searching for safe places where fugitives from the ghetto might be able to go into hiding. He was on friendly terms with the paediatrician and director of the 'Lopselis' orphanage, Petras Baublys, who, after arranging with great difficulty for the baptism of Jewish children in Catholic churches and using forged papers, succeeded in registering them as foundlings. Mother was able to get news back to Chaim to the effect that Dr Baublys was ready to accept several children from the ghetto.

In the course of his work as an architectural historian, Vladimiras Zubovas had made a wide range of contacts among members of the clergy. In 1943 Teofilius Matulionis was appointed bishop of the Kaishiadorys diocese, and in April was put in charge of the affairs of the episcopate in general. These circumstances were to have a direct bearing on the events concerning my rescue. On instructions from Bishop Matulionis, it was decided that I should be hidden in the Benedictine Convent in Kaunas. The care of me was to be entrusted to Sister Angélé (Agota Misiunaite). Danute and Vladimiras Zubovas pushed the pram containing me through the streets of occupied Kaunas and, at some distance behind them, my mother followed.

In a letter sent to V. Zubovas by Bishop Jonas Jonys, who often used to visit the convent, he wrote, 'We were enraptured by the beauty, alertness, suppleness and vitality of this child. Sister Angélé took great delight in the little girl, used to carry her about, tell her fairy tales and put her to bed in her own room … Sister Angélé remembered that at the moment of parting with her daughter, Estera's mother wept bitterly and kissed the girl, and all the nuns, witnessing the scene, cried as well. When she left, Estera wiped away her tears before long and started playing the piano, despite hardly being able to reach the keyboard.'

The same evening, when I was put in Sister Angélé's bed, the German police knocked at the door of the convent. I was hidden in the attic, but the Germans did not enter the convent on that occasion and, after making a fuss, went away. The nuns realized that it was unsafe to keep me there. Wrapped in a sheepskin coat like a baby doll, I was taken in a horse-drawn farm cart to Chiobishkis' children's home, close to Kaishiadorys, which was under the aegis of the Benedictine Sisters.

By this time there were five little girls and boys of Jewish origin among the children in that orphanage (see Figure 16: Estera Elinaite is in the second row, sixth from left). I was told that I very soon became a favourite with the convent staff; my vitality, pretty appearance and musical talent won everyone's heart. The framework of my day was now the orphanage timetable and the rites of the Catholic Church. The world that now surrounded me and especially the music to be heard during the church services, snatches of which I would always be singing, made the most lasting impression of all.

Evidently an informer eventually gave away the fact that there were some Jewish children being sheltered in the Chiobishkis orphanage; armed policemen broke into the home and demanded that the children be handed over to them. One of the nuns managed to hide me without it being noticed, but the rest of the children were taken off by the police.

Soon after that the nuns took me to the Kaishiadorys church, where they hid me in a room in the bell tower. One of the children who had been led off by the police blurted out that there had been another dark-eyed little Jewish girl as well. To clarify this situation, the Mother Superior of the convent and the parish priest were summoned to the police station in Ukmerge. During her interrogation, Mother Superior Liucina (Rozalija Rimshaite) turned to her fellow-countrymen in the name of God, appealing to their conscience, and asked them to return the children. She also promised that she would give the children back, including me, if the Germans demanded it. Then a miracle took place: the children were given back.

Thanks to this amazing combination of circumstances and the courage of Mother Superior it proved possible to save all five children. When the Germans withdrew from Lithuania my mother began looking for me in Kaishiadorys Cathedral. Bishop Matulionis told my mother that I was safe and sound in the Chiobishkis orphanage.

Mother was greatly moved by the bishop's attention to me, when he told her about my musical skills and that they should be developed. It was already dark and my mother wanted to go to Chiobishkis, but the bishop would not let her. The following morning she set off barefoot, since her shoes had worn out by then. The director of the Chiobishkis orphanage was glad to welcome my mother, but she did not want to cause distress to the other children, and at first did not approach me.

One evening, mother went carefully to the room, in which the children had already been put to bed, so as to have a peep at her miraculously saved daughter from a distance. I remember well that when I caught sight of her on the threshold, I leapt to my feet and asked her in Lithuanian, *'Ar tu busi mano mamyte?'* ('Will you be my Mama?'). Mother gave a slight nod of her head and tears welled into her eyes. She quickly left the room.

We left Chiobishkis on foot. We had a journey of fifty kilometres in front of us before we would reach Kaunas. Peasants passing on carts piled high with hay helped us to reach the main road leading to Kaunas. Units of the advancing Red Army were moving along it in enormous numbers. After the quiet of the monastery, I found the clatter and din of the vehicles deafening and scary. One army vehicle pulled up: soldiers with hot dirty faces, which were happy and welcoming, hoisted us into the back of one of the lorries. Eventually we entered liberated Kaunas.

For a long time I was reluctant to admit that I was Jewish. I used to pray several times a day and protested when my parents explained to me why Jews should not make the sign of the Cross and that I, Esther, was a Jew. It was clear that the children in the orphanage had been taught deliberately that being Jewish was something bad and dangerous. Time moved on and the depleted Jewish families, which had survived, slowly started to regain their faith in life and in the future. Mother kept the promise that she had made to Bishop Matulionis. At the age of 5 I started studying the piano in my mother's class in the Kaunas music high school.

Later our family moved to Vilnius, where I continued to study music. My debut at the age of 9 was with the Vilnius Radio Symphony Orchestra. That marked the beginning of my success-ful career as a pianist. In 1956 I went to Moscow to continue my education at the Central School of Music. From the age of 11, I had dreamt of becoming a pupil of the great pianist and teacher, Heinrich Neuhaus. This dream was to become reality in 1958, in Moscow's Tchaikovsky State Conservatoire. My concerts, given in many towns of the USSR and beyond, were warmly accepted by the public and praised by the critics.

After emigrating to Israel in 1973, I continued to give concerts there and in Europe. I included in my repertoire works by Mikalojus Chiurlionis, whose family had played a crucial part in saving my life. His great-grandson and pianist, Rokas Zubovas, and his pianist wife, Sonata Zuboviene, have on several occa-sions taken part in my master classes, which I gave at the Heinrich Neuhaus Foundation in Zurich, of which I am the artis-tic director.

My daughter, Ilana Yellin-Panov, was a classical dancer. She organized and was general director of Panov's Ballet Theatre in Ashdod, Israel. Ilana's husband is the world-famous dancer and choreographer, Valery Panov. In October 2008 their son, Tslil Meir, was born; his name in Hebrew means 'shining sound'. Ilana told me that the name had been chosen in honour of my playing. 'When you play them, sounds begin to shine,' she explained.

Switzerland, 2009

EDITORS' NOTE

Ilana tragically died in December 2009, when she was only 42.

24. I Always Celebrate My Birthdays

Hasia Aronaite-Gitlin and Volodia Katz

My father, Chaim Aronas, moved to Kaunas from Jonava, a small Lithuanian town, and worked in the famous Kapulsky shop and café. There he met my mother Michle, née Katz, who was also originally from Jonava. Both my parents were Communists.

Figure 48. Michle Aronas, mother of Hasia Aronaite-Gitlin.

I was born in 1936 in Slobodka; two and a half years later my brother Motele was born. When the Germans invaded Lithuania, father's parents and three of his brothers were killed in Jonava. My parents tried to retreat to Russia, but were stopped by Lithuanians and forced to return to Kaunas. I remember very well the long and tiring journey we made on foot. Our cart turned over and German soldiers helped us to put all our belongings back in order.

When we reached Kaunas, we found our home occupied by our former housemaid; she did not let us in. It was a German officer who ordered her to leave our apartment. In the cart accident I had badly wounded my leg. It was bandaged, and whenever my parents left our apartment, they used to hide money and jewels beneath the plaster. Once, when my parents were not at home, several Lithuanians came in. They searched every corner of our house, but found nothing. Eventually they undressed me, tore my plaster and took the money and jewels. They beat me and then left me there naked and frightened.

Although our house was in Slobodka, it was not within the ghetto borders. We were forced to move to the ghetto. I was a very agile and mischievous child. At time of the 'selection' during the 'Great Action' I constantly moved from one column to another until a German soldier shouted, 'Stay still!' Eventually we were selected to join the 'good' line, but my Uncle Moshe Aronas, his wife and two children were sent to the Ninth Fort.

I can remember my birthday celebrations in the ghetto and even remember receiving a very special present from the neighbour's son: it was a bandage glued with pieces of coloured paper to wear as a crown on my head. These days I always celebrate my birthdays; if we could celebrate it in the most terrible conditions of the ghetto, it is a *Mitzvah* and duty to celebrate now when we are free and well.

From our house we could see Jews being led to the Ninth Fort. I also saw the escape of prisoners from this fortress; one of them, our relative, came to our room. My mother was terribly anxious: if he was found, we would all be punished by death. After maybe only a day my father led him somewhere else.

When my parents went to work, they always left us some food on the table. My father used to say, 'The food does not belong to the one who gets to it first, but to the one who waits patiently.' I always sent my younger brother first, and then reminded him what our father would say.

Though my mother protested, my father joined the anti-fascist underground organization. He would let me distribute proclamation leaflets in the ghetto. I was a naughty girl and would play snow fights with the neighbours' children, with the leaflets hidden under my dress. Motele was a much more responsible boy; he would pull me by the sleeves saying, 'Come on, we have chores to do.'

During the 'Children's Action' Motele was hidden in a bunker together with several other kids. They were discovered by the Germans, led to a laundry and there burnt alive, while the distraught parents were forced to watch their execution. My father told me, that when the fire caught Motele, he shouted, 'Mother, Mother, when I burnt my finger, you would blow on it so it would not hurt!'

My mother ran towards him to throw him out of the fire. A Ukrainian policeman struck her with the handle of his rifle. She lost consciousness and suffered a bad backbone injury in her fall. My mother never recovered after this incident.

I was smuggled out of the ghetto twice; I think at that time I was already aware of what was going on. The first time there was an arrangement with a woman who lived in the central part of Kaunas. She was paid generously for hiding me.

I was told to crawl under the barbed wire of the ghetto fence at a strategic moment and to walk in a certain direction where a Lithuanian woman would be waiting for me. After successfully getting past the fence I walked in the darkness until suddenly a strange woman called to me. She brought me to another woman's apartment where I was hidden for some time. I remember that if there was a round-up, I would be locked in a basement. I was only 6 years old, but I sat there quietly talking to rats that wandered around me. I do not think I was afraid! Today I am afraid of spiders, insects, you name it!

I did not stay in that apartment for long. One day I heard that a Jewish girl had been discovered and killed together with a Lithuanian woman in this neighbourhood. I ran to my 6-year-old cousin Cilia Katz who was being hidden nearby with another Lithuanian family. I told her, 'We are going back to the ghetto.' We walked a long way through the Kaunas streets, and it was evening when we reached the ghetto. I stood close to the fence and saw my mother come out of our house. I called to her. She looked around but saw nothing in the darkness. She entered the house and told my father that she thought she had heard me calling. My father thought this was nonsense, but Mother insisted that he should go check outside. I called him and he saw us. I chose the right moment to slip under the wire fence; Cilia crawled next. She was a little bit clumsy and tore her new coat on the barbed wire and cried bitterly.

Cilia Katz disappeared for ever during the 'Children's Action'. She was exactly my age, the daughter of Hanah and my Uncle Yosef Katz. Yosef was a very good carpenter. Before the war he built a wooden house in Slobodka. The house is still there, but Yosef, Chana and Cilia are not with us. Only Volodia Katz, the youngest son in this family, born in the ghetto on 21 September 1941, survived.

After receiving a shot of Luminal, Volodia was smuggled out of the ghetto in a suitcase. It was agreed that a Lithuanian carpenter whom his father had known for many years would transfer him to a priest. Volodia stayed with this priest for some time but fell ill and was transferred to Dr Baublys, who ran an orphanage and saved many Jewish children. Volodia stayed at the Baublys orphanage until the end of the war. Dr Baublys was able to keep him because he was not circumcised.

Before the liquidation of the ghetto, a group of about seventy Jewish men and women, including Volodia's parents, escaped to a forest, and hid there in a bunker which they had dug for themselves. A man who was paid to take care of the food supply turned out to be a traitor. The group was surrounded by the Gestapo and burnt alive. There were only three survivors, who were not in the bunker when the incident occurred.

My father was asked by the underground leaders to stay in the ghetto and not to join the detachment. He passed his days in a workshop but at nights he would sew boots for the partisans. Once during a meeting of the underground group to which he belonged, Dr Kutorgiene told my father that he was lucky to have come that day: a shelter had been found for me.

Dr Kutorgiene was a most courageous and noble woman. Endangering her own life she would enter the ghetto to arrange contact between the underground members and the kind

Gentiles who were willing to rescue Jewish children. This time they were talking about a monastery in Zhemaitija. My father asked me if I was prepared to leave the family to go there and I agreed. My mother was against the arrangement, but my father persuaded her. When I think about it now, I am surprised at myself. How could a girl at that age agree to leave her parents and go to an unknown place with complete strangers? The realities of the ghetto presumably made us mature enough to understand these situations; we felt the dangers and behaved in a way not typical of normal children's behaviour.

This time, just a day before the 'Children's Action', I was carried out of the ghetto in a sack of potatoes and transferred to our contact. She led me to a location in Kaunas, from where orphan girls were taken to the Girenai nunnery, located near the town of Reitava. I remember how petrified I felt on this journey. I was warned not to speak in Yiddish. During the long journey by train to this orphanage I was afraid I'd get my languages mixed up, so I kept silent.

I was registered in the orphanage as Maryte Radzevichiute. As far as I remember, I lived there for almost two years. I mostly worked in the kitchen, and because I worked well and very fast, the adults praised me and often gave me extra food; I was clever enough to share it with other girls. During my leisure time I would knit, a skill I had learnt at a very young age. I understood very well that I was different, and using wits beyond my years, I bribed other girls with extra food and knitted clothes. All the orphans in the nunnery were supposed to pray every evening. I would pretend to pray, but actually every evening I'd repeat to myself, 'I am Hasia Aronaite, my father is Chaim, my mother is Michle, my brother is Motele', and so on.

When the front approached our nunnery, all the nuns escaped, leaving us without any supervision or food. We would wander through the buildings and garden, abandoned, cold, hungry and dirty. At the end of 1944 a young Jewish man in Soviet Army uniform appeared in the orphanage; he had heard there might be a Jewish girl being hidden in Girenai. He talked to a priest and then met me, asking me who I was. I told him the words I had repeated so many times in my 'prayers'. He wanted to take me to his relatives in Rietava, but I refused to go. He also posted a notice to the Kaunas synagogue notifying my whereabouts. This man was later killed by Lithuanian bandits, called *'Zhaliukai'*, the so-called 'forest brothers'. According to the descriptions I heard later, this young man was probably Shmuel Peipert.

My mother died in Stutthof from disease and starvation. My father was released from Dachau, mobilized into the Soviet Army and came back to Lithuania only in 1946. He found the notice in the synagogue and went to collect me from Rietava. By then I was living with Peipert's relatives, who had eventually persuaded me to leave the orphanage. I remember I was lying in bed and saw my father's reflection in a mirror. I jumped on him with joy, asking, 'Where are Mom and Motele?' 'We will talk about it later at home', was his reply.

Father took me to his home, where he was living with a woman called Malka. Once we went to Vilnius to see my aunts Sonia and Riva. I saw a woman in the window and was sure it was my mother. I ran towards her shouting, 'Mama!' However, when I got closer I saw it was Aunt Sonia, who resembled my mother. My father married Malka and adopted her two daughters. They had another daughter together. To this day we all maintain a very warm and close relationship. However I never called Malka 'Mother'.

My father was the most kind and generous person. Despite Mother's reservations, many people would stay with us for couple of days in our crowded room in the ghetto. After the war friends and even strangers could find shelter and a meal in our house; my father helped others as much as he could. He used to give pocket money for sweets to the small children from the Jewish orphanage and money for cigarettes to the older ones. He especially supported those who wanted to study and helped others find employment.

I went to a Jewish school where I was the favourite pupil of Sheinale Gertneriene, our beloved teacher. I was married, very young, to Yakov Gitlin and we had two children. We emigrated to Israel in 1972. Yakov passed away comparatively young; he neglected his health, would not complain and by the time he went to see doctors it was too late, he had advanced cancer.

I am not lonely. My children and five grandchildren are with me through the hard times. I am very close to Volodia Katz, whom I regard as my brother. When Kaunas was liberated, Volodia was taken from the orphanage to Vilnius by his aunt Ida

Figure 49. Jewish School in Kaunas, 1947. First line: first from left: Liuba Fuks (hidden child); second: Lyusya Borstaite; middle: Sheinale Gertner; next to her Mika Rosenblum and Ester Elinaite; first from right: Gidon Sheftel. Second row: just above Gertner: Yakov Taft (with collar). Top row: fourth from left: Hasia Aronaite; sixth: Matias Taft.

Shapiriene. She had returned to Lithuania from Russia. A journey to Vilnius by train was the first event Volodia remembers in his life. They travelled to the sound of shelling and bombardment, the war was still going on.

Ida had a son, Folia. Tragically, he found a grenade that exploded and killed him. Ida was completely broken by this event and was not able to bring up Volodia: she gave him to the Jewish Orphanage. Later he was transferred to the Lithuanian Orphanage, where he lived till he graduated from high school.

Volodia regards the time spent in the orphanage as the worst period in his life. He ran away several times, but was brought back. He was beaten by the older boys until he had to learn to fight and defend myself. Eventually he became one of the strongest boys there and often defended the weak ones. He became a carpenter, like his father. His first son was named Yosef after his late father, and the second, Chanan, in memory of his mother.

On 21 September 1972, his birthday, Volodia's family came to Israel, where he immediately started to work as a carpenter. Eventually Volodia's family settled in quite well. His sons served in the Israeli Army and both graduated from university, one in electronics and the other in civil engineering.

Ashdod, Israel, 2008

25. My Sister's Name was Ruth

Ilya Levy and Tamara Ratneryte-Kadishaite-Levy

ILYA

When Yaska (Yakov Zilberg) involved us in this project we were in the apartment of our mutual friend, Israella Blat. She and her sister Liba, also survivors of the Holocaust, were saved by righteous Lithuanians, in the Telshiai region. Until that evening, we never talked about our past. We were busy and happy building a future.

Tamara and I first crossed paths in the beginning of 1945 when I was 5 and Tamara was 4 years old. Tamara lived in the Jewish Orphanage established immediately after the liberation of Kaunas from the Germans. My mother sent me to the kindergarten that had opened in the orphanage. Naturally, neither of us remembers if there was any hint of the future friendship. Very soon we were 'separated' when my family moved to Vilnius in 1945. In Israel in the early 1970s we were invited to a meeting of the children of the Kaunas Jewish Orphanage. There somebody pointed out to us that we had attended the same kindergarten.

TAMARA

Until I found my birth certificate in the Kaunas archives, I did not know when exactly I had been born. I believed it was in the ghetto, but I learnt that I was actually born in January 1941, not actually before the war. My father, Shimon Ratner, was a building engineer contractor, a partner of Bagriansky in a small private firm. My mother Judesa, née Zeigarnik, worked as a kindergarten teacher.

So I was just a baby when my parents were forced into the ghetto. Ida Shateriene was a liaison officer whose duty it was to keep contact with Gentiles who were willing to help save Jewish children. V. Zubovas mediated between the ghetto underground and Dr Baublys, the director of an orphanage in Vilijampole. It was agreed that Jewish children would be brought there one by one and left as if they had been abandoned. This 'joint venture' was extremely dangerous for both sides.

Figure 50. Shimon Ratner, his eldest daughter Rut Ratner (Tamara Ratneryte-Kadishaite-Levy's sister) and uncle Aharon Zeigarnik, just before the war.

The story of how I was smuggled out of Kaunas Ghetto is described in the book '*Ir be ginklo kariai*' which means 'Unarmed Fighters':

> One autumn evening in 1943 in a small room in the ghetto where Ratner's family was living, Ida Shateriene patiently waited until the 2-year-old Tamara would fall asleep. There were fence guards on duty who would cooperate and the adept child-smuggler, P. Shateris, was ready to act. Most important, Dr P. Baublys knew that on that very night a child would be left on the porch of his orphanage, which

was located just a few streets away from the ghetto. Trustworthy nurses were scheduled to work on this particular night. But Tamara would not go to sleep and the operation was cancelled. All the logistics had to be rearranged and rescheduled for another night.[1]

A nurse called Berlovichiene gave me a shot of Luminal, and I fell into a deep sleep, was put into a big suitcase, and Ida carried me out of the ghetto into the night and through the dimly lit streets of Kaunas. She put the case on the porch of the orphanage, rang the bell and waited, hiding in the darkness. It was agreed that the nurse in charge would come to collect me. Several long minutes passed, but nobody appeared. In such a situation every minute lasted an eternity. A lorry with German soldiers passed by; fortunately they did not pay any attention to the parcel on the porch. In desperation Ida decided to take me back to the ghetto, but fortunately the door opened and the nurse collected me. Later Ida learnt that the delay was due to some unexpected guests who were visiting Dr Baublys; they could not take any risks by attending to the child at the door. Dr Baublys could not trust all the members of his staff, but there were at least two nurses, P. Vitonyte and E. Uborevichiene, who helped him in all his dangerous missions.

Several ghetto children were smuggled out by Ida Shateriene in this way and kept at the orphanage of Dr Baublys; he saved many Jewish lives during the war and was awarded the title of 'Righteous among the Nations' at Yad Vashem; a tree was planted in his memory in the 'Forest of the Righteous'. My father, who was an active member of the ghetto anti-fascist underground organization, was shot during an attempt to join a partisan detachment; it is likely that a Lithuanian lorry driver gave him away.

It was only in Israel that I learnt from my mother's cousin, Dov Alroy (Zeigarnik), who had emigrated to Palestine before the war, that I also had an older sister; she would have been 6 years old when we entered the ghetto. Together with my mother she was sent to Stutthof where they both perished. I do not have any memories of my parents and sister.

Many years later, when I looked for information about my family at Yad Vashem Holocaust Museum, I was astonished to find that my sister's name was Golda-Ruth. Without knowing this, eight years before, we had named our Israeli-born daughter

Ruth. Maybe this name had been subconsciously dwelling in my memory.

Ida Shateriene, who managed to escape from the ghetto and join a detachment, knew where some children were being hidden. After the liberation of Lithuania she collected us from Dr Baublys and placed us in the new Jewish Orphanage; I was the youngest child there. They gave me the best bed to sleep in, which had belonged until then to Ruth Ben David, also a Kaunas Ghetto 'hidden child', and the oldest girl there. Naturally she was not happy and from the start Ruth did not like me. But soon her attitude towards me changed and she became my friend and protector. All this I learned at the meeting of children of the Jewish Orphanage held in Israel in the late 1970s, when our former teacher, Malka Pogotsky, a member of Kibbutz Masarik, introduced Ruth to me. Ruth's parents perished and Malka subsequently smuggled her through the Soviet borders and brought her to Israel in 1946.

Dora and Avraham Kadishas, who had known my parents well before the war and did not have children of their own, took me on several occasions from the orphanage to their home. When they were sure I liked it there, they adopted me; that was at the end of 1946.

I only vaguely remember my life in the orphanage and the first visits with the Kadishas family. It was supposed to be a secret that I was not the Kadishas' biological daughter. It was only when I was 18 years old that Professor Liolia Aizinbud told me the names of my real parents, but asked me not to tell my mother that I knew the truth. In fact, from a very early age I had felt that I was not their child; after all, I was nearly 3 years old when I was smuggled out. I remember that at the age of 10, after an intensive search in our house, I found a document saying I was adopted, but I said nothing and just went on pretending.

My adoptive father, Avraham Kadishas, was an engineer and a very intelligent and highly educated, warm, kind and distinctive person. He died from a heart attack when he was only in his fifties; I loved him very much. My mother, Dora Kadishiene, was regarded as a very good paediatrician. She worked mainly from her own office, one of the few who dared to keep a private practice throughout the years of the Soviet regime. I followed in her footsteps, studied medicine and became a paediatrician. My mother Dora passed away when she was about 96 years old, and was strong, retaining her memory almost to the end.

ILYA LEVY

I was born on 30 May 1940 in Kaunas to Sheina and Shmuel-Yaakov (Yankale) Levy. During the First World War, my father's family was forced by the Russian czarist government to evacuate to Russia, where all his relatives died from typhus.

My father Yankale was a teenager when he made his way back to his village alone in the vain hope of finding some relatives. He lived in the village until he went to Kaunas to study photography, where he was taken into the household of his teacher. My mother, Sheina Baron, was born in the small town of Gelvoniai to a poor tailor's family. At the age of 16 she left her parents and moved to Kaunas. My parents met, fell in love, married and too soon found themselves in the ghetto.

Figure 51. Yankale Levy, 1938.

I can remember that in our room in the ghetto there was a secret door through to our neighbours. The door was blocked by a footstool with a pail of water on top of it. When somebody knocked at the door my mother and I crawled under the footstool to the neighbour's flat. I can also remember my third birthday party; Mother made pancakes from carrots and invited the neighbours' children.

Figure 52. Dr Elena Kutorgiene. From the personal Ernestas Kutorga archive.

My father, Yankale Levy, was one of the bravest and smartest liaison officers for the ghetto underground and the detachment. In the book *Unarmed Fighters* he is described as follows: 'Short in stature, hunchbacked, leaning on a stick, with a long moustache and a pipe in his mouth, a typical old Lithuanian man, he would wander around the streets of Kaunas, without arousing the suspicion of the police.'[2] To be on the safe side, my father carried a passport in the name of Antanas Gudauskas, a farmer. Father was a cool, but very energetic officer and so he was always sent to perform the most dangerous tasks.

One of my father's many duties was to look for trustworthy people who would agree to harbour the ghetto children; he was involved in the rescue of many ghetto inhabitants. Eventually, with the assistance of Dr Kutorgiene and her son Dr Viktoras Kutorga, he found a family willing to keep me, a 3-year-old boy. A local woman named Emilia Vasiliauskiene took charge of delivering me to the childless Petkiavichius family. This couple would have preferred to adopt a girl, but when they saw me – a blond-haired, blue-eyed boy – they compromised. They prepared documents that stated that I was an abandoned Polish refugee child; I was baptized and given the name Aleksas (Aliukas) Petkiavichius.

Figure 53.
Dr Viktoras Kutorga. From the personal Ernestas Kutorga archive.

My mother visited me twice. The first time was a couple of days after I had been brought to the Petkiavichius family. They told my mother that had she come a day sooner, they would have asked her to take me back. I had cried non-stop and spoke only Yiddish. Fortunately Petkiavichius knew some German and could communicate with me and calm me down. I remember how my adoptive parents were disappointed that they had received a boy instead of girl: they even dressed me like a girl and forced me to sing and dance.

Now that they knew I was safe, my parents joined a partisan detachment. Several days before they escaped from the ghetto my mother came to see me once more. I remember this visit very well; I recognized my mother although she was disguised as a beggar. She stood behind the entrance of the house looking at me; I already understood that I shouldn't talk to her.

I saw the burning ghetto from the Petkiavichius' house as the Germans liquidated it.

The last incident I remember from my time with the family was when Petkiavichius chased me with a belt in his hands, because I did not want to eat soup with pork in it. This chase resulted in a broken leg when I fell down from the porch. I was taken to the hospital; this took place a few days before the liberation of Kaunas by the Red Army. I can remember lying in the bed with a stretched leg. When shells began to fall in the vicinity, everybody who could move fled and only a few patients were left in the huge ward. Then, suddenly, my mother appeared.

Several days later, when I recovered and a plaster was put on my leg, Mother took me home; Petkiavichius was angry with her. He came to us drunk and shouted, accusing her of 'stealing' me; Petkiavichius hoped my parents would not survive, and that I would stay with them forever.

Father was killed just a few days before liberation. He and Shlomo (Solomon) Abramovich, were sent on a reconnaissance mission. They entered a small manor, but the owner of this manor alerted the Germans; the manor was surrounded by German troops and in the confrontation my father and his friend were shot.

Petkiavichius' wife visited us once after we moved to Vilnius, but it was my last meeting with a member of this family. We did not keep in touch after that.

I graduated from the Kaunas Polytechnic Institute in 1962. My friendship with Tamara was renewed during our student years, and in 1965 we married and settled in Vilnius. My mother Sheina married Yakov Bloch who had fought in the 16th Lithuanian Division. His first wife and three children were killed in the small town of Daugai. He and my mother had a daughter, my half-sister Masha; Yakov Bloch later died when we were still in Lithuania.

In 1972 we emigrated to Israel with our two children, Rafael and Asia, two grandmothers and my half-sister Masha. I started to work immediately as an engineer in *Mekorot*, the institution responsible for water supply in Israel and eventually held a high managerial position. My mother passed away aged 94. Tamara was a highly respected paediatrician in Ashkelon, loved both by her small patients and their parents. Besides Tamara's clinical work she was for many years in charge of medical services for the southern districts of the General Health Fund, responsible for provision of medical care to 120,000 people.

Until we became involved in the project on the hidden children of Kaunas, we never talked about our past. We were busy and happy building a future.

Kfar Sava, Israel, 2009

NOTES

1. S. Binkiene (ed.), *Ir be Ginklo kariai* (Unarmed Fighters) (Vilnius: Mintis, 1967), p.120.
2. Ibid., p.116.

26. The Prayer of an Innocent Girl

Ada Feldstein-Levner

I was born on 13 March 1938 in Kaunas. My father, Lev Feldstein, was a young surgeon and oldest son of Tzemach Feldstein, the principal of the Hebrew School in Kaunas. My mother, Sara Aronovsky, was the youngest daughter of a very wealthy and successful businesswoman, Esther Aronovsky. We lived on Laisves Avenue, the central street of Kaunas, in my grandmother's three-storey house and we were a happy family.

Figure 54. Sara Aronovsky-Feldstein and Lev Feldstein, parents of Ada Feldstein-Levner.

I remember a few images from my time in the ghetto, such as houses, streets, the River Neman. I know that I almost died from pneumonia. My father worked in the ghetto clinic as a surgeon.

Most probably my uncle, mother's eldest brother, Liolia Aronovsky, warned us about the planned 'Children's Action'. I was told that I was in a refuge, together with my future husband, Edik Levner, then a 6-year-old boy. After the 'Children's Action' my parents decided that they needed to get me out of the ghetto. They contacted my former nanny, Victorija Jacinevichiute, and she and her sister Elena agreed to save me.

Figure 55. Ada Feldstein-Levner with her mother, Sara Aronovsky-Feldstein.

My father bought a false birth certificate in the name of Rimute Kazimiera Komisaraityte, and arranged, by bribing the Germans, for my passage through Vilijampole Bridge. There he handled me over to my nanny. During the first days outside the ghetto I remember crying non-stop, but little by little I got used to being away from my parents.

My nannies had to keep me hidden and we moved several times in Kaunas and the villages around it. I lived for short periods of time in the city with one of nanny's friends, Mrs Jagminiene, then in a small village, and back in Kaunas with Mrs Starkiene and her two children. My last hiding place was the hamlet of Pazhaislis where we lived in a small cottage; when the front approached we went to hide in the Pazhaislis Convent.

War was so near and everyone was afraid, but I was content there, the nuns would spoil me. They asked me to pray to God to save the convent from bombing. They believed that the prayer of an innocent little girl would be heard by God. The convent was indeed spared from bombing, and maybe my prayers played a part in this. The nuns wanted to baptize me but my nannies refused. War was nearly at its end and they believed my parents might return and that it would be their decision.

During the liquidation of the ghetto my parents were in hiding there but were killed along with countless others. In September 1944, when I was already 6 years old, I was enrolled in school with my false papers. I had continued to live with my dear nannies.

For a few years I waited for my parents to show up like many others. But they never did. These were the days of Stalin and I continued using my false papers although I had my real birth certificate as well. All my friends knew that I was Jewish and they called me Ada. I graduated from high school with honours in my false name, and entered Kaunas Medical Institute, from which I graduated in 1961. It was only when we came to Israel in January 1972 that I made all the legal arrangements and got my real name back.

All the time, until I married Hertz (Edik) Levner in the autumn of 1961, I had continued to live with Viktorija and Elena, who looked after our elder son Lev until we left for Israel in January 1972. My youngest son Daniel was born in Israel in 1978.

I was in constant contact with my nannies all the time, writing and sending gifts. They passed away long ago.

It appeared that in the ghetto we had lived with Edik on the same street. He was born on 18 February 1938 to Meir Levner and Frida Melnikaite-Levner. After the 'Children's Action' Hertz was given away to the Grigoreviches, a Polish family in Kaunas on Savanoriu Street. He was transported to them from the ghetto in a sack hidden among others containing grain, which were sent to the mill. A bribed German guard and his father were on this cart. In the mill the bag was passed to Mr Grigorevichius. Hertz became Edvardas Grigorevichius. Fortunately, his parents survived the German camps and came back for him. The Levners were in constant contact with the Grigorevich family, until they were deported to Siberia in 1947, like many others in Lithuania at that time.

For twenty-one years we lived in Netanya, Israel and were very happy there. In October 1992 we moved to live to Toronto, Canada.

Toronto, Canada, 2008

27. I Asked If It Was 'Safe' to Know Her

Ahuva (Liuba) Peres-Gold and Shalom Peres

These memoirs are a combination of Shalom's written text, made by him at the editors' request, and the testimony taken from Ahuva's interview. For this reason, the descriptions do not follow in strict chronological order.

SHALOM

I was born in Kaunas on 6 June 1934 to Eliezer (Lazer) and Shulia Peres (née Budnik). Six years later on 25 September 1940 my sister Ahuva (Luba) joined our family. Our mother, I believe, was born in Krekenava, on a farm (at least this is where her parents lived) and went to school in Panevezhys; Father was born and educated in Kaunas.

On the first day of Germany's invasion our family became part of a large stream of refugees moving towards Russia. Some had horse carriages, but most of the people, including us, were on foot. There were also menacing flights of German planes forcing the crowds to hide in the ditches and fields. I believe that in this chaos our father became separated from us.

While we hid in a barn, we heard a knock at the door. There was a German paratrooper announcing the 'liberation of the territory' and telling us to go home.

As we were walking back to Kaunas we encountered a convoy of Soviet troops driving toward Russia, but they had no place for us. They also told us that if they were confronted by Germans they would have to surrender, since most of their weapons and even their bullets were stolen. Continuing our march toward Kaunas we saw some wounded people in the roadside ditches: torn off limbs, blood, cries for help.

Our mother found herself alone with two children in the ghetto. Father arrived in Kaunas a year after we separated. During that year he lived in a number of ghettos, from each he escaped. He hid in a few villages in Belarus. His main asset that assured his survival was his skills in mechanics, which he had acquired when in Soviet Lithuania he had to abandon his profession of many years as a travelling salesman. He could fix cooking pots for farmers, old soviet cars for the Germans, and so on. After my father's return for a while we had plenty of visitors, who asked my father whether he had met their missing relatives.

One of our father's last jobs was at some place outside the ghetto, where on that fatal day he had to inflate the tyres of a truck or bus. While pumping air, Father saw that the required pressure had been reached and stopped the pump. But his guard indicated that the meter showed low pressure (Father believed that when he had gone to the washroom, the guard had turned back the needle for fun), accused him of attempted sabotage and ordered him to continue pumping until it showed the correct pressure. As a result the tyre exploded and the rim hit my father in the legs, breaking each of them in two places. He was taken to the ghetto hospital where they operated on him without anaesthetic; these were good doctors, but they had no medical supplies or equipment.

As it became obvious that the ghetto would eventually be liquidated, the residents dug underground hiding places with ingenious secret entrances. In our house the entrance was in the kitchen floor, under the iron protective plate in front of the stove. Yet while they built their hiding place, my parents didn't put all their faith in it. So they started to search for means of survival outside the ghetto.

Our family was lucky that my mother had the necessary qualities for these circumstances. She had a relentless drive and belief in her ability in finding a solution. In addition, her physical advantages, non-Jewish looks and command of the Lithuanian language provided her with the freedom to move around, once she took off the yellow stars and slipped out of the work column.

Father had four brothers and two sisters in the Kaunas Ghetto, some with spouses and children. When they heard of my parents' plans to dispatch their kids to different locations from themselves and from each other, they said they wouldn't do it, that they'd rather the family shared the same fate. My parents, on the other hand, said that it would be better if at least someone survived, rather than nobody at all. They considered and accepted the fact that if only the children survived they might have been converted to Catholicism (*goyim*). For our parents even this outcome was preferable to being dead. As fate had it, our parents' decision turned out to be the right choice to have made, because from my father's family, only one brother and one sister survived; not one of the spouses or children saw the end of the war.

AHUVA

All I know about my family during the war and about my rescue is what my mother told me. Father never spoke about his experiences during the time of occupation or about the fate of his parents. It was too difficult for him to recount.

For years I never shared my story. Only recently I wrote some of it down at the request of my grandchildren.

During the 'Great Action' our family was sent to the doomed line, the 'fast track' to death. One Lithuanian policeman grabbed and dragged my mother and me from this column and pushed us to another; people in this one could live a little longer. We discovered later, that this policeman had been our neighbour before the war.

Mother slipped out of the ghetto on several occasions in search of trustworthy people willing to provide us with shelter from the Germans, the Lithuanian police and collaborators. Shalom believes it was Aunt Nesia (Nehmod) Budnik who heard from someone that the priest Bronius Paukshtys helped save Jewish children. So Mother went to see him. Not believing her to be Jewish, he gave her some Old Testament text to read in Hebrew. Mother had attended the Hebrew Gymnasium in Panevezhys, so she read the text fluently and thus could convince him of her authenticity.

I was the first to be smuggled out. I was left with Paukshtys, who had arranged my transfer to Dr Baublys' orphanage.

SHALOM

By the way, getting Ahuva out of the ghetto was quite an adventure. Since Ahuva was still a baby, my mother took her to the ghetto gate in a bag (I have no idea how she was kept asleep or quiet). The Jewish policeman knew of her plan to go out of the ghetto. She waited the whole evening, but there was no opportunity, and she returned home with Ahuva. She repeated the same routine the next evening, and this time she was lucky. A German car broke down within view of the gate. So the policeman ordered the Jews around the gate to run to the car and push it; this was what my mother needed. She soon left the car, removed her Star of David, and grabbed a horse carriage to go to Paukshtys. Pretty soon they heard an order to stop, and a mounted Lithuanian policeman started interrogating her. When he saw her bag, he asked what was in it. She answered that it was something innocent (such as grain or clothes). He ordered her to show its content to him. And at this critical moment another policeman shouted to him that he had stopped the wrong carriage (they were in pursuit of some criminal), and so he left without seeing Ahuva in the bag! That was quite a combination of bad luck (being stopped for the wrong reason), and then good luck (being saved just in time)!

AHUVA

Some months later my mother had a nightmare. In her dream, she saw me bald and my naked body full of purulent ulcers. She woke up with an urgent feeling that she must go to the orphanage. Although she might endanger both of us, nobody could dissuade her from visiting me. The priest Paukshtys arranged that she could see me from a distance through the fence of the orphanage. As it happened, I was recovering from measles. I was very thin and my hair had been shaved. Mother told me that I noticed her, pointed with a finger in her direction and said, 'There is my mother!' and ran to the edge of the garden.

SHALOM

Next it was my turn to escape from the ghetto. Before leaving I was taught some words in Lithuanian, and my new identity, Jonas Petronis; a matching false birth certificate was issued by Paukshtys. I spent a few days alone in a room in his house. Being alone for the first time in my life, with no knowledge of their language, felt very painful. A few days later my mother came for a visit, during which I begged to be taken back to the ghetto. It is obvious that my request was not granted.

Then I was taken to Marijampole, to an orphanage belonging to Paukshtys' church, the Salesian Society, sometimes known by the name of their founder, Don Bosco. There for a while I played the role of a deaf mute. I was most anxious to conceal that I was circumcised and feared that I would talk Yiddish in my dreams. Otherwise I followed the daily routine of other boys: kneeling in bed to pray in the morning and night, and going to church every week. Sometimes after everyone was asleep the director would take me to her room for a conversational lesson in Lithuanian. When she finally decided that I was sufficiently fluent, she announced that she was taking me to a 'doctor'. She obviously didn't take me to a doctor but upon our return from our walk, she announced to the kids that I was 'cured', that is, that I could now speak.

One day in the orphanage, the director told me secretly that the new ball given by some donor for us to play with had in reality been sent by my mother. This was obviously good news, that they were still alive.

I remember that most of the other kids were attending school and had homework, but since I was 'cured' after the school year had already commenced, I would only be going to school the following year. Nevertheless, when some of the other kids had problems with their arithmetic, I would come out with the right answers despite my lack of schooling, and pretty soon I was considered the resident 'expert'.

AHUVA

After our mother had smuggled us out, she started to look for a shelter for her sister, our father and herself. Father could not wander on the streets of Kaunas because of his obvious Semitic appearance. A German or Lithuanian policeman would immediately have arrested him. Mother wandered in the Kaunas suburbs looking for a hiding place and could feel comparatively safe. After a quite desperate search it seemed she had found an adequate location in some village. She made an agreement with the house owner: she would rent a basement in exchange for some belongings as payment. Mother brought the 'payment' and it was agreed that our mother and father would arrive the next day. During the earlier visits in that village my mother was presented to the neighbours as the owner's cousin living in

Kaunas, and who planned to move in with her in the village.

After she brought the 'payment' Mother slept there since she planned to return home by boat the next afternoon. Early in the morning her 'cousin' left the house for some errands. A couple of hours later a passing neighbour asked my mother, how serious was the argument with 'her cousin'? Realizing that this was something important, Mother admitted to a non-existing small argument and managed to 'fish' out some crucial information, namely, that her 'cousin' had gone to the village head and told him that my mother was Jewish. He promised to inform the Germans about it, but left it for later in the day, since he didn't believe her story. In the meantime he told this 'funny crazy invented story' to his wife, who repeated it to the neighbour who spoke to my mother. My mother laughed at it, but obviously left the house soon after the neighbour departed. She was so shocked by this situation that for a while she didn't know what to do. Finally she did take a boat to Kaunas. And during an inspection of documents, thanks to my mother's 'typical Lithuanian' looks, she was not even asked to show her papers.

Eventually mother found shelter for my father and herself. Father spent all his days in a small suffocating basement and only at nights could he breathe fresh air. Mother worked as a tailor in Gentiles' homes, mostly receiving food instead of money. She started to feel that it was too dangerous to keep me in the Baublys orphanage, so she brought me to their hiding place in the village. In order to somehow feed me better, Mother used to take me with her, and I would play in these houses while she worked, sewing clothes. The visits were stopped after I uttered several words in Yiddish out loud. Till then I had not spoken at all.

SHALOM

Once while crossing a street one of our orphans got hit by a vehicle. He was taken to a hospital and never came back. I don't remember what we were told about it, maybe that he had gone to heaven. It was only after the liberation that I heard that he was killed in the hospital when they saw he was circumcised. I never suspected that there was another Jew there. There may have been more!

In addition to the director, there were other personnel,

including a few girls (maybe nuns) in their late teens. I had a little argument with one of them, to which I didn't give much thought. At some point after liberation I found out that the girl with whom I had argued had gone to the police to inform on me. Perhaps they did not completely trust her. And since they were busy with the evacuation, going to investigate only one possibly Jewish boy was a somewhat lower priority.

Since the front was getting closer, Marijampole was being bombed. Someone in the director's family had a country property. She decided that it would be safer from bombs there, and off we went, on foot. I only remember that this 'long march' lasted less than a day. According to the neighbours, the Germans came for me just hours after we had left for the village; it was a close call. And it was too much trouble for them to find the village and go and search for me there.

After the orphanage moved to the village, farmers visited to select kids to adopt. Some of them were suspected of just searching for cheap labour. For some unknown reason, most of them wanted me. The director, knowing that I might still have living parents, would dissuade them with all kinds of invented stories about my health. Soon she found a better solution, sending me daily far into the field to look after the cows. I would leave the house early in the morning and return late at night. This became my daily routine seven days a week. It didn't change even after I saw the Soviet soldiers, although that was encouraging.

After Kaunas was liberated, my mother confided to a Lithuanian neighbour to being Jewish and told him about her family. As she mentioned a son in the Marijampole orphanage, he started asking whether I was such and such age, such and such size, such and such colour of hair, and then stopped. She managed to squeeze out of him that he heard that such a child had been killed: he was talking about the Jewish child I mentioned already, the one murdered in the hospital. We had enough common characteristics to fall under the same description. Mother was quite convinced that I was dead, in which case she wanted to find my burial place. On the other hand, since it was only a rumour, she did harbour a little hope.

The moment she learned about the liberation of Marijampole, she went there. She managed to find the location of the orphanage. But there were, obviously, no kids. With difficulty she managed to find the orphanage in the village. Looking around she saw children playing, but not me. That only confirmed to her that the rumour was true. Being afraid of hearing confirmation that the story was true, she sat down at a bench. Finally one of the nuns, who probably thought that my mother was looking for a child to adopt, also sat down at the same bench. My mother asked how many boys they had, and then whether there were any Jewish ones. At that point the nun had a good look and asked, 'Are you the mother of Jonas (maybe Jonelis)?' I don't think it is necessary to describe my mother's feelings upon learning that I was still alive.

As usual, I had continued to spend my days in the field until that day when I was called to return urgently to the farmhouse. There I saw my mother sitting on a bench. I immediately recognized her but I was still afraid to show it. On my arrival at the orphanage I had been coached to deny knowing my mother, should I be questioned. So when the director asked if I recognized this woman, my first answer was negative. When she asked me to look again I asked if it was 'safe' to know her. Only when she assured me did I jump into my mother's arms.

AHUVA

Several days after the liberation, my mother managed to get an apartment in the central part of Kaunas where we lived till our emigration to Israel. My first clear memory from childhood is of Mother carrying me to a new flat and putting me on the sofa in a dark room. All the members of our core family were saved, but still there was a lot of sorrow in the house; grandparents, brothers, sisters and many other relatives and friends had perished.

After the war I went to a Jewish school, which was very soon shut down (see Figure 15: Ahuva Liuba Peres is in the third row, fifth from right). A new wave of anti-Semitism began. In the Russian school I was quite unhappy until I started to speak Russian fluently. Later I flourished: I was young, strong and pretty, so I became a leader and the queen of the class. I was very good at different kinds of sports: skiing, ice-skating, cycling and especially at volleyball.

The years 1957–59 were a period of repatriation of former Polish citizens from the USSR to Poland. Many Lithuanian

Jews took this opportunity to emigrate to Israel, fictitiously marrying these formerly Polish citizens, since the Polish leader, Gomulka, allowed them to leave Poland. Persons entitled to Polish citizenship arranged fictitious marriages with Jews for money. Shalom married in this way but fell in love with his so-called 'wife', and their fictitious marriage became a genuine one. Thanks to Shalom's marriage, our family received permission to leave the USSR.

After eight months in Poland we moved to Israel. I remember how shocked I was by my first impression of Israel: sand and stones instead of the trees and grass of a Lithuanian landscape. I wanted to become Israeli as soon as possible, but I felt Israeli only when I did my Army service. After my compulsory service, I was employed by the Army until my retirement.

In 1962 I married Shmuel Gold, who was among the refugees who made *Aliya* to Israel on the famous *Exodus*, and we had three children. In 1985 my parents and my husband died. Several years later I met a widower with four children. Together we built a new warm and friendly family made of our seven children and fourteen grandchildren. The last blow of fate was when my handsome and gifted son, Ziv, was killed in a car crash, leaving behind a wife and a child. In 2004 my daughter gave birth to our youngest granddaughter, by this restoring some joy to my world.

SHALOM

After liberation from the Germans, I went to the primary Yiddish school. Being over 10 years old I was in a hurry to catch up and graduated the four grades in two years. From there I continued my education in a Russian secondary school. A good part of my first year in that Russian boys' school was traumatic. In most cases I didn't understand the teachers' questions and instructions, and as a result my responses often seemed funny to the Russian classmates, if not stupid.

As a result of irregular schooling during the war, some of the Russian boys were quite a few years older and bigger than me, and more than one of them harboured strong anti-Semitic feelings. So they used to beat me up on a regular basis. I dreaded to go home after school, since very often somewhere on the way a group of these older kids was waiting to torture me. I was asking my father to come to school to pick me up, but he refused, saying that I must learn to fight! Luckily for me, a couple of months later someone in my class organized a wrestling competition, and I unexpectedly took second place. This brought me so much respect from the other boys that the beatings stopped.

I wanted to continue my education in Leningrad, but every Leningrad Institute rejected me. I ended by returning to my city of Kaunas and being accepted by the Faculty of Electrical Engineering of our Kaunas Polytechnic Institute.

Within a couple of years after Stalin's death the political atmosphere significantly improved. We lost the fear of political persecution, and even started telling some political jokes. This false feeling of freedom ended up costing me dearly. In the fall of 1956 we had a faculty *Komsomol* election, and as a joke I and a couple of friends crossed out the nominees and wrote in (with our left hands) the names of Eisenhower, Dulles, Adenauer, Ben-Gurion and Gomulka. Unfortunately, they discovered the 'jokers' months later. There was an open *Komsomol* 'court' where they claimed that such political jokes led to the Hungarian revolution and, as a punishment, I was expelled from *Komsomol* and from the university. I did graduate, however, a year later.

Our family took the first opportunity to leave that country. The opportunity turned out to be repatriation to Poland, and then emigration to Israel. We lived in Israel for over six years, and in 1966 left, together with my wife Alexandra and son Amos (born in Poland) for Canada. In 1968 our daughter Belinda was born in Montreal.

I don't remember now what exactly led me to the subject of Bronius Paukshtys. But I seem to remember that after the war we attended the court hearing against him. Then I remember him visiting us after his return from Siberia. Thinking about it made me feel guilty about going through long stretches of life without a thought about the person who saved my life.

It turns out that after returning from Siberia, Paukshtys couldn't get his position back. He was receiving some help from the church, but it seems not enough. So to earn a living he had to 'shlepp' around Lithuania and make money by preaching in various small churches. Unfortunately, by the time I got this information, Bronius was already dead.

Some of my vivid memories:

Selling yeast, which someone in our family must have smuggled into the ghetto.

People rushing home after an 'action'. They presumably did this for two purposes: to protect their belongings or to collect the goods of the people who were taken into the 'bad' column for themselves.

Mother and I meeting someone on the street who told us that my father had arrived. My mother thought the guy was crazy! But then someone else came with the same news. As we rushed home there was a crowd surrounding it. It was so large that we needed help to get in. There were people who wanted to know whether my father had encountered any of their lost relatives.

Father in the hospital bed with weights stretching his legs by pulling his feet. Holes were made through his heels, metal rods were inserted, strings were attached to both sides of each rod. These strings went over pulleys and were attached at the ends to the hanging weights.

My desire to go back to ghetto despite mother telling me of the 'Children's Action' which took place just a few days after I was taken out.

In the orphanage in Marijampole:

Being afraid that I might talk in Yiddish in my sleep. The fear caused me to wet my bed.

Showering with other boys, making sure they didn't see I was circumcised and discover I am Jewish.

Being taken by foot together with other kids to the Catholic church every weekend.

Being bitten by a guard dog, which was released from its leash. This may have caused my lifelong fear of dogs.

Even when I saw the liberating Soviet soldiers speaking Russian, I still continued as if nothing had changed. After all, what if the situation reversed again?

For a few days upon our return to Kaunas and living with just my family, I continued to kneel in bed and pray to Jesus, although there was no logical reason for it. Obviously I was scared of losing the Lithuanian/Catholic identity that had saved my life and I could not part with it until I was absolutely sure that the Germans were not coming back.

Montreal, Canada, 2009; Haifa, Israel, 2009

28. From Darkness to Light

Rivka Shlapobersky-Strichman

In 1996 representatives of the Spielberg Fund, who initiated the archiving of Holocaust survivor's stories, asked to interview me. I wondered what I could share about my childhood, and to my amazement found I could gather only a few blurred recollections. Actually, there was nothing to tell. The publishing of testimonies by Yad Vashem, the Holocaust Museum, enabled me to read other accounts and I decided to start investigating my past. What had happened to me? What had I been through? How had I survived? What became of my parents and who had they been?

First I opened the *Keidan Memorial Book*.[1] This book was given to me by my relatives and had been in my home for many years; the same relatives gave me pictures of my parents. I was so moved when I found a whole chapter describing events in my life and the people who had helped me to survive. After reading the book I went in search for more.

I became acquainted with Sara Weis, who introduced me to the Society of Lithuanian Jews in Israel and to a group of people who survived the Kaunas Ghetto in their childhood. Everybody I spoke to helped me get more and more information.

In the story about my rescue, written by my aunt Rachel in the *Keidan Memorial Book* I learnt that as a child I had spent some time in the Brides of Jesus Convent. From the Lithuanian Embassy I learned that there are three monasteries with the same name. I called one of them. A nun named Klara answered the phone; her Russian was good. Klara had been deported to Siberia by Russians, where she spent ten years. I told her I would like to visit Ponevez (Panevezhys), the town where I grew up and to find out about my past. She was happy to meet me and promised that the convent would help me in my search.

On my visits to Lithuania, I found a lot of material in the archives in Kaunas, such as confirmation that I had been born in a private maternity hospital, my parents' wedding certificate, the official registration of my father's company and the income-tax dossier and even a rental contract and the plans of the apartment in 12 Palangos Street, where my parents lived before the war.

During our first visit, my husband and I spent several days in the monastery; the authorities provided us with a car and a nun acted as our driver so that we could visit many places where I had been in my childhood. We visited the orphanage where I most probably grew up.

We met Yehuda Ronder, whose brother Chaim Ronder helped Aunt Rachel to find me after the war. Yehuda had dedicated his life to hunting and bringing to justice the Lithuanian fascists who took part in the genocide of the Jews. Together with Yehuda we travelled to Kaunas and visited the places my parents had lived in. We went to Kedainiai (Keidan in Yiddish) as well and Yehuda, familiar with the town, showed us all the places related to Keidan Jewry, including the houses where my grandparents, father and Uncle Zodek Shlapobersky lived.

In 1941 in Kedainiai behind the Catholic cemetery at Datnuva Road, a mass grave had been dug. The young and strong were rounded up in batches of sixty and forced to undress, while machine guns were aimed at them. The dead, the wounded and men still alive were buried in the pit.

There were attempts at fighting back. Among the second batch was my uncle, Tzodek Shlapobersky, a man of about 40. He had been an officer in the Lithuanian army and had taken part in the fight for Lithuania's liberation. He had also been in charge of the fire brigade and was a city councillor for many years, and was friendly with the Lithuanians. A German officer was behind the massacre. According to the testimony of Mr Silvestravichius, one old Jewish man refused to take off his clothes. A Lithuanian named Raudonis tried to force him to get undressed. Tzodek Shlapobersky pulled the Lithuanian into the pit and began strangling him and sank his teeth in the Lithuanian's throat. Then he grabbed the Lithuanian's pistol and tried to shoot the German officer, but missed. Shlapobersky was pierced by the bayonets of other Lithuanians and his body was cut to shreds; his sister Anna, his wife and two children were killed in the same incident.

Raudonis was taken to hospital where he died, and the Lithuanians accorded him an imposing funeral. A number of addresses were held in which the Lithuanian bandit was described as 'the last victim of Jewish power'.[2]

During my visit to Lithuania, some vague episodes from my early childhood started to emerge: I am in a lorry at night and endless electricity wires...Sleeping on two chairs instead of bed ...The noise of planes and flashes of light in the sky, while we are hiding under the bed...

Another picture repeatedly comes back to me from my life: I am holding on to the wooden boards of the floor, when all of my body is suspended in the hole of the toilet, which was in the yard of the monastery. I started to shout as loud as I could. A nun who passed by pulled me out and washed my legs in a puddle. The nun told me I should not tell anybody I went to the toilet alone, otherwise I would be punished. During my visit to Panevezhys I found this toilet in the orphanage, but now it is a brick building instead of the wooden one.

In addition I recalled coloured eggs, and the nightly ceremony of kneeling in front of a cross and mumbling some strange words I could not understand.

I interviewed a lot of people and travelled to Lithuania three times. The story of my past started to emerge and thus I was able to build the following picture in which, I am sure, there are still many gaps I will never be able to fill.

I was born in 1940 to Feige, née Feivelson and Eliyahu Shlapobersky. My mother was the daughter of Eliyahu Meir Feivelson, the rabbi from Kupishkes. He published a lot of articles and a number of books. From records, I discovered that he was among the founders of *Agudat Israel* (Society of Israel), a clericalist political party of Ultra-Orthodox Jews, founded in 1912, as well as of the *'Yavne'*, a chain of religious Zionist schools in Lithuania. Mother graduated from the Yavne Teachers' College and became a headmistress in a school in Panemune.[3]

My father Eliyahu Shlapobersky was born in Kedainiai, one of eleven children in the family. Father's family owned a windmill. They were non-observant. After completing his studies and having obtained his professional qualification as a chemist, my father opened a private business. I still cannot understand how my grandfather, the famous conservative rabbi, could agree to the marriage of his daughter with a secular man who played the mandolin. (Mother's sister married a rabbi).

I was smuggled out of the ghetto either at the end of 1942 or at the beginning of 1943, before the Children's Action. My parents handed me over to a Lithuanian policeman (possibly for payment) whose wife was my parents' neighbour before the war. They gave him my birth certificate and the address of my uncle, Harry Shlapobersky, in South Africa and asked him, promising a generous award, to send me there, if they did not survive.

Figure 56. Feige and Eliyahu Shlapobersky, 1939?

The Lithuanian policeman transferred me to his family in the village. I was kept in the kitchen in the company of a stout lady and a large stove; there was a nice sitting room in the house with lot of lights, but I was not allowed to leave the kitchen. I remember I felt deeply insulted by this treatment, as if I was an inferior creature compared to the other inhabitants of the house. Much later I understood I was a hidden child and the people who rescued me were afraid that their neighbours would see and report me.

When the Germans retreated, Shmuel Peipert, a young Jewish fellow and an officer in the Soviet Army, who was wounded and released from battle, returned to Lithuania and sought out the Jewish children hidden in the villages. He reclaimed them with money and transferred them to orphanages. One day the stout woman led me out of the kitchen to the sitting room; a man in uniform was standing there. She told me that my father had come to take me back. For one simple reason I agreed immediately to go with him. I just wanted to escape this kitchen were I had been imprisoned for so long.

Peipert placed me in an orphanage in Panevezhys that belonged to the Brides of Jesus Convent. Naturally we were given a Christian education; we learnt all the Christian rituals, and I was named Eva. From time to time Peipert used to visit me and bring me candy; I referred to him as '*tevialis*' (Daddy). Once he came with a photographer, took me on his lap and told me, 'Look there, a bird will come out of the camera.' A photographer covered his head with a black sheet and I sat tense with expectation. But no bird appeared. I saw only a blitz of light. Unfortunately this photo of Peipert with me on his lap was lost in one our movements from one place to another. During one of Peipert's attempts to reclaim a child, Lithuanian nationalists murdered him.

My parents perished in the liquidation of the ghetto; I could not track down people who could tell me about their last days. I became acquainted with my parents at the later stages of my life only through photographs. I was not fortunate enough to know the love of a mother or a father's embrace.

In 1945, my aunt Rachel Shlapobersky-Levin was liberated from Stutthof and returned to Kaunas. By chance, she was informed by Chaim Ronder that her niece had survived and was being kept at the Brides of Jesus Convent in Panevezhys. She went to the convent to collect me. With all my might I resisted the attempts of this lady whom I did not know to take me away from my home and my friends. Eventually I was obliged to go with her and soon we moved to Vilnius.

My aunt married Jermiyahu Ratner, a man who had survived the Klooga concentration camp. We were a complicated family: a small girl and two adult people who had just returned from the horror and suffering of the ghetto and the concentration camps. I grew up in a home full of tears and the terrible stories of my foster-parents about what they had gone through. I avoided being at home when my parents were there, looking for refuge outside in the school, with my friends and in activities of the Young Communist Movement, *Komsomol*.

One rainy day in 1959 my aunt told me that there was a good opportunity for us to leave Lithuania. Since Jermiyahu Ratner had been a Polish citizen before the war, we were entitled to move to Poland, his homeland. My aunt was happy and told me with excitement that from Poland we could move easily to Israel. I was shocked, for me this news came like a thunder bolt; I strongly opposed us leaving the USSR. I attended the Russian school, all my friends were Russian and I was educated in the ideals of Communism. Stalin, the 'sunshine of the nations' was our father, and Russia was our Motherland! What did I have to do with Israel!? Eventually I had no choice and we emigrated to Poland. There I studied Civil Engineering at the polytechnic in Wroclaw. It was difficult since I could not speak the language. We stayed in Poland about a year, till our relatives organized our visa to Israel. In 1960 I emigrated to Israel with my aunt Rachel and her husband.

Despite the warmth and attention of distant relatives, early settlers in Israel, who cared for all my needs and even helped me enrol in the Polytechnic Institute, the Technion in Haifa, I felt like a stranger in Israel. I did not understand the language, different to any languages I knew before, and did not like the Israeli ways and manners. It was difficult to bear the heat and the behaviour of the local people. I will never forget my first journey by bus to the Technion. All the seats in the bus were occupied by male students; they stared at me but no one gave up his seat. I stood alone in the middle of the bus, embarrassed. Never in Lithuania and Poland had I encountered such rude behaviour. I thought: 'What am I doing here? I do not belong to this place and to these people.' I wanted to leave, but I had no means and no place to go.

During my first days in Israel, when I was still living with my relatives, I was 'advised' not to speak of my past. This advice suited me very well, I did not want people to pity me. I blocked out my whole past and took no interest in my roots. Throughout my student years I was extremely busy with my studies and overloaded both physically and mentally. It was not at all easy to study without knowing the language and without friends. However, then my life happily changed when I met Yakov Strichman, who became my husband. I graduated from the Faculty of Civil Engineering and Yakov graduated as an industrial and management engineer.

We started a new life together relying on ourselves alone, with no substantial help from anybody. We worked very hard to bring up our two children, Liora and Eliran, and to build our life; we did well in our professional careers. Eventually my children left home and I retired. The atmosphere in Israel had changed. There was more openness about the Holocaust and those who had survived it were speaking out. I suddenly found myself exposed to the period of my life that till now I had repressed. Unfortunately my aunt Rachel and her husband Jermiyahu passed away and a lot of information was lost with them.

Our daughter gained a PhD in Molecular Biology and our son is a lawyer. Our legacy is our two grandsons and two granddaughters.

Haifa, Israel, 2009

NOTES

1. J. Chrust (ed.), *Keidan Memorial Book* [Hebrew] (Tel Aviv: Keidan Association in Israel, with the Committees in South Africa and the USA, 1977), p.229.
2. David Wolpe, *The Destruction of Keidan* (Johannesburg: Keidaner Sick Benefit and Benevolent Society, 1950); The Association of Lithuanian Jews in Israel, *Lithuanian Jewry. Vol 4. The Holocaust 1941–1944* [Hebrew] (Tel Aviv: Reshafim, 1984), p.346.
3. Association of Lithuanian Jews in Israel, *Lithuanian Jewry. Vol 4*, p.132.

PART FOUR

IN THE COUNTRYSIDE

29. Letter to My Grandson Idan

Dan Vaintraub

My dear Idan!
Today you asked me how it was in the Holocaust. I saw you, a gentle soul, hesitating to ask, trying not to hurt me.

Maybe it is time to tell you the story of a child from the ghetto. It all starts with the stories of my mother, Helena Vaintraub, born Girshovich. My father, Haim Vaintraub, who also survived this hell, reluctantly refused to speak about it until his death in May 1993. Only after his death my mother started to recount her ghetto stories; sometimes the details would differ, but the main events remained the same. Over the years, her stories merged with the few memories I had preserved deep down in my own head, hidden in the dark corners of my mind and reluctant to surface.

I was born on 10 November 1938 (the very night of *Kristallnacht*) and I was nearly 3 when we entered the ghetto. I was 5 years old on 17 November 1943, the day I was smuggled out of the ghetto.

The very first event I remember: it happened when I might have just turned 3 years old. There was a knock at the window, a sign that something ominous was stirring in the ghetto, my mother recalls. My parents got dressed and quickly dressed me. And then I asked in German *'Das Ghetto ist Umtzingelt?'*('Is the Ghetto surrounded?'). How did a thought like this enter the mind of a 3-year-old? Perhaps I had heard the adults talking about this and associated it with a feeling of danger. Perhaps this was the reaction of a child seeing the look of terror in his parents' faces.

It was very difficult sharing my memories with others. Especially difficult was recounting the story of the neighbours' son who was older than me by a few years and who had once teased me in the street. I choke up with tears every time I recall this. Yet I have to tell it here for the sake of that boy whose name I don't even remember but whose voice still hums in my head after all these years. My mother had clothed me in some kind of a dress or long apron before sending me out to play in the yard.

That 6- or 7-year-old boy taunted me for wearing a dress in a song that he made up on the spot, the song that still rings in my ears today:

> *Danke di meidel trogt a kleidel,*
> *Danke di meidel trogt a kleidel.*

This means in Yiddish, 'Danny the girl is wearing a gown'.

I can still hear his voice and I recognize it. Or perhaps I just imagine hearing it. But what difference does it make? That whole family perished. Whether in the ghetto or in the camps my mother could not remember.

The only thing left in this universe of that little boy who played in the streets of the Kaunas Ghetto is the song that he sang that autumn of 1941 which for sixty years has been preserved in the memory of another little boy.

I remember another chilling event that took place in the street. I was outside when I saw a beautiful wagon with nickel trimmings. I was thrilled by the sight of this car and started running so as not to lose sight of it. And then I caught sight of my mother standing at the entrance of our house, and she is mortified, there is a look of terror on her face that I will remember till the day I die. My mother recognized that the man in the convertible car was the ghetto commander.

The brigades were groups of several hundred men and women whom the Germans would lead to slave labour outside the ghetto. After removing the yellow star my mother slipped away from the brigade. She went to meet Maryte, a Lithuanian lady who was a relative of my nanny. They were going to finalize the details of how to rescue me. On her way to meet Maryte at the arranged place she suddenly spotted the history professor who had taught her at the university. Before she could even contemplate the danger that was posed, the professor lifted his hat in a gentlemanly manner and said, 'Good luck Girshovitciute', which was mother's maiden name.

On 17 November 1943 I was smuggled out of the ghetto and straight into my nanny Mariona's arms, after Father had bribed the Romanian soldiers who were in charge of watching the gates.

I remember a day when I was playing with Nanny Mariona's knitting needles (I do not remember her surname). One needle represented Russian cannons and the other the Germans, and I was aware back then that the Russians were good and the Germans were bad. To hide the Russian cannons I stuck them inside the hay mattress but pushed too far and lost them inside; I remember Mariona being angry with me. This happened in Aleksotas, at the home of a Lithuanian couple, relatives of my nanny.

We were there until the spring of 1944 when my parents escaped from the ghetto. The River Neman separated the ghetto from the suburb where I was hiding and my parents crossed this river in a boat. Father had bought the boat from Gentiles in exchange for the family house in the very centre of Kaunas. An interesting fact: they kept the paper signed by my father all through the years of the communist era until the disintegration of USSR and Lithuania regained its independence – and then claimed the property for themselves.

Figure 57. Dan Vaintraub (stands, taller boy) with the Kulikauskas' children, in the village of Ziulkine near Kaunas, summer 1944. Photo taken by a neighbouring farmer, who hid Dan's parents, in order to persuade them that Dan was alive.

So my parents moved in with my nanny's relatives, but then they decided to move Mariona and me away to live with her other relatives in a tiny village called Zuikine. They were afraid that a little boy my age might behave with less caution in the presence of his mother and that this might endanger us all.

I have an amusing memory of being in the village. One goose got into the habit of biting me on the backside, he would creep up behind me and attack; it must have happened three or four times and has stuck in my memory.

In my new home I was given the name Antanas and the master of the house, Mr Kulikauskas, pretended I was his son. He and his wife became my adoptive parents and insisted I call them 'Mother' and 'Father', even when we were alone. Their children didn't know that I was Jewish, they were told I was the son of relatives and that I had been orphaned. Sometimes five or six German soldiers from the anti-aircraft unit located nearby would sit at our long wooden farm table and my adoptive father would bring homemade schnapps and fresh bread, while the soldiers would bring preserved food, which may have been their battle rations. Sometimes we would be called to join them at the table, and sometimes Kulikauskas' children would play with the soldiers at their military post and I would go with them. My 'father' would urge me not to go saying, '*Do not go there* and, if you do go, keep quiet'.

One day a high-ranking German officer came for dinner and we all sat at the table. The drink was flowing. Then the German said something that my adoptive father did not understand; I understood what the officer had said because German had been my first language, and so translated it to my 'father'.

The German officer suddenly sobered up, 'How come this child understands German?!'

My 'father' stroked my head with one hand, and with the other he pinched me hard in the leg. In a mixture of Lithuanian and German he answered, 'Children are always wiser than we are'.

I will never know why the German decided to let the matter drop. Many years later, when the memories began to surface, I felt an enormous urge to find this officer and to ask him if he had known my true identity. On my only visit to German soil, I had to spend the night in Frankfurt. It was 13 September 1993. I went out to feel, to see and to smell Germany for the first time in my life. I skimmed the faces in the street wondering whether this or that man could be him. I peered into coffee shops trying to find the faces of older German men to see if this could be the officer from years past. Only later I did the maths; that officer would have been 40 years old in 1944, by then he would have been 90, if he hadn't met his death somewhere in the war. But I couldn't let the matter rest. Perhaps this was the ultimate expression of the ties between the victim and the executioner.

And finally I remember the thunder of cannons as the front approached. My adoptive mother prayed incessantly, I remember my nanny reciting prayers and knitting, of being rushed to the trenches that the Germans had built for cover. I never understood why the Germans would have cared for our safety. One day when we were all in one trench, a horrified German officer ran in shouting 'Russian planes!' I remember the terror in his face.

I don't know if we stayed in the trench through the night, I don't remember any explosions, I just remember that I felt hunger for the first time since coming to the village. When we emerged from the trench, there were no Germans, there were no Russians and there were no rockets. This was the end of July 1944.

My reunion with my parents was embarrassing rather than happy. It was a few weeks after the liberation of Kaunas by the Soviet Army. I remember myself standing in the middle of the barn facing the sunlit doorway and repeating time and again some Russian dirty words I had recently learned from passing Red Army soldiers, when suddenly I saw my mother's shadow in the doorway.

Because of the strong sunlight I couldn't see her face, but somehow I knew it for sure: this woman was my mother. After a few moments my father appeared in the doorway. Years later, he complained that he couldn't expect any better from a person like me: all that I could learn from a Russian soldier was a couple of dirty words.

Anyhow they took me back to Kaunas where we spent the next twenty-five years together with Itamar and Abigail, my two cousin-orphans who survived the ghetto and were adopted by my parents. I graduated from the Kaunas Polytechnic Institute in 1956. We all emigrated to Israel 1972, where I work as self-employed structural engineer.

I tried many times to organize my memories and put them on

paper. Somehow I never succeeded to do it. Why? Fear? Maybe, but now I am finally able to complete the story. I think that it will be right that you, my dear Idan and your sister Karin will have my memoirs, and will read the life story of their grandfather who was fortunate not to end up as a cloud of smoke from a chimney.

With all my love,
Saba (Grandfather in Hebrew) Dan

Tel Aviv, Israel, 2009

30. The Only Little Black Mouse

Maya Shochataite-Davidov

Before the war my father, Nachum (Naum) Shohat, had been working as an engineer at the rubber factory and my mother, Masha, née Balin, as a secretary. I was born in Kaunas in May 1939. I grew up in a prosperous family surrounded by the love of parents, grandmothers and grandfathers. On a single day all that was shattered. Our whole family failed to be evacuated in time and landed up in the Kaunas Ghetto, where my parents, my aunt Rachel and my uncle Faivele all lived in one room.

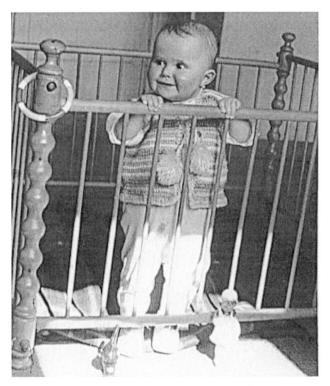

Figure 58. Maya Shohat, a 'hidden child', 1940.

During the 'Great Action' our whole family found itself in the column which was being sent to the Ninth Fort; it was raining and people had to walk an interminable distance. Mother was carrying me all the time. I refused to get down. Despite the fact that my mother was almost collapsing from tiredness, I was not prepared to go to anybody else. It seemed the road would never end. Then suddenly a miracle happened. At some stage the Germans realized that they were losing manpower. The Germans began drawing up a list of the workers they needed and those people were taken out of the column with their wives and children. That was how my parents, Mother's 15-year-old brother Faivele and 16-year-old sister Rachel, who were quick enough off the mark to say that they too were my parents' children, succeeded in returning to the ghetto.

All the remaining members of our family, my grandfathers Eliahu Balin and Moshe Shohat, my grandmother Golda Shohat and uncle Yitzhak Shohat, were killed. Despite the fact that I was too little to understand the whole tragedy, I was gripped by fear all the time. I was frightened to sleep and used to ask my mother not to shut her eyes and to keep looking at me all the time.

Papa was sent to work at the construction site for the new airfield at Aleksotas. When news reached the ghetto that all the children in the Shauliai Ghetto had been taken off and killed, my father realized that the same thing could happen in Kaunas as well. He began to look for people who would be ready to take in a Jewish girl. He was ready to hand me over to anyone who would agree to take me, because it was the only chance for me to survive.

Father shared his thoughts with an engineer by the name of Mil, who was working alongside him. One day a Lithuanian couple were walking past the men engaged in building the airfield. They stopped and started talking to Mil. They told him that they were going from Jurbarkas to the Kaunas station in order to buy a little girl. Their priest had told his congregation that the Germans transported women with their children from Russia to work in Germany. Trains used to stop in Kaunas and many of women used to throw their children out of the wagons in a hope that someone would pick them up. For a certain sum of money guards at the station were prepared to sell those children. The couple had sold their cow and they were planning to spend the money on buying specifically a little girl, since they already had three boys of their own.

Mil told them that he was working with someone who would be ready to hand them his 4-year-old daughter, as long as they did not mind that she was Jewish. The couple met my father and said that they were ready to take a Jewish girl, as long as she did not look very Jewish. It was agreed that they should come to the ghetto fence and he would show me to them. They saw me and agreed there and then to take me; they took me in with a single aim in view, which was to save me, without asking for anything in return.

By then my parents did not have anything left either. It was 1943 and everyone was hungry. Everything that could be exchanged for food already had been. All that my father gave them was a couple of letters. One was addressed to his sister in Palestine and the second to his uncle in New York. He asked the Lithuanian couple to send off those letters, if he and my mother did not survive.

Father arranged with the couple when and where he would hand me over. I was put to sleep and placed in a sack; my aunt bribed the guards at the gate and I was carried out of the ghetto. Mother fainted when her only child was taken away from her. All that happened on 20 November 1943. Neither my parents nor my aunt knew anything about the couple: who they were or what they were. They only knew that it was my only chance of survival.

We went from Kaunas to Jurbarkas by boat. I was still under the influence of the sleeping pill I had been given and the couple did not wake me, because they were worried that I might start crying and asking for my parents. In the village to which they brought me, they kept me at home for a long time, because I could only speak Yiddish. They explained to the neighbours that a German had given them this little girl at the station, who in his turn had gathered her up somewhere, which was why I sometimes used German words when I spoke. They knew that by rescuing me they were putting their whole family in danger.

The woman who became my 'Mama' was called Elena and her husband was Petras Lileika. Their oldest son was the same age as myself. They all called me Maryte, and I became one of the family. I was given everything that their children were given and I was punished for being naughty, just like their children were. I remember that on one occasion I had been up to some mischief and 'Papa' was about to unbuckle his belt to beat me. It had gone missing though. I crawled under the beds, under the table, eventually found the belt under a cupboard and brought it to him. After all that Petras said that he would forgive me that time, because I had found his belt and brought it to him.

Then came 1944, when life grew even more difficult. There was not enough food. One day Petras went into town while Elena was digging in the vegetable garden. Next door to them lived her cousin. All of a sudden that cousin came running over to Elena, shouting that Elena was digging up her potatoes and she would go to the local commandant's office and tell them that they were hiding a Jewish child.

Elena was alone with her four children when she saw her cousin coming back with a German. Her three sons were all fair-haired and I was the only little black mouse. The German pointed his gun at the cousin and asked her to show him which of the children was Jewish. She pointed at me and the German said, 'You're lying. She looks like her mother and I'll kill you for that lie.' This happened at a time when the Red Army was already not far from Kaunas; perhaps the soldier was someone who had some human feelings, or perhaps I was just destined to survive. He came to the Lileika family a number of times, bringing cans of food, milk powder and other produce.

At the end of 1944, the Germans were driven out of the area and the Red Army entered Lithuania. That very same cousin went this time to the office of the Soviet commandant and reported that a little Jewish girl was living with the Lileika family, who were treating her badly, despite the fact that they had been given plenty of money by her parents. After that Russian soldiers came to the house one night, told everyone to get up and dressed and took Petras into Jurbarkas to the commandant's office. Petras had the two letters from my father with him, in which it was stated that he had handed over his only daughter to these strangers in the hope that they would rescue her and that he had nothing left to give them. During the interrogation a woman officer had been present, who turned out to be Jewish. She started crying and gave instructions for Petras to be returned to his home.

Despite the fact that I was convinced that Petras and Elena were my real parents, it would seem that somewhere deep down

I felt that there were things I needed to beware of. When Petras' brother completed his studies at the seminary, a party was held in his honour in the village. During the celebrations one of the guests unexpectedly died and the police were called in. Everyone had been scared. At some stage of the proceedings the guests realized that for several hours it had been impossible to get into the toilet, which was outdoors; they started knocking at the door and pulling at it, but it would not open. Then they opened it by force and saw me in the corner with a sack over my head. The Lileika had explained to me earlier, that I should always hide away from people in uniform so as not to be seen. I had not yet grasped that I did not need to be frightened of the Soviet militia.

When the Lileika family learnt that a Jewish orphanage had been opened in Kaunas, they decided to take me there, in the hope that perhaps someone from my family was still alive and could take me back from there. They arrived with me in Kaunas and first of all went with me to see Petras' mother. She persuaded them not to give me up; she thought it a shame to hand a little girl to the orphanage after they had saved me from certain death over a period of two years. She decided that I should stay with her in Kaunas, while Petras and Elena went back to the village.

We lived on what we managed to obtain through begging outside Kaunas Cathedral. I was small and thin, so people used to take pity on us and gave us money. We used to live on that money and 'Granny' also used it to put together parcels for her other son. Once a month we would go to the prison to visit him; he had been a member of the Lithuanian police who worked alongside the Germans. One of 'Granny's' sons had saved a little Jewish girl, while the other had been working as a policeman.

People who had survived in the camps began returning home. Petras began making enquiries about my relatives, but failed to find anybody. Then he sent off the letters which my father had given him, and he informed my father's relatives that during the war he had rescued this little Jewish girl, but that her parents had not appeared. The letter reached my father's uncle in New York via the Red Cross, who then contacted my aunt in Tel Aviv, who sent parcels to Lithuania and started making plans to enable me to come and live with him.

At Kaunas station Jews used to gather to meet those returning from the camps; each one tried to find about the fate of his relatives. Someone told our relative, Raya Levin, that they had seen Naum and Masha's daughter in Kestuchio Street. Raya found me and started coming to visit 'Granny' but I would always cower away from her. Raya tried to win the hungry little girl over with ice cream, but I refused to respond. When I caught sight of Raya in the yard, I would run to 'Granny' and say that the Jewish woman with the painted lips had come again and I would ask 'Granny' to say that I was not at home.

I remember the day when I was sitting at the kitchen table with 'Granny' and the door suddenly opened and there were three terrible women standing in the doorway. They had shaven heads and were wrapped in blankets. When they saw me they began to shout and cry. 'Granny' realized at once that they were my relatives. She asked me, 'Maryte, who's come to see you?' Like a frightened cat I jumped over the table, clung to 'Granny' and began to call out, 'It's not my Mama, my Mama was young and beautiful. Make those women go away.' My mother had only just returned from Stutthof. She was with Rachel, who also survived Stutthof, and another woman. Mama and Rachel stayed for six weeks in 'Granny's' house but I refused to go up to them. In the end my mother managed to find photographs of my father and the family, and she tried to explain to me who the people were. Some two months later my father returned from Dachau; it did not take so long for me to accept him. Mother must have been able to get me used to the idea that he was my real father. My parents decided to move from Kaunas to Vilnius, because in Kaunas there were too many things that reminded me of their tragic past.

My uncle Faivale, after liberation from a concentration camp, went directly to Israel. Here he was killed during the War of Independence. Rachel tried to escape from the USSR by plane, but was arrested and put in a prison. Fortunately she was soon released. Rachel emigrated to Israel only in 1971 with her daughter and husband David Rubenstein.

I eventually graduated from the Kaunas Medical Institute, married Kalman Davidov and left for Israel. We have two children and four grandchildren. I worked for many years as a doctor and was a highly respected GP in Haifa.

Haifa, Israel, 2008

31. Two Mina Steins

Mina Stein-Wulf

Noa, my eldest granddaughter asked me in 2006, when she reached the age of 9, to give a talk in her school about what had happened to me during the Second World War. For years I had not spoken about it, I had not wanted to remember. My late mother, Raya Stein, who died in 1983, hardly ever talked about that past so full of horrors. Almost everything I have put down on paper I know from my sister Izana Levit. When I read through what is written down I cannot stop my eyes filling with tears.

My mother had nine brothers and sisters. Her father, Hirsh Stein, had been a businessman. He and five of my mother's brothers and sisters perished during the war. Mother had obtained a place to study at the chemistry faculty of Vienna University, but when my father proposed to her, she abandoned those plans. Many years later, I followed in my mother's footsteps and graduated in chemistry from the Technion in Haifa. In 1925 my mother married Max Stein.

Father was a very erudite man: he knew many languages, including Hebrew and Esperanto. He worked as an economist for various trading companies. In 1929 Izana was born and I, Mina, in 1937. I was called Mina in remembrance of my grandmother. My official name was Manuela, which my father had chosen, because he was a supporter of the Republicans during the Spanish Civil War.

The atmosphere in our home prior to the war was happy and life was very comfortable. We lived at 3 Zamenhof Street on the bank of the River Neman. Izana was sent to study in the Schwabe Gymnasium.

Before we had to move into the ghetto, my sister Izana used to stand in a queue at a food shop 'for Jews only'. Despite being little more than a child, Izana was made responsible for the family's 'queuing'. One day the Lithuanians suddenly started seizing people standing in those queues. Everyone started running off in all directions and Izana ran off too till she found where to hide in a wooden toilet in someone's back yard. She waited there until things went quiet and she was able to make her way home.

Even before the family was moved into the ghetto, our father, with Vulia (Wolf) Peper, the husband of my aunt Vera, was arrested by Lithuanian collaborators ('*Baltaraisciai*') wearing white armbands: Father came home again, but Vulia did not. My aunt said to our mother, 'Of the two who were destined to die, it's good that Max has survived, because he has children who need looking after.'

In the ghetto our family was allocated a room in a four-storey brick house referred to as the 'Red House'. There were five of us living in that room: my parents, Izana, my favourite aunt Adela and me. One day, Izana and I set off with our mother to visit Grandfather Hirsh in the 'Small Ghetto'. We were stopped on the way by guards and they would not let us pass. It turned out that people were being rounded up that day: our grandfather and Aunt Vera were taken off to the Ninth Fort and shot there. It is terrible to think that, if we had been allowed to continue our journey, we would no longer be among the living.

In 1943 rumours were spreading in the ghetto about an imminent round-up of children. My uncle David asked his close friend from pre-war days, Zaborsky, to help rescue my cousin Mina, born in 1938. Zaborsky was given some valuables and a large sum of money to look after till end of the war. He was offered a part of the money in return for rescuing me. Zaborsky, who had been only too happy to be a friend of a rich Jewish family during the good times, refused, adding cynically, 'In any case she would die.'

Mina's father, Liolya Stein, another of my mother's brothers, was asked to save a small girl called Anya Levinson. Liolya arranged for Anya to live with Antosia, the maid who had worked for Max (mother's favourite brother) and Lea Stein before the war. Max and Lea had been arrested as 'bourgeois elements' by the Soviets and deported to Siberia a few days before the German invasion. Max had left his son Arie in the care of his brothers. Antosia was asked to hide Arie, but she had refused, saying she was afraid to take in a 'circumcised boy'. Efforts to save Arie failed and he was killed during the 'Children's Action'.

Figure 59. Stein family. Standing, left to right: Mina Stein-
Kotkes's parents, Liolya and Bunya; Aunt Vera; Izana Stein; and
Max Stein, father of Mina Stein-Wolf. Seated: Aunt Lea Stein
(pregnant with Arik) with Mina Stein-Wolf. In the hammock:
Raya Stein.

Antosia was prepared to take in a little girl though. Later someone informed on Antosia. She had not known Anya's surname
and had used Liolya's surname while being interrogated. Little
Anya had started begging people to leave her alone. She cried out
to Antosia, *'Mochute gelbek!'*, which means 'Mama, save me!', but
the Gestapo men took her off and she perished.

When we heard what had happened, my father tried to

persuade Liolya to go into hiding, but he did not take the advice
and went off to work as usual. Jewish Polizei Tanchum Arnstam
arrested Liolya at work; Izana saw Arnstam lead him off. Bunya,
Mina's mother, was arrested at home. She was seen for the last
time in the prison, when she sent greetings to her loved ones.
After the war Arnstam was convicted and shot for his evil deeds.

Mr Jonas Januliavichius cooperated with the Gestapo, but still
was our father's loyal friend. He offered to rescue me and Izana.
Januliavichius refused to accept any payment or presents. He
suggested to our father that he should save him as well, but
Father refused to leave the rest of the family alone.

It was decided that just I should go; I was six and a half at the
time. Saying goodbye to my family was very hard. I remember,
as if it was yesterday, how my father stood me on a chair and
fastened my winter coat. It was made of sheepskin and had beautiful embroidery on the outside. Father taught me how to behave;
I had to remember that I was a Russian girl called Manya.

On 7 January 1944 I was taken out of the ghetto. It was a very
cold day and the main gate on Varniu Street was being guarded
by Germans and Lithuanians, so there was no chance of taking
me out while they were still around. Three times Jonas had come
to the gate to collect me, but it had proved impossible. He was
standing there bursting with impatience and my father went up
to the German guard and said loudly, 'You see what a pleasant
and beautiful language German is. In German you would say,
"*Bitte, warten Sie*", while in Lithuanian it sounds so brash, "Wait,
Jonas!"', Jonas realized then that he had to go on waiting. When
the next shift of guards came on duty and there were the 'right'
people at the gate, my father led me through and put me into the
cart in which Januliavichius took me to his house at 3 Daukanto
Street in the centre of the city.

There I spent the first two weeks. I behaved nicely and always
helped with the housework. On only one occasion did my father
manage to come and see me; I was dressed in a little blue suit
specially made for me and given strict instructions not to call my
father 'Papa', so that no-one would realize I was Jewish. As I
dusted the furniture, I whispered into his ear, 'When's Mama
coming?' When my father went back into the ghetto, he wept like
a baby. It was the first time that he had ever been seen crying, and
that was the last time I ever saw him.

In the Januliavichius family they spoke German. There was a boy in the household, probably a Russian, whom they had taught to speak German and I used to answer him in Yiddish. This frightened Jonas and his wife, as they knew it would be disastrous if anyone should hear me. So Januliavichius decided to send me to the village of Mishkuchiai, where his mother and sisters lived.

Life was not easy for me in that village. Children had to grow up quickly and take on all sorts of duties on the farm; I used to feed the pigs, the cows and the geese. The cows would be taken out to graze in the meadows after haymaking. The only shoes I had were dark blue ones with laces: they were too small for me. When I went out into the fields I would put them on so that my heels were treading down the backs, which made me look like some sort of clown.

On one occasion one of the pigs went missing; I tried as hard as I could to find that pig but failed and returned home with one pig too few. I was beaten with a strap and sent back out barefoot to look for the lost pig. While I was looking for it, this time at the nearby bog, knowing that pigs liked mud, I suddenly bumped into it. The pig began to squeal very loudly, and in my fright I fell over into the mud. I can still remember that wild squealing and how frightful I looked, all covered in mud.

It is likely that my Jewish mind was still ticking over even in those hard times. My parents used to send me suitcases with clothes from time to time, and there were a few books as well. I could already read at that stage and loved reading: my father sent me to a teacher in the ghetto, mainly so that I should learn to read and write in Russian. I used to give away the clothes to other girls in the village so that in exchange for each garment they would look after the animals for me, while I lay at the edge of the field reading books.

A little later on, my cousin Mina joined us, once again with the help of Januliavichius. She was four and a half at the time. Father had carried her out of the ghetto in a sack of potatoes; the guards had been bribed, but for the sake of appearances they had stuck their bayonets through the sack taking care not to do Mina any harm. Mina's parents were still alive at the time, but they did not live long enough to know that she had reached the village safely.

Mina was still wetting her bed at night and this made the

couple who had taken us in very angry. We slept under the same blanket. Once I took the blame for the wet bedding, so as to spare Mina a thrashing. I was severely beaten with a stick. Mina was a very pretty little girl with blonde hair and blue eyes. German soldiers often used to drive into the village, but she never aroused their suspicions. I even remember one German soldier playing with Mina and putting her on his knee.

The food in the village was always the same, but at least we did not go hungry. For breakfast we were given a mug of milk and black bread and for dinner and supper we had dumplings. Sometimes we were given a piece of bread with pork fat. We never sat around idly though from morning till night. When the Russians were about to enter Lithuania, Mr Januliavichius disappeared. Long before that he had told my father not to look for him after the war.

The last of Januliavichius' attempts was to rescue Izana. Izana had already been dressed up in a black coat with a fur collar, so that she would look more grown-up, and Januliavichius was preparing false papers for her in the name 'Danute'. He was delayed, however, and, by the time he arrived, the ghetto gate was shut tight.

A few days before the ghetto was liquidated, Mother asked Uncle David to let Izana take shelter in his bunker, but he refused. He told her that there was not even room for a pin in there, as it was so crammed with people. It turned out that his refusal saved Izana's life. The Germans blew up the bunker and none of the people, including Aunt Adela Stein, who had been hiding there, survived.

Father met his end in the Dachau crematorium; Mama and Izana were transferred to Stutthof. From museum documents we have since discovered that Mother succeeded in having herself registered seven years younger than she really was and Izana as two years older than her actual age; this move probably saved both their lives. From Stutthof, Mother and Izana were transferred to various work camps. Even when they could sense that defeat was round the corner, the Nazis went on forcing these women to cover long distances on foot, but one day the guards just abandoned them and ran off. The women managed to make their way to the deserted Turin camp, where Russian troops later found them.

Mother and Izana were liberated in January 1945, but they were held up in Poland for two weeks. There they learned of our father's death. It was also the time when Izana fell ill with pneumonia and only just pulled through. They were then taken to Grodno in Belarussia, where they had to spend quite a long time. The only reason why my mother and Izana went back to Kaunas at the end of 1945 was to reclaim me.

In July 1944 artillery shelling of the village by the Russians began, and Mina and I had to sleep in the cellar on its damp floor. We used to lie on one half of a blue blanket and cover ourselves with the other. At the end of my stay with them, the Lithuanian family had sent me off without any help, without any directions or instructions. I had put on two sets of clothes: one of them had been the 'sailor suit' with the pleated skirt. I took with me my favourite brown teddy bear under one arm and under the other a live hen as I set off to Kaunas. When I told my granddaughter's class about my experiences, one of the questions asked was, what had I done with the chicken?!

After walking a few kilometres, I came across a 14-year-old Jewish girl on a horse-drawn cart. She had gone into hiding of her own accord in a Lithuanian household in another village. She realized I was Jewish straightaway and she suggested we should make our way to Kaunas together. She took me directly to the Jewish Committee, which had been set up in the town immediately after the liberation. It was there that my aunt, Anya Koc (née Langleben), found me, and I lived with her for a year. Later on, my father's brother, Mark Stein, took me to Moscow. He used to call me Ella: the name Mina sounded too Jewish to his ears, Manuela was too long and Manya seemed too Russian.

From there my mother fetched me home in 1947. She had been unable to do so before that, because she had not been able to obtain a permit from the authorities to travel to Moscow. I lived without my parents for three and a half years. We moved to Vilnius, where my mother worked first as a waitress and later as a bookkeeper.

The Lithuanian family had kept my cousin Mina on in their household; they thought that Mina would stay with them for always. Eventually someone appeared in the village in Red Army uniform. It was Nosen Levit, the husband of Mina's aunt Musya. The couple adopted Mina and she came to live and grow up in the care of her aunt.

In 1958 we left for Poland and from there, Israel in 1959. My father's sister, Rebecca, had been a Zionist. She had departed for Israel in 1919. Our father had visited her in 1935; he had liked Israel, but our mother had not been prepared to leave her family behind in Lithuania. Rebecca met us when we arrived. Settling down in Israel was not easy at first; our mother had to work very hard, but she always made sure that we did not go short.

Izana married in 1950, she has two children, five grand-children and two great-grandchildren. I married in 1964. For many years Mother helped us bring up our children, so that we were able to study (I studied chemistry) and acquire a profession. She was always cheerful, energetic, surrounded by friends and she never complained about anything. She died quietly and suddenly, not getting in anyone's way or making things difficult for others.

I am retired now and have two children and five grandchil-dren. I work as a volunteer in an organization that provides advice and practical help for inexperienced people trying to cope with the maze of bureaucracy. Mina graduated from the Vilnius University and became a paediatrician. She married Filip Kotkes, and the Kotkes family emigrated to Israel in 1972. Mina worked as paediatrician till retirement several years ago. The Kotkes have three children and four grandchildren.

Raanana, Israel, January 2009

32. Pesahl, a Wonderful Child

Lilit (Lyda) Yoffe-Davidson

When the Germans entered Lithuania we were living in Panevezhys. I was aged 2 at the time and my father, Leiser Yoffe, was working as a doctor in the hospital there, and my mother Yulia (née Segal) as a dentist. The Germans drove all the hospital staff out into the street and demanded that the Jews and Communists be identified. The only person who was not betrayed that day was my father who was loved and respected by colleagues and patients alike.

We fled to Kaunas, where we soon landed up in the ghetto. My father worked there as a doctor but my mother was sent to work outside the ghetto. Lithuanian friends of my parents, who were members of the anti-fascist underground, made contact with them and used to send food into the ghetto with my mother's help, and Mother in her turn kept them informed of what was going on inside the ghetto (see Figure 30). With the help of those friends we were all able to escape from the ghetto and go into hiding until the end of the war.

Certain episodes from our life in the ghetto have etched themselves on my memory: how my mother cried when my father told her that her parents and younger brothers had been killed. There was another episode when I was in the kindergarten. One of the children asked a nanny which foot he should put his shoe on. 'On your left foot,' she had replied. The boy then asked what he should do with his second shoe; I thought to myself, what an idiot he must be. Those children were later taken away to certain death together with their nanny, who refused to abandon them.

Hardly a single day goes by without me remembering Pesahl, a wonderful child, who had been a neighbour in our cramped flat in a dilapidated wooden house in the ghetto. Little Lord Fauntleroy in person, he had an angelic face and heart and he behaved like a noble adult. My parents later confirmed the impression I had had of him as a little girl of 3 or 4. One day a group of us children was playing in the main street of the ghetto and we saw a man with one leg moving about on crutches. We all began to laugh and then suddenly came Pesahl's voice, exclaiming, 'And if that had happened to you?!' Pesahl died, like most of the children in the ghetto, and I never knew his surname or how old he was.

And then I remember well July 1944. The Germans were retreating and the Russians were advancing, moving through the village where Mother and I hid during the last year of the occupation. My mother had to pretend to be 'a Lithuanian refugee from the nearby town'. When she said goodbye to the peasant for whom she had worked in return for shelter, she told him that she was a Jew. He replied, 'Do you think I didn't realize?'

We managed to scrounge a lift into town in a lorry that was full of cheerful soldiers and I heard my mother mutter to herself, 'Has that idiot managed to survive or not?' I realized that she was very worried about my father, who was staying in the house of my nanny Anna in Kaunas. Most of the time he spent in a cupboard, only coming out at night to breathe some fresh air at the window.

Our reunited family, complete with nanny, was allocated a spacious flat by the Soviet authorities. My parents both had jobs, and parcels from Israel from my father's sisters started arriving. What a treat it was to have needles and thread!

I knew that my father's sister had died with her husband in Kurshenai and that Mother had lost two brothers in Rokishkis and that we had no other relatives left, apart from those in Palestine. I could spend whole days looking at the photographs which my parents had managed to salvage, despite all the ups and downs of the war they had experienced; they showed my parents in the circle of their large family, young and carefree. I was only 5 or 6 at the time, but each night I used to have a nightmare about the Germans chasing after my grandmother, my grandfather and my mother's younger brothers, whom I used to think of as my own brothers. One night I imagined that I was standing with a cudgel and lashing out with it at my nightmare with all my strength, so as to drive it out of my mind once and for all: the nightmare never came back. Then I decided that I would grow up to be a doctor so as to invent medicine that would bring my grandfather and grandmother back to life.

By means of my fictitious marriage, we came to Israel in 1958 through Poland. I graduated from the Hadassah Medical School and worked as a dentist. I am married and have two children.

Ever since I can remember, I have wanted to prove to everyone that I had been worth saving.

Jerusalem, 2009

33. Abandoned in the Forest

Boris Dvogovsky

My father, Moshe Dvogovsky, and mother Riva, née Kweskin, always dreamed of going to Israel, and were on a waiting list for a certificate to emigrate to Palestine. Father was active in the left-wing Zionist movement. He played football very well and was a member of the *Hashomer hatzair* football team. Unfortunately, the course of history in Lithuania destroyed their dream. We were finally to arrive in Israel more then 30 years later...

I was born on 9 July 1941 in Kaunas at the Jewish Hospital. The Germans had already occupied the town. My parents realized that registering delivery of a baby posed an immense risk, so Mother left the hospital immediately after my birth. Father's parents and his brother Zundel were buried alive by Lithuanian collaborators in Butrimonys during the first days of the occupation.

In 1942, my parents escaped from the ghetto. For a time they hid in the surrounding woods, until they came across a group of partisans. There were two conditions for membership: children were not permitted, and arms had to be acquired independently. The leader of the partisan group, called 'For Soviet Lithuania', took it upon himself to settle me with a family in the countryside, within the partisans' area of activity. The terms were made clear to those who had agreed to adopt me that if anything were to happen to me the village would be burnt down. This family was in fact under enormous pressure: they were afraid of the Nazis, if I were to be found, and of the partisans, who would retaliate if this occurred.

I was made to sleep on a wooden bench at the home of the Lithuanian family; my daily diet was a piece of bread and yogurt, and I was shaved bareheaded to conceal my dark curls. Occasionally my parents would come to visit. It is difficult to describe the joy that came with our brief reunions, but this joy was always overshadowed by the bitter dread of an imminent, unavoidable separation. My parents would be haunted by the sound of my sobbing even as they re-entered the woods; with every parting, there was the recurring fear that we would never see each other again.

The Germans were hunting for partisans, Jews and Communists among the local population, and the family with whom I lived understood that if a Jewish child were to be found, they would inevitably be killed. They dressed me in old torn boots and put a coat over my naked body. On a frosty November night, only 2 years old, I was given a piece of bread to hold in my hand, taken to the forest and abandoned there. No one knows how long I walked through the woods. Partisans returning from an operation found me half-frozen and hungry. They recognized me and brought me to the camp where my parents were based. The fate of a Jewish girl, Miriam, who was being hidden by neighbouring Lithuanians, turned out to be more tragic. She was murdered even before the Germans had entered the village.

I remained in the camp for a few months. It was impossible to get me out since the camp was surrounded by Germans and was constantly under fire. When the situation calmed down, I was taken to another Lithuanian family, the Duniavichius household, and stayed there until liberation. Acquiescing to my mother's pleas, military superiors gave her a horse and carriage and permitted her to go and fetch me. This was a perilous task; the woods harboured many active groups of armed Lithuanian Nationalists, the '*Zaliukai*' ('forest brothers'). Mother however still managed to reach the village and find me. We were lucky; both my parents survived and rescued me.

Mother's youngest brother, Benishke, was shot in 1944 for smuggling food to the ghetto, he was 14 years old. My maternal grandfather Baruch (I am named Boris in his memory) and grandmother Chaya also did not survive the ghetto.

Following the war, I attended the Jewish school for two years (see Figure 46: Boris Dvogovsky is in the top row, seventh from left), and after it was closed went to the Russian gymnasium. I graduated from the Minsk Medical School. My first wife died young from cancer. I emigrated to Israel in 1987 with my two sons, where my parents and my post-war sister Fruma now lived. In Israel I remarried and worked as a GP.

Bat Yam, Israel, 2009

34. My Playmates Were a Cat and a Hen

Julius Neumark

After the First World War my grandfather, Leon (Leib) Neumark, together with three Jewish partners had founded '*Nektaras*', the company consisting of two breweries, a spirit factory and a yeast factory, built on an estate which my grandfather had bought from a Polish noble. The name of the estate was '*Antanavo dvaras*'; this estate also had a small castle and a park of twenty-two hectares. Grandfather died before the German invasion of Lithuania. His second wife, my grandmother, Pauline (Pesa) Neumark, née Grossmann, was murdered in the Kaunas Ghetto in March 1944.

My father, Philipp (Shraga) Neumark, was born in Telsiai, where he attended *cheder* until he was about 10 years old. Then he studied in the Hebrew Shwabe School in Kaunas. He was a member of '*Beitar*', a Zionist World Movement, and in '*Hachschara*', a Jewish youth leadership and education programme. He studied in Berlin and in Vienna, where he graduated from the University of Economics. He met my mother in Vienna and married her in 1936. From 1936 to 1940 he was employed as manager at Grandfather's company. After the occupation of Lithuania in 1940 by the Soviets, Grandfather's property was confiscated, but my father remained as a manager.

I was born on 19 July 1940 in Kaunas about three weeks after the Soviet occupation of Lithuania. My mother, Gisela (Gittel) Neumark, née Neumann, was a bookkeeper. My maternal grand-father had been a soldier in the Austrian army during the First World War. In 1938 he escaped from Vienna to Lithuania, and was murdered in March in the Kaunas Ghetto.

My family's attempt to escape to Russia in June 1941 failed, and we found ourselves in the Kaunas Ghetto. Father, a member of the Jewish police, was in contact with the underground movement. Mother worked most of the time at the airfield in Aleksotas. She was able to hide me during one of the 'actions'. While Germans and their Lithuanian collaborators searched the houses, my mother put me into the toilet while sitting on it,

Julius Neumark

pretending she had diarrhoea, and she behaved as if she was ashamed when somebody opened the door.

When I was 18 months old I was put to sleep with barbiturates and my father smuggled me out of the ghetto. By means of connections with a Lithuanian priest, Father found a couple who would hide me in their home. The names of these foster parents, very loving people, were Jonas and Elena Beliajevas (Belia jev).

I have memories, typical for a small child, of their home where I was hidden in the attic. My playmates were a cat and a hen and I looked every day to see if the hen had laid an egg. If so, the egg was cooked and I was always allowed to eat it. Since I was hidden all the time and nobody in the neighbourhood knew that I existed, besides a friend of my foster mother, Agnes Zhylaitis, they did not need to change my identity. I also remember that I never wore shoes in the hiding place, because after liberation when I was given my first shoes, I refused to put them on. I could not walk in them.

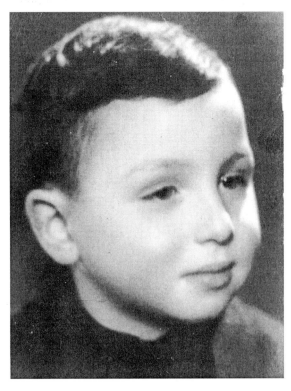

Figure 60. Julius Neumark, a hidden child, 1944.

My mother, grandmother and father with his colleagues had escaped shortly after his mother and father-in-law and many elderly Jews were killed. They lived on a farm and whenever a stranger came, they were hidden in a deep ditch covered with hay and branches. My parents came immediately after liberation to pick me up from my foster-parents; we remained in close touch with them all the time until we left Lithuania in 1946. My foster-mother died shortly after liberation. I remember the funeral and how my mother told me at her grave that now Elena would sleep for a long time.

We moved to Vienna, because my mother was entitled to be repatriated from Lithuania to Austria as an Austrian citizen. From 1946, owing to the political situation of Stalinism, we had no contact with Jonas Beliajevas until about 1965. Then I got in touch with him and regularly sent him parcels until he died.

After the liberation my father obtained a job with the new government of Lithuania, but he decided that we had to leave as soon as possible, because of his history as the son of a 'capitalist' and member of a Zionist movement. With false papers he was able to join us in Austria. Father lectured at the university, wrote a thesis about the economy of Lithuania and became a Doctor of Economics in 1947. He was a member and at one point in charge of *'Beitar'*, a chief editor of a Zionist newspaper founded by Theodor Herzl, *'Die neue Welt'* until 1949, and a manager in different Jewish organizations. Father died in August 1986 and my mother on 1 February 2008 in Vienna.

I graduated from the University of Vienna Medical School, certified in anaesthesia and intensive care medicine at the University Hospital of Vienna. In 1992 I became the chairman of the Department of Anaesthesia and Intensive Care and director of the operating centre of a new hospital, the SMZ-OST.

Vienna, Austria, 2009

35. Left with Mother's Handkerchief

Moisejus (Mika) Rosenblum

I was born on 13 March 1940 in the town of Kaunas to Anatolij Rosenblum, son of Moisei and Raya Rosenblum (née Kenigsberg). My father was a civil engineer and architect, who later worked as a professor at the Kaunas Polytechnic and the Vilnius Institute of Civil Engineering. On the second day after the war began, my parents tried to move out of the path of the Germans. They put me in a pram and decided that they would set off on foot along the Jonava road to the north. It soon became clear, however, that this plan was not going to work. The fact that the Germans had advanced more quickly than expected or the potential dangers of all kinds of violence made my parents turn back. A peasant agreed to hide us in his hayloft. On the third day he came, looking deathly pale, to warn us that we would have to leave: Lithuanian fascists were on the rampage and if they were to find us, he would be bound to get killed. We succeeded in making our way back to our flat without any setbacks. Not far from Kaunas we turned off the road to have a drink of water in a smallholding bordering the road. The woman who owned it warned us that we should not approach the town from that side, since terrible things were happening near the Vilijampole Bridge. She led us over a hill to the other side of the town.

In Kaunas bandits were going from house to house. They were searching through and plundering all the Jewish flats they could find and then taking people away to the Seventh Fort. An enormous number of our friends were killed there. The Lithuanian rabble had not touched our house, since it had been taken over by the German '*Ortskommandatur*'. A German had already taken up residence in one of its rooms. It is worth noting that my parents had a good command of German.

My father was apprehended on the street, precisely at the time when mass shootings were taking place at the Seventh Fort. He was taken there, with a group of other Jews, three times; this group was not accepted there because of 'overflow' in the Fort.

They were held in an enclosed basement with low ceilings that was part of the Security Department during the time of Lithuanian independence (the building was one that my father had constructed) and then three days in the open air in the prison yard. They were not given a crumb of food all that time. On one of those days my father and a group of other people were taken into the yard of the headquarters of the Lithuanian 'partisans' on Mishko Street. There they were made to stand with their faces turned to the brick wall, while their escort guards lined up opposite them with their rifles at the ready. The command was given for them to prepare to fire, but then it was called off. When much later my father took me to see the spot, I asked him what he had felt at that moment. He said that he had not felt anything, but I could not believe that. He thought that the Germans had decided not to shoot everyone, because they did not want the trouble of having to deal with the corpses afterwards. On 10 July they were all released and my father returned home. That was when he learnt that a couple of Lithuanian ruffians had ransacked our flat.

When the resettlement in the ghetto was being organized, my father was called upon to take part in drawing up the plans for it. In Avraham Tory's book, *Surviving the Holocaust: The Kovno Ghetto Diary*, he cites a document which laid down the rules to be observed during resettlement in the ghetto and which had been drawn up and signed by my father on 22 June 1941; Father was referred to as a member of the committee set up to organize the resettlement in the ghetto.

In the course of two weeks, at the beginning of September the Germans surrounded specific areas within the ghetto, which they would then proceed to search house by house. They would take anything they pleased out of those houses: clothes, linen, clocks, jewels and valuables, furniture, china, fur coats, typewriters, carpets, dress materials, pianos and so on. While these searches were going on, the Germans would kill one or two people in every third or fourth house they came to. Young women were often made to take off their clothes and sometimes they were raped as well. Our quarters were naturally also stripped bare. The Germans then issued an order to the effect that people had to hand in all their valuables at special collection points: gold, silver, precious stones, good quality fur coats, fabrics, electrical items and so on. They promised that those who failed to do so would be shot, and not just the people directly concerned but also a hundred others living in their neighbourhood. My parents, like the vast majority of people, duly handed over all the valuables they had.

During the large-scale 'action' that took place on 28 October 1941 SS-Rottenführer (master sergeant) Helmut Rauca, carried out the 'selection' of the people, sending some to the right and others to the left with a casual gesture of his hand. Our family landed on the 'bad' side. My father rushed over to the head of the Jewish ghetto police, Mikhail Kopelman, to seek help. Kopelman and his wife, the actress Evgeniya Gidoni, had been close friends of our family before the war. Kopelman managed to obtain permission to move us, together with my mother's parents and a few of our close friends to the 'good' side.

In the ghetto my father was assigned to building work at the airfield and later he was involved with planning and design. He told us how, when he asked a German official for some remuneration after completing some design work, the German casually suggested the firing squad, evidently believing that he would end up shot dead sooner or later anyway. Another incident from that period was the occasion when my father was caught moving out of the work-team group for a brief moment, so as to drop into a shop to buy some bread. As a result he was cruelly beaten by the guards escorting them. Later he showed me where all this had taken place in Kaunas.

Sometimes my mother succeeded in being able to absent herself from the ghetto, managing to find some extra work. I remember my mother working as a cleaner in a house in the suburbs, and I was with her as well. Obviously she had been trying to find some kind of refuge for us. I still remember an incident from our life in the ghetto, when I was standing next to the house and the children started pushing me towards two German soldiers who were walking past. Nothing untoward happened, but the terror I had felt at the time was something I never forgot.

At the end of 1943 my parents, on learning about the round-up of children which had taken place in the Shauliai Ghetto on 5 November, decided that I could not stay in the ghetto any longer. An agronomist, Antanas Midvigis, whom my mother had come to know in circumstances of which I was unaware, agreed to help us. He took her and myself to see Vincas Voboliavichius, who had a smallholding in the village of Saliai. It turned out that the Voboliavichius family was not able to take in a Jewish child, because the village was quite a dangerous one. He already had two small children of their own, one of whom was a new-born baby. All that remained for us was to go back to the ghetto.

Figure 61. Moisejus (Mika) Rosenblum in the Ghetto, 1943.

Vincas and his wife Helia, however, took it upon themselves to find another 'safe house' for me. One day Vincas turned up at the appointed place to meet my mother with good news. Monika Lukoshiavichiene (née Valionyte), Helia's sister, who lived in the village of Maironishkes not far from the Ninth Fort, had agreed to take me in.

We had to go through the gate in the barbed-wire fence near which there was a railway wagon used by the guards. The spot was brightly lit and I had been warned that there would be 'bad men' in the wagon. I had been told that I had to be very quiet so that we would not be heard. The guides at the gate had obviously been bribed and we got through.

We walked along in total darkness, keeping off roads. Sometimes we could see the lights of passing cars in the distance. On one occasion my mother and I fell into a large pit, but I did not let out even a squeak. As far as I know, we were making our way to the house of the Zubov-Chiurlionis family. From there we were taken on a cart to Monika's village. I can still see before me the dark streets of Kaunas and the ride in the horse-drawn cart of that night, as if it was yesterday. It is possible that what I recall is in fact connected with some other episode; unfortunately, there is no means of checking out the details any more.

Vladis (Vladimiras) Zubov and his wife Danute Zubova-Chiurlionyte lived in a house of their own on Zhemauchyu Street. My father had known the architect Vladis Zubov since before the war. During the war that couple, and also Danute's mother, Sofia Chiurlioniene, helped my parents on several occasions, sheltering them sometimes for several days. The Zubovs were unable to take us in for long, since German house searches in the centre of town were commonplace. The names of Sofia Chiurlioniene, Danute and Vladis Zubov, who saved many Jews during the war, are written for ever in our hearts. It should be noted that various people at various stages during the war helped us; my father mentioned five families outside the ghetto who used to give my parents shelter and other assistance. It is clear that all such help was at the risk of their lives and those of their relatives. It was only compassion towards those who were being persecuted that made them disregard the very great danger.

In Monika's house I was put to bed and my mother lay down beside me. She told me later on that I had been given a sedative, Luminal. When I woke up, my mother was not there any more. I can still remember my despair at that moment. Mother's handkerchief, which I had been holding, I kept for a long time and used to press up against my face.

Figure 62. Sofia Chiurlioniene-Kymantaite. From the personal Moshe Rosenblum archive.

Figure 63. Vladimiras Zubovas. From the personal Moshe Rosenblum archive.

Figure 64. Danute Sofia Chiurlionyte-Zuboviene. From the personal Sofia Ligija Makuteniene archive.

On Christmas Eve of 1943 a large group of Jewish prisoners escaped from the nearby Ninth Fort. One of them made his way into the smallholding where I was in hiding in search of food; he went on his way soon afterwards, but obviously someone had noticed and reported him to the authorities. A few nights later the Lithuanian police turned up out of the blue and started searching the place. Everyone was already in bed when they came. I remember first seeing shadows outside the window and the light from their torches that dazzled my benefactors, and then terrible knocking at the door. It took a long time before anyone answered the door. It was clear what lay in store for the family if they were to discover me. Monika (or Aunt Nika, as I used to call her) grabbed hold of me and tucked me into her own bed: she lay down half on top of me, so that my head was under her arm, on which she was propping herself up. I could see everything that was going on in the room. For some reason nobody turned any lights on and I could see the light from the torches, which were being shone into the cupboard and under the beds by the black figures of the men. When they left Aunt Nika collapsed unconscious.

When my mother heard about what had happened she decided that the Lukoshiavichius family would not want to let me stay on any longer, but they did not refuse to keep me with them. I stayed with them for a total of eight months, until the liberation.

There was another dangerous incident, from which certain scenes are still imprinted in my memory. A German soldier was billeted in the house where the Lukoshiavichius family were hiding me. He was given a bed in the large spare room, and a safe hideout was set up for me in the back room adjoining his. Under the table, which stood in the corner of the room, using panels of plywood, they made a 'kennel' for me so that I would be out of sight. I slept there and they brought me my meals. I had to keep very quiet. How long I stayed there I do not know: I think it was probably several days. On one other occasion Monika's husband, Bronius Lukoshiavichius, took me out to the hay-making. When we came home at the end of the day, he put me on top of the cartful of hay. Bronius made a special dip in the top of the pile of hay, like a little nest for me. On the way we bumped into a local policeman, who waved to us to stop and embarked on a long conversation. I did not give myself away then either.

When I was living with the Lukoshiavichius family, my mother came secretly to visit me once. When she started talking to me in Russian as usual, I announced that I only spoke Polish, the language I spoke with my Lithuanian family; before joining them I had not known any Polish.

I had been taught that, if any German should catch sight of me by chance, I should start shouting out that I was ill. Everyone knew that Germans were very afraid of becoming infected. One fine day, when I was out in the yard, a man on horseback in military uniform came riding in. I dropped down on the ground and tried to hide behind a flower bed. I can still remember what those flowers looked like. When I realized that the man would be able to see me anyway from his vantage point on horseback, I fell to the ground and began shouting, just as I had been taught. It turned out to have been unnecessary: the man was the first Russian soldier I had seen after three years of dark horror.

My parents and my mother's parents remained in the ghetto until 29 March 1944. By that time it had already become very difficult to get out of the ghetto. All the people being led out were counted and there were more guards round the ghetto than before. Still my parents succeeded in escaping and were hidden in the Voboliavichius family's smallholding for four months, and who asked nothing in return, acting out of pure human kindness, until the Red Army arrived.

After the war and for as long as my parents were alive, they maintained warm, sincere and really close ties with our rescuers, who were survived by Vincas and Helia (Helena) Voboliavichius' two sons, Bogdanas and Janushas, and the three daughters of the Lukoshiavichius' family, Alina, Tenya and Nelya. I also have a family, two sons and grandchildren. None of this could have happened, if it had not been for them. I am a civil engineer. In Lithuania I worked as a planner for construction projects and later as a teacher at the Vilnius Institute of Civil Engineering, and now in Israel as the chief designer of a construction firm.

Ashdod, Israel, 2008

PART FIVE

SMUGGLED IN A SACK

36. Just Another Baby 'From the Train'

Mika (Michka) Karnovsky-Ash

I was born on 13 June 1941, delivered by my grandmother, Cerna-Beile Sandler, who was a midwife. On 16 June my maternal grandparents and my aunt Lea Sandler were deported to Siberia. The shock of all this stunted my mother's ability to breastfeed. On 21 June my mother, Gita Karnovsky née Sandler came out of hospital, a day before the war began.

The Germans soon entered Kaunas. My father, Grigorij, an engineer, was working with Mendel Kamber, building military fortifications for the Soviet Army, somewhere in the provinces. When they heard about the outbreak of war, they both hurried back to Kaunas to their families.

In Kaunas a Soviet officer caught sight of Mendel Kamber, whom he knew before, and asked whether he could drive. On hearing a positive response, he ordered Mendel to get behind the wheel of his vehicle and would not listen to any objections or explanations. Mendel was ordered to catch up with the retreating Soviet Army. That was why Mendel did not reach his family and did not know that his wife was pregnant.

Father came home and, alongside his relatives, experienced all the horrors of the ghetto and the camps. My mother had been studying biology, but before the war she had not worked in her chosen field: she had travelled wherever her husband had been sent and kept the accounts.

Our family went to live with my paternal grandmother, Anna Osipovna Karnovsky. She had been a widow since the time of the First World War; she had lost her husband in Kharkov when Lithuanian Jews were forcibly evacuated on orders from Russia's czarist government. She was a very strong character, an enterprising and intelligent woman. She had managed to survive that forcible evacuation and eventually returned to Kaunas with her three children, Grigorij, Nina and adopted son Otto. Now she was the first person to have sensed the grim times ahead and had taken pains to lay in reserves of food for the whole family. This made life for our family a great deal easier, at least in the early days.

My aunt Nina was married to a rich Kaunas Jew called Yakov (Kuba) Gudinsky. Later he would serve in the Jewish police; he was a good man and helped as many people as he could. Kuba was a well-known contractor in Kaunas and he had many connections among the engineers of the town. With one of them, who used to live in Slobodka, he had swapped flats. A Lithuanian engineer moved into Yakov's flat at the end of the central avenue in Traku Street, while my parents, grandmother and the Gudinsky family, Kuba, his wife Nina and their 2-month-old Rina, moved into the Lithuanian's small house inside the ghetto area.

One episode was recalled by the family regarding the time between their old life in the town and the move into the ghetto. Mother had to cross the whole town on foot from Traku Street to Slobodka with luggage and a pram, and Lithuanians were pushing her off the pavement onto the roadway right under the wheels of the carts, since the road was already teeming with traffic and crowds of people being herded into the ghetto.

On the same floor of that small house in the ghetto, apart from the Gudinskys and the Karnovskys, there were two other families. One of them was the Rabinovich family with an 11-year-old son, Muki Rabinovich.

The Jewish Council and the Jewish police had, in the opinion of my mother, played a very positive role in the life of the ghetto, keeping order, attending to hygiene issues and sharing out any 'benefits' available as fairly as possible. For example, in the initial period in the ghetto, there were two cows, and each baby had been issued with 100 grammes of milk. Very soon the cows disappeared and there was nothing to feed me with; I was at death's door. My mother actually heard her mother-in-law telling Nina that she could not understand why Gita was so agitated about the baby, as her days were obviously numbered. Father used to exchange valuables for 50-gramme lumps of butter, which he would then smear over his stomach and bring into the ghetto. Out of that butter they used to make some kind of drink for me.

There was a man in the ghetto called Teddy Blumenthal who had at one time been married to my mother's elder sister Ester. He was regarded as one of the 'representatives of German culture'. He had been born in Riga and had studied engineering at a German university. The Germans took him on to work as one of their translators and that was how he had access to important information. The Germans started bringing Jews from Western Europe into the Ninth Fort and then shoot them without further ado. Teddy was involved in sorting out their possessions and he managed to pinch some 'Nestlé' powdered milk for me.

Before the so-called 'Intellectuals' Action', when about 500 of the most educated people in the ghetto were lured by a false promise of the Germans to enlist for 'interesting work', it was Teddy who warned my father and Kuba Gudinsky not to let themselves be 'recruited'. During the selection process on the day of the 'Great Action' Teddy warned as many people as he could which side of the square they needed to move to, right or left. It is possible that my family was saved thanks to him.

At the end of 1943 it was decided that I should be smuggled out of the ghetto into safer hands. A friend of my father had known a childless family before the war: the husband was German and the wife Russian. They had already taken in one child 'from the train', namely one of the children handed over at railway stations to local inhabitants by Belarussian, Ukrainian or Russian young mothers, being deported to Germany for forced labour. That much the authorities would allow.

Father and his friend negotiated with Karolis and Evdokija (Dunya) Greize, who were simple, semi-literate people; they agreed to take me in. The members of our family were arguing amongst themselves as to whether they should hand over the baby or keep me with them to share the whole family's fate. Muki Rabinovich's mother, for instance, did not want to hand over her children to anyone. Luckily, my mother opted for the desperate and courageous step of parting with her daughter.

I was handed over the fence to Karolis in a sack of potatoes, after Nina had first given me an injection to make me go to sleep and then bribed the guards. I had fair hair and grew up speaking only Russian, which meant that Karolis and Dunya could tell the neighbours that I was just another baby 'from the train'. Mother met my rescuers on a number of occasions, but then she decided to stop doing so, because it might only expose everyone to extra dangers.

Nina and Kuba entrusted their daughter Rina to the

Garkauskas family, who had children of their own. This family clearly had some links with the Russians and it was perhaps as a result of this that Germans came to search their house one day, looking for leaflets or weapons. They did not find anything and were just sitting there drinking, when Garkauskas burst out while drunk, 'You come looking for leaflets and don't even notice that there's a little Jewish girl right under your nose!'

Nina and Yakov heard about what had happened when they were hiding in the dugout known as '*malina*', the 'raspberry patch'. They tried to get Rina back from Garkauskas, but he refused to hand her over. I explain this by the fact that Garkauskas must have been frightened for his own children, who would then all have been shot, if he had not given Rina up to the Germans. As it was, only he was arrested and taken off to prison. That was how Rina Gudinsky perished.

In 1969 Garkauskas turned up at our flat. He had heard that the Gudinskys had survived and gone to Australia where they were prospering. Garkauskas asked us to tell them that he wanted some money. I can remember how I started to shout at him, 'You traitor, you were responsible for the death of Rina, how dare you after all that ask for anything, get out!' My Lithuanian acquaintance, Valdas Zheromskis, who happened to be in our flat at the time, threw out the uninvited guest.

After the ghetto was disbanded, my mother was taken to Stutthof and my father to Dachau. By some miracle they both survived. The family had paid some Lithuanians in Kaunas to hide my paternal grandmother. Mother, who had given up hope that any of her local relatives might have survived, gave those Lithuanians the address of some of her American relatives.

After the liberation Nina and Yakov Gudinsky came out of hiding and straight away went to fetch me from my rescuers, who had looked after me out of the kindness of their hearts, without taking anything for it. They were simple folk and quite old by then. Unfortunately, despite all the efforts of our family, they were deported from Lithuania to Central Asia, because the husband was German. We used to correspond with them and send them parcels.

My cousin Rachel Blumenthal Josef had been saved by one of the Baublys brothers. After the liberation she went to live with Gudinsky as well. To this day she cannot forgive herself for what she feels was a 'betrayal' of Baublys. I have only vague memories of the time I spent with the Gudinsky family. I remember I used to call Nina 'Mama' and Kuba 'Papa'.

My father was liberated from Dachau and made his own way back home with some other Jews along rivers and eventually reached Kaunas. The Gudinskys learnt that my father had survived and told me that my real papa would be coming to find me. I remember sitting in Father's arms. He said to me, 'We'll go and wash now and then we'll go to bed', to which I responded by asking, 'Papa, why do you say "We" when you're talking about yourself?' And father had replied, 'Because I'm big'.

A few months later Father learnt that my mother had survived as well and we waited impatiently for her to arrive. She came back to Kaunas and, when walking out of the railway station, she met a Jew whom she knew and who took her to where my father was working. The two of them walked home together and in the garden I was out playing with Ilana Kamber, who lived nearby. Father asked my mother which of the little girls was Mika and she recognized me straightaway. Father told me, 'That's your Mama. She has a doll for you.' I do not remember if I felt any particular excitement or agitated emotions at the time.

My mother tried for many years to bring back her parents from Siberia, but with no success. My grandmother died in Yakutia and Grandfather Rafoel only came home after Stalin's death in 1955; a mere two years later he died. My Aunt Lea and Uncle Yehuda had been allowed to leave Siberia earlier.

I graduated from the Kaunas Polytechnic Institute, married Josef Ash and in 1973 left for Israel, where I practised the profession for which I had been trained. I have three children: two daughters, Viki and Bela, and a son Uri, whose twin brother Giora was killed while doing his military service in the Israeli army. My father died in Lithuania, but Mother is still alive today. She is now 94 years old and completely independent, in relatively good health and very alert.

Kiron, Israel, February 2009

37. A Pit beneath the Bed

Josef and Aviva Gilis

Girsh Gilis, a jeweller and watchmaker, and Chana, née Levner, a housewife, had three sons: Peisah (1926), Izya (1928) and myself, in August 1938. When my mother was pregnant with me, she was prepared to have an abortion, but her brothers intervened, 'Don't do that, he'll bring you good luck!'

My paternal grandfather, Peisah, had been a jeweller and watchmaker in Kretinga. After his death my grandmother (I do not even know her name) had taken over the business and with the help of her sons made a success of it. One of her local customers had often taken items from my grandmother to sell for her. Not long before the war she stopped trading with him, because he had begun to keep the money for the goods entrusted to him. He blackmailed her, but my grandmother was adamant: she stuck to her guns and would not give him anything else. According to eye-witness accounts, after the German invasion, this man came to my grandmother's shop, beat her and took her to the place where Jews were being killed. There he buried her alive.

Our family owned a plot of land near Kaunas. A Russian Old Believer, Konstantin Samokhin, asked my grandfather, Moshe Levner, to sell him the plot adjacent to his own land. Grandfather refused, which made Samokhin very angry. As he left he said, 'You'll live to regret this.' On the second day of the war my grandfather, my uncle and father were all at home. When he saw Samokhin with Germans out in the yard, my father ran off and hid on the landing of a neighbour's house. The mistress of that house realized that my father was hiding from the Germans and drove him out, shouting as she did so. The Germans caught my father, took him back into his own house, found my grandfather and uncle as well, and led them all off to the Seventh Fort, where they were shot. As soon as the Germans left, some Lithuanian neighbours broke into the house and stole everything they could take.

Another uncle, Henekh Levner, was a strong imposing man and could turn his hand to anything. He was also a very fine cook; the commandant of the ghetto took him on to work as his family's cook. During the 'Great Action' my mother was sent to the Ninth Fort. Henekh came out looking for us, running round shouting and calling for my mother, but could not find her. He realized that things were looking very bad. Trembling with fear, he rushed to the Gestapo officer Rauca. Henekh beseeched him, lying that his own wife and children had been sent to Fort Nine and begging Rauca not to send them there. Rauca said, 'Fetch them back. Take a Lithuanian policeman with you and look for her.' Henekh turned to one of the Lithuanian policemen, promising that he would pay him fifty marks for his trouble.

They began looking for my mother in the long column of people, running about like lunatics, calling out, and asking people if they had seen her. Mother was half-stunned by everything going on around her. In her hand she held a little bag in which she had been keeping her money and valuables 'for a rainy day': she did not realize that day had already dawned. When Henekh eventually found her, he grabbed this bag from her hands and gave it to the Lithuanian policeman. This made my mother very angry, she had no idea that the money had been used to buy her own and her children's lives back.

As early as the age of 3 I began to understand what was going on around me and to remember it all. The first thing I remember is how I spent all my time in the bed of my grandmother Simha; she had ten children and they were all in the ghetto. The children often used to visit her, bringing her an apple or a piece of bread. She did not eat what they brought but fed it to me. Only when I was no longer hungry did she eat what was left over. Grandmother Simha eventually died in the ghetto.

My mother, uncles and aunts would go out to work every day into the town. My eldest brother, Peisah, was employed by the Germans as a driver. He offered our mother the opportunity to drive us all out of the ghetto, but she refused.

During the 'Children's Action' I was hidden first in the attic under the broken tiled roof. A few hours later I was taken into a pit that had been dug out in the room, where my uncle Meir Levner lived. To get into the pit, we had to pull out the drawer containing bed linen from under the divan, remove its plywood base and then, under that, open up the small door in the floor and climb down into the pit. The pit was cramped, with a very low roof and it was cold. I sat there with my mother and cousin, Edik Levner. Mother made sure that we did not make any noise.

The pit was only a metre square and there was not enough air; a pipe was fixed up leading out of the pit, through which we took it in turns to breathe air. Each person felt they had to wait too long until it was his or her turn. After a few hours we heard Germans come in looking for children. They asked Uncle Meir whether he was hiding any children, saying that if they found them, he and everybody else would be shot. Down in the pit we heard someone open up the base of the divan and start throwing out the bed linen. According to Uncle Meir, who had been standing in the room, numb with fear, the policeman accompanying the Germans did not bother to lift up the plywood base of the divan and informed the Germans that there was no one hiding in it. We remained in the pit for two days. All we had to eat or drink was water and a little bread.

Things calmed down in the ghetto by the third day and people started being led out to their work places once again. What could still be heard however was the heart-rending cries of those whose children had been taken off. Uncle Meir took my mother and me back to our flat. The neighbour from the adjacent room, a shoemaker, caught sight of me, safe and sound, and began shouting and screaming, 'How can that be? They killed my daughter and he's still alive!' He went straight to the Gestapo to complain.

As soon as the neighbour had left, my mother took me back to Uncle Meir, who in his turn, ran over to his sister Riva. Her husband, Zalman Baikovich, was in charge of the ghetto's food store. Zalman used to send a cart out of the ghetto into the town with empty barrels and sacks on it, which would then be brought back containing food. Uncle Meir got in touch with a 'kind' SS officer, whom he knew well and paid him 20,000 marks, just to make sure that the next day when the cart would be driven up to the gate by its Jewish driver Lourie, he would sit on the open floor of the cart, where I would be hidden, to ensure that no problems arose at the gate. A Lithuanian woman would be waiting in the town on a deserted street to take charge of me.

Early in the morning of the following day, I had to curl up and be placed in a large bag, which was then locked, but a crack was left open, so that I should not suffocate. The bag was taken over to Baikovich's house. It would have been dangerous to actually take me into the house, because Baikovich's daughter Shulamith was hiding there. I was taken out of the bag and placed in an empty sack, which was left two metres from the house where there were some empty barrels. I lay there for four hours without moving, gripped by horrible fear. I could hear the steps and voices of the nearby Germans. When the cart drew up, empty barrels were loaded on to it and the sack with me in it was stowed in one of them.

Lourie, the cart driver, was sitting on a high seat. He placed his feet in the barrel that contained the sack with me in it. The German sat down on the floor of the cart and we all drove out of the ghetto without any problems. A young Lithuanian woman, as arranged, met us. She lifted me out of the sack where I had been lying curled up. It was several hours before I could stand upright again. I was all of five and a half.

Meir himself managed to escape, but my uncle Haim Levner, who served in the Jewish ghetto police, was shot later on for refusing to help the Nazis carry out another of their round-ups.

I was kept in this woman's house for a week, but then she took me to Zhemaitija, to a village called Grazhuriu, near the town of Kvederna, to stay with her sister Barbora and brother-in-law Jonas Balchinas. They had no children of their own. That was at the beginning of April 1944. By this time I was so used to going hungry that I often turned food down. I found it impossible to eat. Realizing that I had lost my appetite, Jonas used to make me drink a small glass of home-made vodka every day. My appetite soon came back. I got used to Jonas and followed him about wherever he went. After a while I began to call Jonas 'Father' and Barbora 'Mama'.

In Jonas' house there also lived Barbora's sister Stefania, an uneducated woman who could not even write, but sincere, kind and friendly. She grew fond of me and used to treat me like one of the family. I remember clearly how some Germans who came into the farmstead treated me to some chocolate and I said '*Danke schön*'; the Germans were surprised and asked how I knew German. Jonas explained that I had grown up in Königsberg. When the fighting was close to our village, Stefania used to take me into the woods and hide out there with me, until the danger was past.

Not only did Jonas grow crops, but he was also a server in the village church. For many years he had known the priest there and had complete confidence in him. He asked the priest for help, so as to keep me and his own family safe. The priest was a kind, humane man. He found a space for the right year in the book in which he recorded marriages and births, and registered me as Vytautas Balchinas. The priest wrote me out a birth certificate. A story was concocted for the inhabitants of the village to the effect that Barbora had gone to Königsberg in 1938 for medical treatment and had been pregnant at the time and given birth there. Since she was still feeling weak, she had come back to the village, leaving the boy with her cousin who was ready to look after him. Only now had she at last brought him home.

Apart from Yiddish I did not know any other languages, but my colloquial Yiddish was accepted in the village as German. The neighbours suspected that I was Jewish, but by this time the front line was approaching ever nearer and nobody gave me away.

When it was all over, my brother Izya came to the village to fetch me back. Izya was 16 years old at the time. From him I learnt that Peisah had perished in Dachau a few weeks before it was liberated. Izya had managed to escape in a group of about thirty prisoners when the ghetto was set on fire. They were chased, some had been killed, but Izya survived, pretending he was shot dead. Izya was hidden by the mother of his friend, Alfonsas Rudminaitis. Jonas and Barbora tried hard to persuade Izya to leave me with them, because, after all, times were hard. Izya did not agree though: he said that we needed to be in Kaunas and wait there, since our mother might soon be coming back from a concentration camp. However, in Kaunas there was nothing to eat, so in the end Izya returned me to the Balchinas home.

Our mother had been transferred to Stutthof, where three times she had succeeded in running out of the row of prisoners destined for the crematorium into the 'correct' queue of people. She had also survived the 'March of Death'. After the liberation she came to fetch me.

I was 7 by then and Mother was 52, but she looked desperately old and I did not recognize her. I used to say, 'What does that Yid woman want with me? Take her away!' Jonas and Barbora persuaded my mother to stay and live with them, saying that there would be enough room and food in their new house.

My mother stayed on there for a few weeks, so that I could get used to her; she devoted all her time and attention to me. She used to tell me about our old home and various little details soon began to resurface in my memory. Eventually I realized that Chana was my real mother. After that she took me back to Kaunas.

Life in Kaunas was difficult and my mother had problems trying to feed us. When Jonas found out, he harnessed his horse, loaded up a cart with sacks of food and brought it to mother, covering a distance of 165 kilometres.

My mother was an energetic and enterprising woman. She started baking rolls, which she sold at the market. It was hard to come by any kind of food and her rolls sold out as fast as she could bake them. Our room was soon full of sacks of flour and sugar. Under the bed little sacks containing money were kept. There was a good deal of it. But in 1947 the old currency was replaced with new notes, which made everyone's savings worthless. It had also become dangerous by then to bake rolls and sell them privately: the Soviet authorities were coming down hard on all forms of private enterprise. In the meantime someone had told us that the Balchinas couple had died.

In 1990 I was paid a visit by a well-known Lithuanian journalist, Birute Vishniauskaite. I told her about my earlier life and asked her to find out whether anyone from the Balchinas family was still alive. This was what she found out: Barbora had indeed died in the early 1950s, but Jonas had lived to the age of 105. After the death of Barbora, Jonas had taken a second wife, her sister Stefania. All those years he had hoped to see us again. He had finally died not long before the journalist made her trip to his village. Now the only person from the family still alive was Stefania. In 1992 I visited Stefania. She was 88 at the time and was very glad to see me. She lived in a house on her own. I helped her to prepare firewood for the winter and hired people to help her out in the house, leaving her a large amount of money.

When I visited her again a week later, she complained that she could no longer find the money. We searched the house, but there was no money anywhere. It turned out that poor illiterate Stefania could not read the amounts on the notes and had handed the people she needed to pay the whole pile, just saying, 'Take what you are due.' Soon after that Stefania died. Jonas

Balchinas, Barbora and Stefania have been recorded as 'Righteous Among the Nations'. My conscience still troubles me to this day with the thought that I did not do as much for the Balchinas family as I might have done.

I draw a clear distinction between those Lithuanians who are rampant anti-Semites and those who during the war were putting their own lives in danger by rescuing Jews. Since Lithuania became independent, I have been going back every year to visit those who helped save me and my relatives, assisting and paying them the respect they deserve. This gives me a real sense of satisfaction.

In 1948, at the age of 10, I went to school for the first time. As a young man I was a keen sportsman, a skilful motorcyclist and tennis player, and competed in Lithuania's team, before going on to become a tennis coach. Later on I studied and worked as a coach in the Kaliningrad Education Institute. I married Aviva Feller, whom I had known ever since I had first gone to school.

Aviva, born in 1940, was taken into the Kaunas Ghetto as a child. After the 'Great Action' Aviva had been very ill and her mother had said at the time, 'It would be better for her to die a natural death than to be killed by the Germans.' Her father, Dr Feller, insisted, 'I am going to make her better.' He got hold of some medicine and did indeed make his daughter better. Ever since then, one of Aviva's heart valves has not functioned properly, which is even more of a problem now. When Aviva's father had learnt that there was going to be a round-up of children, he went to see Doctor Elkes, a head of the Jewish Council, but did not find him at home. Aviva's father talked to the doctor's wife, and asked her to help take his daughter out of the ghetto and into hiding. She replied, 'What is going to happen to all the children will happen to your daughter as well.' That statement, undeniably true, which underlined how all were equal before God, seemed harsh and unfeeling to Aviva's father at the time. It left a searing wound in him and was something he could never forget. Aviva's father could not rest and when he went out into the town with his brigade, he made contact with Jonas Vainiauskas, a stage-set designer, whose children he had treated before the war free of charge. He asked the man to hide Aviva; Jonas and his wife Onute immediately agreed. Aviva was brought out through a hole in the fence and taken to Shanchiai, a suburb of Kaunas.

I came to Israel in 1972 with Aviva, our daughter Simona and my mother. I was able to obtain responsible posts. I joined the Labour Party, and became an active party worker. Today I am a pensioner and I no longer take part in any political activities. Aviva completed training as a nurse and worked in Israel in her chosen profession.

Netanya, Israel, 2008

38. There's a Yellow Dog Running By

Rina Joels-Parason

I, Rina Joels, the second daughter of well-established Lithuanian Jews, Benjamin Joels and Malka Joels-Kaplan, was born in 1940, when my elder sister Bella was 5 years old. My father owned a grocer's shop on the central street of the old city of Kaunas. He had three brothers: Shlomo evacuated with his family to Russia, where his wife died but he and his daughter Masha survived. Father's second brother, Shmuel, died in a concentration camp, but his wife Hanah and her 10-year-old daughter, Riva (Riva Knobel), survived the camp and came with her family to Israel. Father's third brother had gone to live in South Africa long before the war and we all lost contact with him.

Figure 65. Benjamin Joels with daughters Rina and Tal in the Ghetto, 1943. Photo taken by Hirsh Kadish.

I was a mere 10 months old when my family was driven into the Kaunas Ghetto. We lived in a small room with my maternal grandmother, Uncle Reuven Kaplan and Aunt Berta. My grandmother perished in the ghetto; Uncle Reuven miraculously survived Dachau and came by way of Italy to Israel.

In 1943 my father succeeded in contacting a Lithuanian family by the name of Sinkiavichius, who agreed to save me and my sister for payment. My father used to go on a cart to work in the town, and he bribed one of the guards at the gate so that he would not check the cart. Twice attempts to take us out of the ghetto failed because the 'wrong German' had been on duty at the gate; on the third occasion he did manage to get through. When the cart drew level with the Lithuanians waiting on the pavement, Father threw out a sack of potatoes with me in it, fast asleep after being given a sedative. My sister had been given instructions to cross the road as quickly as possible to join the 'Uncle' and 'Auntie' standing on the pavement waiting for us. My father heaved a sigh of relief when he saw the peasant pick up the 'sack'. The two of us stayed with that Lithuanian family for a while, but it soon turned out to be dangerous, because Bella and I used to speak Yiddish to each other. One day, I was running after a dog and, although I was surrounded by Lithuanians and in a place where Germans sometimes appeared as well, I shouted in Yiddish, 'There's a yellow dog running by'. It was decided to separate us and I was sent to a village to live with the Sinkiavichius family's grandmother, an old Lithuanian peasant, who by then had gone to live in the farm (*dvaras*), which had been purchased not long before using money obtained from my father.

The farm was in a village not far from Kaunas. My sister Bella, meanwhile, was living with young representatives of the Sinkiavichius family and growing up with their two children on the Green Hill. Gradually I forgot my Yiddish and began speaking only Lithuanian: even my name was changed, I started being called Jadviga (Jadzike). As far as I know I was not baptized or officially registered with a new name.

In July 1944 the ghetto was disbanded and everyone who was still alive was transferred to concentration camps. On his way to Dachau my father jumped out of the moving train with Shlomo Yarmovski, after they had removed some boards from the floor of the goods truck. Yarmovski settled after the war in Zürich. In 1973 he visited Israel and called on us so as to tell me about his last conversation with my father. Despite the fact that the two of them had been shot at, they had not been wounded. For safety's sake they had decided to go off in separate directions. According to Yarmovski, my father had told him that he would try and get to the Lithuanians who were hiding his daughters. They said goodbye to each other and ran off in separate directions. My father never reached us. He probably died while on his way to find us. After the war my mother looked for him, turning to all sorts of organizations, but there was no information about him anywhere.

I stayed in the Lithuanian household until 1945, when my mother and Aunt Berta returned to Kaunas from the concentration camp and came to fetch us straight away. Naturally I did not remember anything about her: she looked like an old woman to me. We had even been taught, most probably to keep us safe, that one had to be frightened of Jews, because they 'would put you in a sack and carry you off'.

It was only after long conversations and repeated meetings, in particular after I had met up with my sister again, who reminded me of little familiar details from that life long ago, that I at last threw my arms around Mother's neck and agreed to go with her. It took a good deal of time and effort before I finally felt part of the family again, and 'real life' could be resumed. Of course there were all sorts of amusing incidents after that. I was told how, if I had forgotten to say my prayers before going to bed, I would cry out in the middle of the night and look for my little crucifix on the wall. When I failed to find it, I would remember that my life had changed and that I was back together again with my mother and Bella. The time that had been disfigured by the horrors of war, which happily for me I had not understood, was fading into the past, but leaving one gaping wound open for ever – the loss of Father.

I know that at the end of the war our mother stayed in contact with the Sinkiavichius family and helped them financially. Quite soon after the war the grandmother of that family which had taken me in died. Shortly after that her daughter, who had taken my sister in, died of cancer, and in circumstances that remain unclear, her husband was killed by the Russians. The younger members of that family have since moved and so we have lost touch with them.

I graduated from the Kaunas Medical School, where I became friendly with many other Jewish students and developed my own sense of identity. In 1961 our mother suddenly died. In 1962 I married Moshe Parason. In July 1973 we at last came down the steps of a plane on to Israeli soil with our two sons. Thirty-five years have passed since then, and we are both still working as physicians. We have restored the family to life, the line has continued. Our parents, if they were alive today, would be proud of us.

In 1986 I learnt by chance from the evening news on TV that George (Hirsh) Kadushin, who had once been imprisoned in the Kaunas Ghetto, had come to Israel from the USA. Being a photographer by profession, he had taken pictures of the ghetto Jews with a hidden camera. An exhibition of his photographs from that period had opened in Tel Aviv's Museum of the Diaspora. Naturally the whole family went to see the exhibition. To my delight and astonishment we discovered on the walls of the museum several photographs of my relatives: my father, my mother, my aunt and myself with my sister. I treasure these photographs as the only precious memento I have of my father and mother from that time, all that is left from that childhood ruined by the war!

My sister, Bella Joels-Tal, was a civil engineer and came to Israel with her husband and two children in 1972.

Haifa, Israel, 2008

39. The Potato-Sack Siblings

Maxim Broyeris, Alik (Peretz) Dvoretz,
Genia Kaltinovsky-Zalishansky and Masha Muller-Hathskelzon

Four young families lived in one apartment in the ghetto, the Broyeris, Dvoretz, Muller and Kaltinovsky families. They were all tailors by profession, so it was probably not by chance that they went to live together. Four children, one from each family, survived. They were nicknamed by one of the parents, 'the potato-sack siblings'.

MAXIM BROYERIS

I was born on 1 January 1941. My mother, Reizel Ring, was from Pabrade, a small town near the border with Poland, where her parents owned a small shop. Their relations with their Polish neighbours were friendly and peaceful.

My father, Sleime Broyeris, was born in Shauliai. My parents met and married in Kaunas, where both worked as tailors; they were not poor but lived modestly. Father believed in communist ideas, although he was not officially a member of the Communist Party; he was imprisoned for a short time in Lithuania for his political activities. In prison he learned the Russian language; he liked to read and was strongly influenced by Soviet literature. He named his eldest son Ilya, after Ilya Erhenburg and named me Maxim, after Maxim Gorky.

Ilya spent the summer of 1941 in Pabrade with our grandparents, Leiser and Beila. In the very first days of the war, the Polish neighbours of my grandparents came to their house in search of money and jewels. They probably found nothing, so they set the house on fire. My grandparents and Ilya were burnt alive. My parents tried to escape to Russia, but because of the severe bombardment were forced to return to Kaunas.

In the ghetto we lived in a small house together with several other families. My parents told me that I would regularly go to the Dvoretz's room because they always had food. Father worked at the airfield in Aleksotas and my mother in a stocking factory called '*Silva*'. She met a woman there who was willing to take a Jewish boy. She did not ask for money or goods but made one condition: the boy should not be circumcised. The guard at the fence was bribed and I, then a 3-year-old boy, was smuggled out of the ghetto in a sack of potatoes. As agreed, somebody picked me up and carried me to my rescuers, the Bargauskas family.

The Bargauskas family lived in a village called Michamedviai where they had a farm and owned a small shop. Jonas and Marione Bargauskas had three children of their own: two daughters, Danute and Aldute, and a son, Petras, who was hand-icapped. I was treated well in this family, exactly as the other children were. I spoke mainly Yiddish, but soon I began to forget Yiddish and speak Lithuanian. Nevertheless I was kept hidden from strangers' eyes. I was baptized and named Albinas Bargauskas. I called Mr Bargauskas by his first name, Jonas but, when I spoke to his wife I called her '*Pone*' (Mrs) Bargauskiene.

I remember several episodes from this period. All the family used to pray at certain hours. I was not forced to pray, but I remember Mrs Bargauskiene saying to me, 'Always tell the truth. God sees and hears everything, and whoever lies will be punished.' And I asked her, 'How can God hear us and see us from so far?'

I remember how frightened I was when I saw a German soldier sitting on the fence of the Bargauskas' farm, picking apples from a tree. Petras and I hid together in the attic: he did not want to be sent to labour camps in Germany and I was taught to avoid any contact with other people. When the front line approached, our village suffered severe bombardment and the nearby match factory was bombed. Everybody ran to a shelter in the garden. I was left alone on the porch of the house: I was afraid to run in the darkness.

Meanwhile, my father managed to escape from the ghetto to a partisan detachment, where he fought, together with Boris Dvogovsky's father Moshe. Their brigade took part in the liberation of Kaunas from the fascists, and together with the Soviet Army entered the city in August 1944. Immediately after the liber-ation of Kaunas my father took me from the Bargauskas family. However, he was then mobilized to the Soviet Army with other members of the detachment. He had to place me in the Jewish orphanage where I was to spend several months. I remember that food was scarce, mainly porridge, and Mrs Bargauskiene used to visit me and bring some food. After several visits, she was asked to stop visiting me, because the other children were jealous.

I had a friend in the orphanage. Together we dug a hole in a corner behind a pile of logs, and we would hide there when somebody unfamiliar came to the orphanage. It was only when my mother returned from Stutthof that I went to live with my parents again. Our family maintained a friendly relationship with the Bargauskas family; I spent my summer holidays there and joined their children in everyday activities, looking after the cow, horse and pigs.

Pone Bargauskiene did not support the Soviet regime and used to say that Hitler and Stalin were the same thing. The Bargauskases lost almost all of their property when the Soviets returned, but fortunately were not exiled to Siberia.

Later, when both Mr and Mrs Bargauskas had passed away, I asked Aldute, their eldest daughter, 'Why did your parents rescue me, endangering all the family?' Her simple reply surprised me, 'Petras was disabled and a man would be needed to work the farm in the future.'

I did not experience anti-Semitism personally, maybe because I did not look like a Jew, but I heard a lot anti-Semitic expressions. My schoolmate told us proudly once that his father had tortured and killed Jews during the war. 'When I am grown up, I will kill Jews too,' he said. I graduated from Kaunas Polytechnic Institute as a mechanical engineer, married Salia Bychovsky, a medical doctor, and we emigrated with our first daughter to Israel in 1972, where our second daughter was born. During all the years in Israel we worked in our professions and liked what we did. Our daughters and three grandchildren all live in Israel.

I am grateful to God that I am among the saved and feel blessed to live.

Or Yehuda, Israel, 2009

ALIK (PERETZ) DVORETZ, TOLD BY HIS WIFE,
GUTA VINNICKAYA-DVORETZ

Alik's grandfather, Yosef Dvoretz, was persuaded by his relatives to return from Denmark, where Alik's father, Shimon Dvoretz, was born, to Zarasai in Lithuania. He was told that he had inherited property and money there. Yosef did not find any fortune in Zarasai, and died before the war, leaving behind children and a wife, Shimon's stepmother.

Two of Shimon's sisters emigrated to Israel before the war; Shimon moved to Kaunas. After he settled there, he invited his bride and friend from childhood, Chaya Pen, to join him. They were both professional tailors and did very well.

During the first days of the German invasion, all the remaining members of the Dvoretz family and the extensive Pen family were killed by Lithuanians in Zarasai. Shimon and Chaya tried to escape to Russia, but were caught by Lithuanians together with many other refugees. Men and women were separated, and both groups were led to the forest to be executed. Chaya was in the sixth month of a pregnancy.

At the very last moment, when they were sure they were going to die, a German officer appeared and ordered the Lithuanians to let the prisoners live: men were taken to an unknown destination and the women were imprisoned in a barn, kept there like cattle for several days and then sent back to Kaunas.

Fortunately Chaya found her husband in Kaunas. Their baby was born on 13 October 1941. A Jewish doctor, most probably Reiza Galah-Zisman, attended at the birth, and the child was given the name Peretz, in memory of his maternal grandfather who had perished in Zarasai.

Shimon had excellent manual skills and the German officer who was his superior in the workshop very much valued him. During one of the round-ups, Shimon was caught. Feiga Abramovich saw him being led to the Ninth Fort and immediately informed Chaya, who ran to the same officer who then ordered the Lithuanian policeman to release Shimon. His life was saved once more.

The underground representative informed the Dvoretz family that Peretz was next in turn to be smuggled out of the ghetto. He arranged a meeting in Kaunas between Chaya and Peretz's future adoptive parents. Chaya concealed the yellow Star of David on her coat with a big shawl, slipped out of the ghetto and went to meet a Lithuanian man to make all the necessary arrangements for smuggling Peretz out. While she hurried along the street, a strong gust of wind revealed the Star of David on her coat. Suddenly a stranger grabbed her and whispered, 'Are you mad! You could be caught and killed.' It was Mr Svigris, the man she had arranged to meet.

Figure 66. Peretz (Alik) Dvoretz, 1945.

The childless Svigris family agreed, for some reward, to take Peretz. Dvoretz's neighbour, Aaron Muller, a member of the partisan detachment, took on the mission. After Peretz was given a shot of Luminal, he carried him out of the ghetto in a potato sack. Aaron Muller managed to smuggle his daughter Masha to the orphanage of Dr Baublys in the same way. After the war Aaron Muller called them 'the potato-sack siblings'.

Peretz had blond hair, and was not circumcised, but from the age of 10 months already spoke only Yiddish. For the first three months he cried a lot. Mr Svigris' brother served in the Lithuanian police. He visited his brother and suspected something, but Mr Svigris told him they had adopted a retarded child. They even undressed Alik to prove he was not Jewish. Persuaded or not, the policemen did not report his brother. Peretz was baptized and called Arnoldas Svigris, and this is why he came to be known as Alik, the name he used for the rest of his life. From this period Alik remembered two episodes. He recalled kneeling every night to pray, and once being led to a grave, where, he was told, 'very bad people' called Jews were buried.

Following the liquidation of the ghetto, Alik's parents were sent to different concentration camps. After liberation, they knew nothing about each other's fate. Shimon and Chaya each made their way to Kaunas. They somehow made contact and met amid the chaos of post-war Poland, reached Kaunas together and found Alik.

When Chaya spoke with him, Alik said, 'I do not like Jews, but you are OK.' Mr and Mrs Svigris let them take Alik without any resistance; Alik's parents moved to Vilnius. Mrs Svigris died soon after the war ended. Mr Svigris used to visit the Dvoretz family there, but for some reason Alik did not like his visits and always avoided meeting him, but he was however invited to Alik's wedding. Interestingly, Alik did not know that his real name was Peretz until he was in the seventh grade of high school.

Alik graduated from the Kaunas Polytechnic Institute in 1964. In 1972 we emigrated to Israel. Alik passed away in 2003, when he was only 62 years old, leaving two sons and three grandchildren.

Bat Yam, Israel, 2009

GENIA KALTINOVSKY-ZALISHANSKY

For years I avoided talking about our family's fate, it was and still is too painful; I even refused to see movies related to the Holocaust. But once I was persuaded to see Roberto Benigni's *Life Is Beautiful* and deeply regretted it. I never asked questions, and my parents, especially my father, did not speak about the ghetto or the concentration camps. This story is based mainly on a few things my mother told me.

My father, Michael Kaltinovsky, was born in a small town called Kraziai near Shauliai. Before the war he worked in Kaunas as a tailor. My parents married there, but were unable to enjoy their new life for long. The war began, followed by the Nazi occupation and the ghetto years.

From my father's family, one of my uncles emigrated to Palestine in the 1930s, two sisters managed to escape to Russia, but all the rest perished.

My mother, Feiga, was one of many children in Yoffe's family. One of her brothers fought during the war in the 16th Division of the Soviet Army. Her mother and sister Lea stayed with them in the ghetto; only Lea survived, all the others were killed by the Nazis.

I was born on 3 February 1942 and my mother named me... 'Geto'. Many years later I asked her, 'Why did you give me such a terrible name?' Her answer astonished me, 'I didn't care a damn about a name for somebody who was going to die. Hitler was not interested in the names of the children he would kill.'

At birth I was very weak and frail; I became so ill that the best Jewish doctors in the ghetto did not know what was wrong with me or how to help me. Everybody, including my parents, was sure I would not live long. Fortunately one physician told my parents that I was suffering from vitamin C deficiency; my father found a way to buy injections of this vitamin and I recovered.

When rumours circulated about an imminent children's round-up, a Jewish man told my father about the option of hiding a child with a Lithuanian family. The man had three children of his own, but he could not make use of this opportunity: one of his children was a circumcised boy and his two daughters were grown up and spoke only Yiddish, so they could not pass for Lithuanians.

Mother did not want to send me away, but my father was adamant and insisted on taking this chance. I was given a shot of Luminal and carried out of the ghetto in a sack of potatoes. The guards on the gate were bribed. I was handed over to a childless couple, Stasys (Stanislovas) and Antosia (Antonina) Stankevichius. I was a girl with a typical Aryan appearance; Antosia told my mother how one high-ranking German officer could not help looking at me, such a charming Aryan girl; he even gave Antosia some money to buy me a present.

I was baptized and named Genute Stankevichiute. The only thing I clearly remember from my life with the Stankevichius family is that I used to kneel and pray every night before I went to sleep. Stankevichius' neighbours reported to the police that a Jewish girl was being hidden in this family. The Germans came, looked at my blue eyes and blonde hair, checked my documents and went away assured that it was a false report. However, after this event Stankiavichius moved us to the countryside to be on the safe side.

When the ghetto was liquidated my father was sent to Dachau. In 1945, when the liberating Allied forces were approaching, the German guards fled, and the prisoners of the camp scattered in different directions. A group of hungry prisoners, with my father among them, found some food left by the Germans. Almost everybody ate more than their stomachs could tolerate, many became very ill, and some even died. To my father's good fortune, his closest friend, Shimon Dvoretz, who was physically stronger than my father, took the food from his mouth by force. Father was very weak and so was sent to the American hospital, specifically opened in a monastery in Germany for the treatment and rehabilitation of prisoners of the concentration camps.

Somebody told my father that my mother had been seen in Berlin. Father could not wait in the hospital till he was completely recovered; he left in a hurry to look for her. It is hard to believe how, but he managed to find her in a city as huge as Berlin and in the chaos of the post-war days. I do not know how or why my mother ended up in Berlin after the liberation of Stutthof. My parents were offered an opportunity to go to the West, but they naturally decided to return to Lithuania to find me.

Meanwhile, my father's sister, Rachel, had located me with

the Stankevichius family and insisted on them giving me over to her. The Stankevichius' told her they would only return me directly to my parents but my aunt forced them to give me up.

My parents returned to Kaunas and found out that I had been taken to Vilnius by my aunt; they were upset about the way my aunt had treated the Stankevichius couple, who were most kind and generous people. Not only had they asked for absolutely nothing for rescuing me, but they even gave my parents some money to move to Vilnius and buy a sewing machine, which was so essential for them to start to work again. We maintained a very close relationship with Antosia and Stasys till their death. When as a child I was asked what my mother's name was, I always said, 'I have three mothers: Antosia, Feiga and Rachel'. Antosia was always named first.

After high school I decided to become a nurse. I married Josef Zalishansky and in 1962 our first son, David, was born. In 1971 our family, including my parents, emigrated to Israel, and our second son, Daniel, was born there in 1974. We have three grandchildren.

Antosia and Stasys Stankevichius were awarded the title 'Righteous among the Nations' by Yad Vashem.

Nes Ziona, Israel, 2008

MASHA MULLER-HATHSKELZON

My father, Aaron Muller, was born in 1918 in the town of Utenai, Lithuania. After gaining a tailor's skills he moved to work in Kaunas. In 1940 he married Hannah Fisher, and I was born in February 1942, in the ghetto.

As a member of the anti-fascist underground my father was informed about the 'Children's Action'. Aware of the terrible consequences of the 'actions', my parents decided to take the risk of trying to save me. Father wrapped me, asleep, in a blanket, put me into a sack of potatoes and, followed by my mother, carried me to the fence. Mother would never see me again. Father slipped with me out of the ghetto and brought me to Dr Baublys' orphanage, where he left me, as agreed, on the porch. There was a note in a pocket of my dress with only two words: Maryte Daugelaite. Father returned to the ghetto: for a long time my parents stood in a room staring at my empty bed with tears in their eyes. Later my father would tell me, 'Only the knowledge that you were safe kept us sane.'

Father also succeeded in organizing Mother's rescue; she was hidden by a kind Lithuanian family. However, she could not bear the loneliness of separation from her child and her husband, and decided to return to the ghetto. She perished with her mother and sister in Stutthof.

Several days before the liquidation of the ghetto my father noticed that the Germans were taking not only finished jackets from the fur factory, where he worked, but also all the materials for unfinished clothing. He immediately decided to escape from the factory, crossed the river by boat (it was dangerous to cross the most direct way over the bridge) and went to the village of Eiguliai where he was good friends with the righteous family of Maryte and Kazys Palkauskas. It was not the last time that this family would help him.

Once, when he was wandering in search of food, he was caught by Polizei a long way from the factory; he was led to the Gestapo, which meant an immediate death penalty. Kazys actually succeeded in releasing him at the last moment from the Lithuanian Polizei's hands. Many times he was on the point of being revealed at Palkauskas' house, but all the family members, including the 12-year-old son, helped him to survive.

Immediately after liberation my father went to the orphanage to collect me. He was so excited that he could only say two words: Maryte Daugelaite. 'Your daughter is alive and safe,' he was told by the nurse, who provided him with an address: Kedainiai district, the village of Pikuliaviciai, and the name of my rescuers, the Urnezius family. Father managed to obtain from the Soviet authorities an order to return the child to him. In fact there was no need to use this document; the noble family of my rescuers, despite the enormous pain of losing me, agreed without demur to give me, their beloved daughter, back to my father. It was me who fought, cried and refused to go with this stranger. My foster-mother helped my father to calm me down and carried me in her arms to the crossroads where she separated from me with tears in her eyes.

But another fateful blow was awaiting me. On his return to Kaunas my father was mobilized into the Red Army, and forced to leave me in the Jewish orphanage for another year. Only in 1946 were we reunited, this time until my father passed away in 2006 at the age of 87. Father maintained close relations with my rescuers, and he took care that they were recognized as 'Righteous among the Nations' at Yad Vashem in Jerusalem.

In 1973 our family emigrated to Israel. We have two children and four grandchildren here. I retired a couple of years ago. My husband, Lev Hathskelzon, is still working; he is a respected haematologist in Soroka hospital in Beer Sheva.

Beer Sheva, Israel, 2009

PART SIX

REUNIONS AND LOST IDENTITIES

40. The Tortuous Route to Israel

Dalia Hofmekler-Ginsburg

My mother Perela grew up in a poor family. She had had six brothers and three sisters. My grandfather, Leib (Arie) Radjunski, a miller in Seiriai, and grandmother Zelda (née Arulianski) had worked hard to bring up their numerous children. Michail Hofmekler was born in Vilnius; his father, Motl (Mordekhai), had been a cellist and his wife Berta (née Blinder-Stupel) was a housewife. Michail, my father, the oldest of five children in his family, had been a violinist and conductor of an orchestra. Three of his four brothers had also been musicians.

I was born on 29 January 1939 in Kaunas. My parents had lived well and my father's career was flourishing: he was a well-known musician and as early as 1932 he was presented with a medal from the president of Lithuania for his contribution to the musical culture of his country.

In the ghetto we lived in a house built of white brick; it had six rooms and there was a family in each. In our room we lived with my grandfather Motl and grandmother Berta and in the room next door there was the family of my cousin, Katia Segalson. Mother was a strong energetic woman, ready to take on any kind of work. Apart from other tasks she even used to clean the office of the ghetto commandant, Goecke. She was very pretty and even Goecke was enraptured by her beautiful Aryan features and could not believe that she was Jewish.

My father, on the other hand, was weak-willed and did not want to turn his mind to anything but music. After the round-up of intellectuals the Jewish Council (*Judenrat*) decided that it was best to employ musicians as policemen. As a result of that decision, my father not only conducted the orchestra in the ghetto, but was also a member of the Jewish police, or rather he wore its uniform when he conducted the orchestra. When the Jewish policemen were killed just before the ghetto was destroyed, for some reason the only ones who were not shot were those who were also musicians.

I remember on one occasion some Germans came to our quarters and my mother hid me just in case. When they saw the double bass and the violin in our room, they asked my father and grandfather to play the instruments. Perhaps their playing served to save my life. When the rumours about a round-up of children spread, Mother started taking me with her to work. On one occasion she hid me in a cellar where there was a Jewish boiler man. A German soldier found me there: I can remember to this day how he grabbed me by my collar. I do not know what he had been planning to do with me, but at that moment my mother appeared, she took the German by the hand and said in German, 'Mr Soldier, you probably have children back home and you can understand my feelings. I beg you to let go of my little girl!' The soldier let me go. It turned out that one of the Jewish workers had seen the soldier go into the cellar and had warned my mother in time.

There was no limit to Mother's courage. One day, while she was cleaning Goecke's office, she telephoned a Polish woman called Maria (Mania) Rudzhianskiene, who had worked for the Segalson family before the war. She arranged that Mania would take me in and would then find me a refuge in the village near Jonava. My mother then arranged things with a soldier by the name of Bretter, well known for the fact that he had helped a number of children get out of the ghetto. Bretter agreed to help.

I remember that day well. My mother told me that we would be separated for a while, that I would be going to live with Aunt Mania and that I must be a quiet obedient little girl and not speak Yiddish whatever happened. Then she got hold of a cart and pushed me into a small cupboard on it. After that the cart driver, with Bretter's help, took me through the gate of the ghetto. Later Bretter was severely punished by the German authorities for the help he gave to the ghetto inhabitants.

Mania was waiting for me outside the gate. She brought me to her poor relatives in the village. Those people had allotments and a few pigs and were finding it very hard to make ends meet. I was introduced as Mania's illegitimate daughter. The local priest, a friend of the family, baptized me. I was given the name Yadviga (Yadzya). They also taught me to pray. The people in whose house I lived were frightened that I might be seen and they forbade me to go up to the windows. I spent most of the daytime sitting in a cupboard and only used to come out in the evenings. I learnt to walk past the windows bent double, so that I should not be visible from outside.

I can also clearly remember my constant feeling of hunger. It was not that I was not given food; this family used to share their food with me fairly, but there was very little of it in the house. The old man had no teeth and he only used to eat the soft part of the bread; I would be given the crusts. My favourite dish was nettle soup with potato peelings.

If I refused to pray, which I often did, sensing somehow that their religion was not mine, I was made to kneel on dried peas in the corner of the room. That really hurt and it did not take long before I agreed to say my prayers. Sometimes, I would be punished by being sent to the pigsty. I loved playing with the piglets and ever since that time I have been very fond of animals. When the war was already over, I nearly paid for my fondness for animals with my life. One day in early spring, as I was walking along the bank of the River Neman, which was still covered with ice, I saw a ginger kitten floundering in the water. With hardly a moment's hesitation I jumped in and pulled him out. After that, trouble with my inflamed joints flared up again: at that stage I used to suffer a good deal from rheumatism. I was far less trusting in my dealings with people as opposed to animals. Mania often used to visit me in the country and bring me sweets from town. Sometimes I would be visited by Genute Pukaite as well, the woman who had taken in my cousin, Katia Segalson.

I remember an event, near the end of the war, when I was already being allowed to go outside the house. We heard shots and a terrible noise in the distance and saw frightened German soldiers running past or being rushed away on lorries.

One day Mania came out to the village from Kaunas and said that a Jewish orphanage had been opened, to which surviving Jewish children were being sent. She took me there, not long after the beginning of 1945 (see Figure 16: Dalia Hofmekler-Ginsburg is in the first row, sixth from right). I was physically weak and small for my age and so I was put into the group of the youngest children. Of course, I had no idea about what might have happened to my parents. After the ghetto had been knocked down, my parents had been sent to concentration camps. All the other members of the family had been killed. The whole of my mother's family from Seiriai had been shot during the first few days of the war.

My mother had fallen ill with typhus during the last few days in the camp at Stutthof. A Russian soldier noticed, as he walked past of a pile of dead bodies, that a hand was stirring and he pulled my mother out from the pile. She was sent to a military hospital, where, thanks to a good deal of care and attention, the staff enabled her to recover. Mother was particularly grateful to one of the army doctors, Nina Stepanovna, to whom she felt she owed her life.

I remember that we were very well treated in the orphanage and that we felt truly safe at last. I should like in particular to recall an extraordinary woman called Hana Brava, who was the bookkeeper. She tried as hard as she could to give the children warm kindness. She was always ready to listen to me and to help. In the most difficult moments I used to go to her to get things off my chest. Most of the children behaved as children: they cried a good deal. I was a very quiet child and never used to cry. One of the women looking after us said to me, 'Dalinka, have a good cry, you'll feel better.' My response to that was, 'Mama told me that I shouldn't cry.' It was also difficult to persuade me that it was all right to speak Yiddish again. Chana told me later on that when I walked past windows I used to bend double, so that I should not be visible through them. Indeed I was still frightened even to look out of windows. My village habits were deeply engrained.

One day a letter written in Yiddish from Mama arrived: it had come from the Soviet field hospital and there was a photograph of her in it. Mother looked beautiful in the photograph, as she always had, and I remember that she was wearing a dress made of flowery material. Chana read me the letter and that was how I discovered that my mother was alive. Chana then put the photograph in a frame and hung it up over my bed. After that I did not feel lonely any more. I could spend hours looking at that photograph, but the other children used to look at it too and say, 'That's my Mama'. I did not want to share my mother with anyone and so I took the photograph down from the wall and gave it to Chana for safe keeping.

It took my mother a long time to recover. She wrote letters to friends and officials in Lithuania and discovered that I had been saved and was in Kaunas. As soon as she could walk again, the hospital staff found her some clothes, gave her some food for the journey, bought her a train ticket and saw her off to Kaunas.

My mother knew that her husband had survived Dachau and had also fallen ill with typhus. He had been treated in an American hospital in the St Ottilion monastery in Bavaria. That was where he was found by his brother, Ruven Hofmekler, who had left Lithuania for the United States in 1938. Ruven had joined the army as soon as the war against Germany had begun and served in Germany as a translator. People from Kaunas had recognized him and told him about his brother. That was how the two brothers met up again: the rescuer and the rescued. My father did not want to go back to Lithuania. He did not know that my mother had survived, although he did learn that I had. He made arrangements for me to be brought out of Lithuania: two young men from the organization 'Bricha' ('Escape' in Hebrew), which was working in Eastern Europe so as to help Jews make their way to Palestine, were sent to bring me to my father. One night they came to the orphanage and the women on duty handed me over to them on the basis of the letter from my father. That was how I left the orphanage at night, without even saying goodbye to Chana. Mother's photograph got left behind in Chana's desk somewhere and was lost forever.

That same night we made our way to Vilnius, where a group of Jews had been assembling in a flat. From there we were all meant to be crossing the border into Poland as the first stage in our journey to Palestine. Shalom Kaplan (Eilati) was also in that group. I remember that en route we were given *teigale*, traditional Jewish sweet biscuits to eat.

Meanwhile my mother had made her way to the orphanage but did not find me there; she was told however where she might find me. Our moving meeting took place in Vilnius and I shall never forget it. Just as I was thinking that it was the happiest day of my life, for the first time in years I began to cry: we were together at last. My mother then joined the group of 'fugitives' after first collecting Katia Segalson from Genute. Mother knew that Katia's parents had not survived. When everything was finally organized and we were already on the lorry that was to take us over the Polish border, some border guards stopped us. It turned out that one of the drivers, called Shapiro, had been a member of the KGB.

Shots were fired, which I can definitely remember. Some of the people in the group were killed or wounded and the rest were pushed out of the lorry into the snow and taken to the KGB office. I recall very clearly how we were made to lie down on that very cold night, face downwards in the snow, while a Russian soldier walked past poking us in the back with the point of his bayonet. When I felt the bayonet touch my back I called out, 'Uncle, don't kill me, I want to live!' Ever since then I have been unable to stand being touched unexpectedly in the back: it makes me shiver all over in fear.

In Vilnius we were taken to the prison in Lukishkiu Street, where children and adults were separated; the children were sent to a refuge for the homeless. My mother was sentenced to eight years' hard labour in the Urals town of Nizhnij Tagil. Twelve-year-old Katia Segalson took charge of me. She found out that they were planning to send us deep into Russia. That would have meant that we would have lost any chance of being reunited with our relatives. She decided that the two of us would run away. It was very cold on that January night. Katia had found a tablecloth, which she wrapped round me. That was how we made our way through the streets of Vilnius. Katia had remembered some relatives she had in the city and took me to their flat. Katia's relatives were naturally very surprised to see us on the threshold of their flat, since they were sure that we had left already. Opposite them lived my mother's cousins, Sima and Lyuba Verzhbovsky, and I was handed over to them. During the short period I spent there I managed to cause a fire in their flat. That was not the main problem though: looking after the daughter of an 'enemy of the people', who had tried to escape from the USSR and take two Soviet children to a capitalist country, would be very dangerous. That was why they handed me over to the Jewish orphanage in Vilnius.

Although I was treated very well there, losing my mother the second time round had been a very bitter blow for me. I started behaving badly, often tried to run away, objected violently to having my head shaved, which was essential at that time when almost everyone was suffering from head lice. The worst thing of all though was that I started wetting my bed at night again. Two years later, on the anniversary of my mother's return, the problem vanished.

I began to study in a Jewish school, but in 1948 the school was closed and I had to start all over again in a Russian-language school. In 1950 the Jewish orphanage was closed and I was transferred to a Lithuanian orphanage in Antokol, where I stayed until 1952. Those years were particularly hard for me: I would not say that I was badly treated, but I was the only Jewish girl in an orphanage for Lithuanian girls and I was also still having to attend a Russian-language school. I felt an outsider and terribly lonely.

Although my mother had been given a sentence of eight years, thanks to the efforts of some high-ranking Lithuanians, who knew my father well and valued him, she was released early, two years after her conviction. Weak in health, she would not have survived eight years in the camp to which she was sent, where all the prisoners had to work felling trees.

I never stopped waiting for my mother, convinced that she would return. One day, on the way to the bathhouse, I said to one of the staff, 'Mama will arrive soon.' When we returned from the bathhouse, a woman, who was giving out clean linen, asked me, 'Dalinka, what surprise would you like today?' I replied, 'Mama.' At that very moment Mother came into the room. She was very thin, white-haired and she was wearing a convict's cardigan and padded jacket. Our reunion was very moving.

As a former political prisoner, my mother was not permitted to live in Vilnius. She was not allowed to take me back with her. In Kaunas she had neither a flat nor a job: she kept moving from one friend, including the Voshchin family, to another. Mother used to visit me regularly and sometimes, if she could find acquaintances who would put us up, we could spend a night together.

In 1952 my mother was allowed to take me home with her. By then she had found work and a tiny room in the flat of one of my father's relatives, a musician, named Stupialis. That was when our happy life started. My mother tried to make up for all the lost years, bestowing on me tender care and love without end. I was 13 then, but she treated me like a small child: fed me, washed me, dressed me and would have carried me if she could. Although I found all of that rather embarrassing, these years were nevertheless happy ones.

In 1956 my mother decided to leave for Israel. She knew that my father was there and that Katia had succeeded in making her way to Israel. My father used to write to us frequently. I myself did not want to leave, I was frightened of the unfamiliar and because I was perfectly happy in the little room I shared with my mother.

Throughout the years we spent in Lithuania we had kept in close contact with Mania. Mania lived on her own and we tried to help her as much as we could. We used to share the clothes and other items we received from America and Israel with her. When we emigrated to Israel, we left her everything we had. It did not amount to very much.

On 8 June 1956 we were welcomed in the port by Mother's sister, my father, his brother and Katia with her family. On the occasion of that very first meeting I felt that something was not right between my parents. They only shook hands when they met in the port. It turned out that my father had come to Israel after spending three years in Germany. He had found someone else there. Mother knew about it, but I was terribly angry to discover that the truth about my father had been concealed from me. My mother had done that deliberately; she was worried that if I had known the truth I would have refused outright to leave Kaunas.

In Israel my father was not doing well and could only just make ends meet by taking casual work, so he left for Germany and managed to obtain a very generous pension there; he remained there until his death. While he was living in Israel we did not meet often, relations between us were cool. My father was disappointed in me, because I had not taken up music. As far as our material conditions were concerned, we were very badly off. Mother and I settled in Tel Aviv in her sister's flat, but we were not very welcome 'lodgers'.

During my army service in Israeli Army the only clothes I wore were my military uniform, and I was wearing that uniform when I first met my future husband, Dova Ginzburg, who had been born in Israel. He gave me many happy years and my beloved daughter, Einat. After my army service I studied to become a librarian and worked for thirty-six years in the Ashdod library.

My mother lived with us till the end of her days; her physical and mental health had been completely undermined by all her tragic experiences. She was plagued by constant fears and worries; she could not sleep at night and often suffered from nightmares, which made her cry in her sleep. Only Einat could calm her down. She used to go into Grandmother's room at night, gently stroke her hair and then my mother could relax and settle down again. My mother died in 1981 at the age of 67. My husband died of leukaemia in 1990.

When my first grandson was born, I cried for a long time, worried as to what would happen, when at 18, he would be called up into the Army. Now, when he is actually serving in the Army, I feel much calmer about it all. Now I am a pensioner. I have four dogs and three cats, not to mention various others who call at my flat to be fed. All my animals were brought in as strays from the street. I have loved and felt sorry for animals ever since the war years. I currently live two minutes away from my daughter. Her family is my great joy.

Ashdod, Israel, 2008

41. I Did Not Want to Go Anymore

Katia Segalson-Rosen

Sometimes I wonder why it was me who survived the Holocaust, when so few of us did, and I often try to recall how it all happened. I was born on 2 January 1934 in Kaunas, a second child to Moses-Misha Segalson (19 January 1903) and Chaya-Raya Arulianski (31 March 1904). My given name was Kelly, but somehow everybody called me Katia, a name I carry to this day.

My father was a businessman in men's wear, mainly hats, in which he specialized. He owned a hat factory at 4 Panevezio Street and a shop on the main boulevard of our town, 47 (today 83) Laisves (Freedom) Avenue.We lived in a rented flat in a house made of red brick, just behind the shop, not far from the public park and the opera house; most of the shops on the avenue belonged to Jews. Among them were my uncle Jacob's fur shop, Rosmarin's famous sausages, Kapulsky's cakes, and Gladstein's *Optica*, next to ours. I remember my father having been occupied with his business, but while at home, I felt he belonged to me alone. I adored him!

My mother sometimes helped him out in the shop, but otherwise I remember being at her side a lot. She took me to the Shirley Temple movies, to the museum on Donelaichio Street, and even to the opera and to the ballet *Swan Lake*. She was a person full of life, tall, elegant and always surrounded by friends, meeting usually in one of the cafés, *Metropolis*, *Monika* or *Versalis*, where Misha Hofmekler played the violin. Mother liked driving our car, skating, skiing at Azuolinas, known as *'Petrovka'*, in winter and swimming in the Baltic Sea, where we spent some summers in Palanga, a resort place, and in 1938 or 1939 in Schwarzort (*Juodkrante*).

I remember that summer in particular as a fairy tale with a 'prince', a few years older than me, named Andrei. He was my playmate for collecting amber on the beach, and my escort on the dancing floor for children, with a band conducted by Misha Hofmekler. I don't remember my parents being as religious as my grandmothers were, or if they kept a kosher kitchen, but I do know that we ate no pork. My parents spoke Yiddish and Russian between themselves; I spoke only Lithuanian.

Just before the Soviets entered Kaunas in 1940, we moved into a new rented apartment, in a house that belonged to the Dushnickis at 16 Vasario Street, who also lived there; Tolia, their daughter, was my brother's classmate. With the younger one, Himma, I played with dolls. After the establishment of the communist regime, my father's hat factory and the shop, as well as the one we had in Vilnius, were nationalized and our flat was confiscated. We were transferred to an apartment in a building on Mickevichiaus Street, which we had to share with a married Lithuanian couple and two Lithuanian young women. One of them was Gene (Genute) Genovaite Pukaite, whom I liked very much; she was also very fond of me. My mother was naturally very unhappy in our new surroundings. She didn't know it yet, but for me this was going to turn out for the best.

Figure 67. Katia Segalson with her rescuer Genute Pukaite, 1944.

Summer 1941 approached. My brother Liusik (19 January 1927) was going to a Pioneers' youth camp, by the seashore in Palanga. I, who had just finished my first grade in 'Aushros' elementary school, could join him. I preferred to spend the summer with my grandmother, Taibe Arulianski (née Shachnovitz), in a village Punia (Alytus district), situated in a beautiful landscape, near the River Neman, where we children liked to bathe. On the evening of 21 June 1941, I was sent to her on an army truck, accompanied by a Russian officer, a friend of my parents. Before leaving town we stopped at Laisves Avenue, under the big chestnut trees, to eat a hot dog with mustard and rolls, which tasted delicious.

Next morning, 22 June, the Germans entered Punia. Our life started to change. We were ordered to wear a yellow Star of David, which I considered to be a privilege, and wore it proudly. Grandmother's living room was turned into a military office; we were not allowed to pass through it or use the front door into the house anymore. We had to climb through the window in order to reach our own bedroom, which was in the back. This seemed to me like a game. As a 7-year-old child, I had at that time no special fears and continued my summer vacation at my grandmother's, who still raised her geese, made *Cholent* for *Shabbath* and lit candles on Friday evenings. We could still use the kitchen entrance from the backyard. The only thing that bothered me then was the carrot juice my grandmother made me drink every day, which I hated. But this was only the beginning.

My parents sent Mania (Maria) Rudzhianskiene, a Polish woman who used to work for us, to bring me back to them, as Jews were not allowed to move from place to place anymore. My grandmother believed that nothing bad could happen to us in the country, as 'there will be food'! There were her Lithuanian friends, especially the priest who was her 'dear neighbour'. She didn't let me go and sent Mania back, urging my parents to come and stay with us instead. My parents preferred to remain in Kaunas.

Mania came for me again. It took us many hours to travel the nearly sixty kilometres to Kaunas. She brought me into the ghetto in Slobodka, a poor district across the River Vilija, to which my parents had to move during my absence. This was on the day on which the ghetto gates were closed, 15 August 1941.

Grandmother's optimism wasn't justified. On 8/9 September 1941, all the Jews from Punia and its surroundings, numbering about 1,400, were brutally murdered by Lithuanians and buried in two mass graves near the village Klidziunai, next to Butrimonys. Two of my grandmother's daughters, Frida and Liuba, did survive, thanks to their emigration to South Africa before the war.

My other grandmother, Chaya Segalson (born Svojatitzki), was taken from the Kaunas Ghetto on 27 March 1944, to Auschwitz, during the 'Children's Action'. Fortunately, my grandfathers, Leib Segalson and Kopel Arulianski, were spared the same destiny, since they both had died before I was born. My cousins Liova, Genia, Vova and their mother Liuba, widow of my uncle, Jacob Segalson, ended up in the Vilna and Warsaw Ghettos, and didn't survive.

I will not write much about my years in the ghetto, as a lot has already been written about those times. We, the three of us, lived at 56 Linkuvos Street in a room to ourselves. My brother Liusik had fled from Palanga into Russia, where he joined the Soviet Army. In contrast to the small wooden houses around us, the house we lived in was a white, two-storey formerly private villa. Of all the other families who occupied the other rooms, I remember only: The Hofmeklers: Misha (the violinist), his parents, his wife Perale, who was my mother's cousin, and their daughter, Dalia; Dr Aharon Pertzikovitz, the gynaecologist, his wife Raya, and their son Alik, their sister-in-law Enta with her two children, Davik and Zina Berger; Aya Sauberblat, her mother, grandfather and son Miron; Anna Rosenbaum, her son Bubi and daughter Lilly.

Lilly was older than most of us children, very beautiful, lively, and gifted with a creative imagination, which she used to organize our activities. One of them was a performance she staged in the garage, with us acting before an audience. This garage was usually used for storage or for prayers on some holidays. Our games were mainly with buttons. Each button had a price according to size and kind. We spoke Yiddish or Russian, which I had learned by then. In winter, we sometimes played in the snow. In summer, we were once allowed to go for a swim in the river, closely watched by the guards, yet it was fun.

Misha Hofmekler taught Alik and me to play the violin. I took up sewing as well. We had a big yard, where we grew some vegetables and raised a couple of rabbits. We gave them a full funeral when they died. Food was rationed. We mostly had some sort of soup. By effort and risk, additional food was smuggled into the ghetto from the outside. I remember my mother's disappointment, and mine when, because of my sore throat, I couldn't eat the egg she specially prepared for me. Once, we were given as a special treat some horse meat, which my mother cooked with a lot of garlic. The smell and taste of it were horrible; I avoided garlic for many years.

We all lived in hope for our liberation, while the ghetto population became smaller from 'action' to 'action', especially after the 'Great Action' of 28 October 1941. We were all gathered there from very early morning for many hours to go through the 'selections', performed by German officers, deciding and sending to the left those who were to live, or to the right, the 'bad' side. My father had a *'Jordan Schein'*, a certificate showing that he was a 'useful' worker. He also took under his protection Aya Sauberblat as his sister, with her son, and her mother as his own mother, but he could do nothing for the grandfather. I remember even now the abandoned old man, bewildered and lost in the big crowd. He didn't return with us to the house.

Luckily, most of the children from our house survived the war: Lilly Rosenbaum-Millner, now in Helsinki, Miron Sauberblat, now in the USA, Dalia Hofmekler-Ginzburg, Alik Peretz (Pertzikovitz) and myself now living in Israel.

I think that at the beginning I felt more secure than the others, as my father was the manager of the 'large workshops', located within the ghetto, on Krishchiukaichio Street. He and those who worked there were, so to say, useful to the Germans, and would therefore perhaps be spared together with their families. At the *Seder Pesah* which we held in 1943 at the house of Uncle Samuel Segalson and his wife Raya at 34 Dvaro Street, most members of our family were still alive.

But when rumours spread of an approaching 'Children's Action', my mother somehow contacted Mania and Genute. They were both willing to take me in. I preferred to live with Genute, so Mania took my cousin Dalia instead of me. One evening, some time before the 'Children's Action', I was smuggled out of the ghetto through the main gate, while the guards were bribed. Genute awaited me there and took me over the Vilija Bridge, back to town.

At the beginning I stayed with Genute in Kaunas, at 6 Presidento Street, sharing the bed with her, the room with a friend of hers, and the flat, with Pranute Shpokaite (Prane Juodvalkiene), who was active in rescuing Jews. From time to time some of them stayed with us for a while. She arranged faked papers for me, as an abandoned child of a Russian officer. I was aware that they were not considered to be reliable, especially because of my Jewish looks: dark brown eyes and curly black hair. Most of the neighbours were hostile, which forced me to go into hiding for a few days at some other place. As part of her cover, Pranute used to entertain Germans and Lithuanian policemen. On those occasions I was kept out of sight, yet it was scary. At that time I became 'Katryte'. I was made to believe that I should be happy to have left the ghetto, but very soon I felt insecure, and became miserable and lonely; in spite of Genute's understanding and support, I demanded to go back to my parents.

A meeting with my mother was arranged for us somehow in Gladstein's former apartment; I cried bitterly. It saddens me whenever I think how she must have felt, not being able to take me back with her. This was the last time we saw each other.

I remained with Genute. She found me a friend, a neighbour's daughter named Grasilda Kniukshtaite, who used to come to me after school to play and do her homework. She was very sensitive and discrete, never giving a hint that she suspected I was Jewish, yet she came to my rescue whenever she could. Thanks to her and to my increasing interest in the New Testament, and belief in Christianity, and of course thanks to Genute, things became easier for me.

During most of the days I stayed alone in the apartment, usually reading, as everybody was out at work. Some mornings I couldn't prevent myself from looking through the window for a familiar face, when ghetto labour brigades emerged out of Vilniaus Street and marched by. Occasionally I took the risk and went out with Grasilda or with Genute into the streets, mainly to church. One day I came face to face with my friend from the ghetto, Fruma Vitkin. Both of us got very scared, yet we succeeded in completely ignoring one another.

When the Soviet front drew near, Genute decided it was time

for us to move to her parents, who lived in Radziunai, a village in the Ukmerge district. Though I could not pass as a Lithuanian by my looks, I spoke the language fluently, without any accent. When rumours spread among our neighbours in the village that I was Genute's illegitimate daughter (she wasn't married), we didn't deny them: 'the father could even have been Jewish'.

When the Red Army arrived again at the end of July 1944, I was overjoyed, but not for long. I received the news that my mother was dead, and my father had been deported, his fate unknown. Genute returned after some time to Kaunas, leaving me behind for another year with her parents and three of her sisters: Birute, Albina, whose bed I shared and Regina, who became my friend. Her married sister Aldona Mackeviciene lived four kilometres away, near the church in Taujenai, to which we went on Sundays for mass. The parents cared for me; I felt that they treated me even better than their grandchildren. I regarded them as my own grandparents. They were poor, decent, hard-working farmers, who lived a simple life, mostly on bread, potatoes and porridge, which I liked. We had apples from our trees, and mushrooms, blueberries and wild strawberries from the nearby woods. For me, there was also always a glass of fresh milk and occasionally an egg. I became very attached to a dog, Princas. I felt I was part of the family!

The winter of 1944/45 was very cold with heavy snow. I went to school in the village and graduated from the fourth grade as best in my class. Most of the time there were lice to cope with. My legs were full of sores. In summer I got sick with typhoid. My head was shaved as I was hospitalized for a month in Ukmerge, twenty kilometres from our village, where I nearly died. I haven't realized that at the time, till a priest came to give me the last rites. During this period Albina visited me a few times, bringing cooked apples her mother sent me.

I recovered after all, and came back to the village, only to find out that the place wasn't as safe as I believed. Though the war had already ended in May 1945, things hadn't much changed for me. I still had to hide my identity, as most of the Lithuanians preferred Nazi German rule to the Soviet regime. In the forests around us were so-called 'partisans' who were former collaborators with the Nazis. Indeed, members of the family I loved and who sheltered me helped them as well. One day, as I entered the barn, I surprised Albina and Jonas Perkunas, who was one of them. His head was wounded; I recognized him immediately. He used to come and flirt with Albina from behind the fence, as her mother never let him pass the gate. The reason she gave: 'he murdered Jews'. The minute I saw him I panicked and ran away. No one mentioned this incident, but since I knew the man was around and he knew that I had seen him, I was scared.

Towards the end of August 1945, one early morning while I was still asleep, my brother Liusik suddenly appeared in a Russian army uniform. He was aware of the 'partisans' in the forests and came accompanied by some Russian soldiers, to take me away. He ordered the grandparents to deliver me with all my belongings to the nearby police station in Taujenai, within two hours. This caused a big confusion, as now my real identity was uncovered. Though I was glad to join my brother, I felt very bad about the way it was done. The grandparents felt insulted by his behaviour, which they clearly didn't deserve. I was very sad to part from them, but I felt relieved to leave the village.

Liusik brought me back to Kaunas and he left me with Father's friend, Chone Lipshitz and his wife Katia. They lived on Putvinskio Street in a very small room, yet made me more than welcome. They were very nice people. I stayed with them willingly.

One day I went to the synagogue at Ozheskienes, which was just around the corner, but left disappointed as there was no one I knew. I visited Genute from time to time, who worked at the *Metropolis* restaurant, not far away.

I stayed with the Lipshitzes for about four months, till Perale Hofmekler, who was believed to be dead, suddenly arrived, as if from another world. She heard somehow that my father and her husband Misha were alive in Germany, and came to take her 7-year-old daughter Dalia and me, to cross the border illegally into Poland, with the intention of reaching them. I was happy, looking forward to it.

That event was going to take place between 5 and 6 January 1946. We left Vilnius with many others, on a cold snowy night. Unfortunately, one of the four truck drivers was an informer. We were stopped by gunfire on our way and brought back by Russian armed soldiers to the headquarters of the KGB on Gedimino Avenue. After a long and tiresome interrogation, the grown-ups were left behind and later sent to prison; among them were Perale and my brother.

We children were sent to an orphanage at the end of the day, from which we escaped the next morning. I took Dalia with me to my father's cousin, Dr Ovadia Jochelson, who lived on Traku Street, some blocks away. From there, Dalia was transferred to her relatives. I stayed on with the Jochelsons for a while, after which they put me into a Jewish orphanage at 6 Zygimantu Street, near the river. Yet I continued to attend a Lithuanian school in the old part of town. I also went often to the nearby cathedral. Maybe this was the main reason I felt excluded. Though the staff did their best, the orphanage remained a miserable cold place to me. The food was poor, I had lice and feared my hair would be shaved again. My only joy was the piano lessons I received at the conservatory, where my teacher was the well-known Nadja Dukstulski, who was acquainted with our family from Kaunas.

Katia Lipshitz came to see me from time to time, always with a piece of cake. After six months, she took me back to Kaunas and to Genute at 4 Zhemuogiu Street on *Zhaliakalnis* (Green Hill), where I felt at home again, and yet didn't feel I fully belonged. I was given to understand, that I couldn't visit the grandparents in the village anymore, as that would still endanger me. I overheard a friend of Genute reproaching her as to why she still kept me, instead of turning me over to my 'own kind', now that the war was finished.

Genute's sister Aldona, with husband and four children, Henrikas, Lida, Judita and Faustas, also came to stay with us. We all got on well. While Genute was at work, I used to go for lunch at Katia's. Walking down the Kauko stairs, crossing Laisves Avenue, I also visited our former neighbours, the Gladsteins, who had returned to their original flat again. Grasilda, my friend, was in town as well.

One day, as I went up the Ukmerges-Savanoriu Avenue, I ran into Fruma Vitkin; this time we were both overjoyed. She was the only survivor of her family and lived with Helene Holzman not far from our flat. We visited each other and planned to go to school together. Life seemed to have become normal again.

Just then came a telegram from Lodz, signed by my father, that he was looking for me. It arrived at the Kaunas Jewish

Orphanage, where Hanna Brava was employed. She took the trouble to find me. As I learned later, my father was liberated from Dachau on 1 May 1945. He got married again in Landsberg to Jenia Segal, born Ginsburg, whom I knew as our neighbour from the ghetto. She was a widow, with no children of her own, and a close friend of the Pertzikovitzes. She was liberated from Stutthof. It was she who went to Lodz and contacted the *Bricha* ('Escape' organization), who arranged to bring me across the border. For that purpose she used a diamond ring that was provided for her by Rabbi Abraham Klausner, a chaplain in the US Army. Soon afterwards someone came for me.

I must say that at that time I didn't want to go anymore. I was anxious to start school next day, I loved Genute and felt loved by her, but she convinced me. I was taken by train to Vilnius, brought back and later taken again to an apartment, where we had to wait till we were able to continue. It took us almost three weeks till we could cross the border with false papers of Poles returning to Poland, via Baranovitz, to reach Warsaw and Lodz. It seemed an eternity to me. My disappointment was therefore very great when it wasn't my father who awaited me there, but Jenia, who turned out to be his wife. She was nice; she treated me to hot chocolate, and cleaned me of the lice. It took us another month and another illegal border crossing from Poland to Germany to reach Father in Munich on 28 October 1946. My dream had come true; I was reunited with him after almost three years of separation. Only then did I learn the missing details of what had occurred after my leaving the ghetto.

During the liquidation of the Kaunas Ghetto my father decided to go along with all the others. He survived Dachau with his brother Samuel, his nephews Liusik-Arie and Chone, and his cousin Iliusha Segalson. His sister, Altochke Maliacki and her daughter Lialia, my age, did not survive.

My mother decided to hide with her younger brother Dodik, Dr David Arulianski and his wife Ira (born Gurwitz), in '*maline*'. As the ghetto was burned down and destroyed, not one of them survived. Mother was 40 years old.

On joining my father, I was given new clothing, a full medical check-up and was taken to Berchtesgaden, ironically the resort favoured by Hitler. We stayed in Munich for another two years, in Bogenhausen. My father became a member of the Central

Committee for Liberated Jews in the occupied American Zone of Germany; I went to an established Hebrew school, where the language was mainly Yiddish. In 1947 a summer camp was arranged for us children in the Bavarian Alps at Urfeld am Walchensee and in 1948 at Hartmannsberg. I made new friends, but had difficulties in adjusting to our new form of life. Jenia was an intelligent vivid woman with a lot of good humour. I believe she had the best of intentions, but at that time they did not meet my feelings. I missed my mother.

By that time I also gradually stopped praying and believing in Jesus Christ and Maria, but I always remember the great comfort this belief gave me during my most difficult times.

We came to Israel by plane on 29 October 1948, to start a new life, this time legally, for a change. On our arrival, I was again given a new official name: Carmela. In the beginning we stayed for a couple of months with my Uncle Samuel's family in Tel Aviv. They came to Israel in 1946. Their 19-year-old son, my favourite cousin, Chone, was killed in June 1948, during the War of Independence.

Later on, we shared for some time the small flat of the Pertzikovitz (Peretz) family; then we moved to three other flats, till we ended up in 1950 in our own small house near the Beilinson Hospital in Petach Tikva, where my father secured his permanent job as chief administrator. I went to school in Tel Aviv, learned Hebrew, joined a youth movement and tried to catch up on the years that were lost.

In 1951, I enrolled in the nursing school at the Haifa Ram Bam Hospital. The Peretzes took me under their wings; Dr Aharon Peretz was head of the Obstetrics and Gynaecology Department and became one of my teachers. After graduation I worked for a few years as a registered nurse, and got married to Dan, then an engineering student at the Haifa Technion. We both went to the same high school, *'Tichon Chadash'* in Tel Aviv. We have two daughters (both delivered by Dr Aharon Peretz), Osnat (1956), an architect and town planner, and Raya (1964), a sociologist and statistician. Our granddaughter Maya is 10 years old while I am writing all this, and I often find myself comparing her with myself at her age.

Perale and Dalia Hofmekler arrived in Israel from Lithuania in 1956, the Jochelsons in the 1960s, Katia Liphshitz's family and

Hanna Brava came in the 1970s. Liusik, my brother and his family arrived from the Soviet Union in 1990, but our father didn't live to see him again. He died on 9 October 1969 at the age of 66, and Jenia died on 1 April 1984; by then we had become very close.

I kept in contact with Mania Rudzhianskiene for a long time, till she stopped writing. I have never found out what has become of her. Genute's mother, Maryte-Marijona, died in 1949, her father, Juozapas Pukas in 1966. I will always remember their kindness, and cherish their memory. On 23 May 1967, Genute (Gene) Genovaite Pukaite, was recognized and honoured as one of the 'Righteous among the Nations'; she received a special medallion and in 1985 a tree was planted bearing her name in the 'Avenue of the Righteous' at Yad Vashem. I was very excited when, after many years of trying, I succeeded in 1991, in bringing her on a visit to meet my family, friends, and the holy places of Christianity.

I visited Genute in Lithuania twice, where I felt welcomed by her family and my friends. Though it was more than painful to me to go back and experience the past again, I was very glad I did it, as it made Genute happy. Her only disappointment was that I had stopped believing in God. During my second visit in 1994, she was also honoured by the Lithuanian authorities for saving a Jewish life. This event took place as part of the ceremonies to mark the fiftieth anniversary of the liquidation of the Kaunas Ghetto; she died a few months later, at the age of 82. For me she is an example of courage, decency, kindness and selflessness.

Genute's relatives, whom I regard in a way as my own, and my friends Grasilda Kniukshtaite and Fruma Vitkin-Kuchinskiene, live in Kaunas. In 1999 I went to Lithuania again, this time with my daughter Raya, to visit them, and all the graves and the places 'where it all happened'. Looking back makes me realize how very lucky I was.

EPILOGUE

In addition to Genovaite Pukaite being recognized by Yad Vashem as one of the 'Righteous among the Nations' in 1967, Yad Vashem awarded this title in 2006 to Pukas Juozapas and

Marijona (Genute's parents), Maria Rudzhianskiene, Prane Shpokaite-Juodvalkiene who played an important part in my life, and whom I remembered in my story.

Haifa, Israel, 2007

42. The First Taste of Chocolate

Ariana and Rut Jed (Told by Ariana)

My father, Meir Jed, studied medicine at Leipzig University; there he met Edna Fuks, who soon became his wife. After graduation my father worked as a surgeon in Germany. When the Nazis came to power he was arrested, severely beaten, his jaw was broken, and he was imprisoned. My mother Edna managed to have him released with the assistance of the Lithuanian Embassy and our parents hastily left for Lithuania. My sister Ruth was born in 1939 in Kaunas, and myself, in 1940.

From the beginning of the war our father served in the Soviet Army. His eldest brother, Motl, who was also a surgeon, had not listened to father's advice to evacuate; he told my father that he couldn't abandon his patients, and he was shot in the hospital ward. My grandfather, Aaron Jed, and my father's younger sister, Ester, perished in the Kaunas Ghetto.

In the very first days of occupation, the Gestapo came to our apartment. They tortured my mother, demanding that she should reveal where she had hidden her daughters. Our mother said nothing. Then she was given an injection and died in twenty minutes.

Our aunt Gerta Fuks, Dr Baublys, Professor Mazhylis and many other people took part in our rescue. We were hidden in the ghetto, sometimes in villages and in an orphanage. From that period I vaguely remember several episodes. The most awful episode ran constantly in my memory, but I cannot tell where it exactly happened. I saw how a policeman had snatched the baby from the arms of a woman and had thrown him out through a window. I remember the sound of the fallen body; the woman rushed to the window and having seen her dead child threw herself out to her own death.

I remember how Rut was sent to feed a bucket of fodder to a cow. The cow, on seeing Rut, ran toward her. Poor Rut, who for the first time in her life had faced such a beast, ran away and dropped the bucket. Rut was beaten by the farmer's wife for losing the swill.

Figure 68. Ariana and Rut Jedaites with their aunt Gerta Fuks in
a hide in countryside, 1943.

The children's home, where we had been transferred, was
located near a forest, and there was a big veranda in front of this
house. I remember that we were always hungry; despite this, I
could not eat the 'blood' sausages that they used to give us. Once
I asked Rut why we did not have a daddy and a mum, like the
others. She said, 'Children don't always have parents. You were
brought to me by a stork so that that I would not feel lonely.'

Lithuanians often came to the orphanage searching for Jewish
children. The frightened children would run away to hide in
dark corners, under a table or bed. Sometimes children were
found and carried away. Rut was very clever and had taught me
to stand easy and to look the strangers in the eyes. So we,
blondes, were never suspected of being Jews. People also came to
the home looking for children to adopt. Rut demanded that we
should not be separated. Quite often couples wished to adopt
me, but Rut trained me to bite so as to frighten off potential adoptive parents.

Dr Dugovsky had served in one division with our father. In 1945 he spent several days off in Kaunas. He met a group of children from the orphanage and recognized Rut among them. Having returned to the army he urged father to go to Kaunas to check if it was indeed Rut.

A brother and sister Nemeikshas used to take us from the orphanage to their house. I very much liked visiting there, where we played in the garden. I remember vividly how the door of the Nemeikshas' house opened and our daddy entered. He saw Rut, fell down to his knees, embraced her and began to kiss her, sobbing as I had never in my life seen him do. I was dumbfounded. I was taught that it is necessary to be afraid of 'Russians' with pistols, and here Rut was embracing one. 'Rut why don't you run away?' I shouted. Only now Father noticed me. He asked Rut, 'Who is this girl?' 'It's Ariana,' she answered. Then Father tried to hug and kiss me, his crying renewed with new strength. As I was taught by Rut, I started to bite and kick.

Father offered me some chocolate. 'Take it Ariana,' said Rut, 'it is a hundred times better then sugar.' I liked chocolate very much. I thought, 'What a strange man, he gives away such a tasty thing for nothing.' Later Rut told me, 'I lied to you that we do not have parents. This man is our daddy.'

Father had to return to the army. He left us in the care of our pre-war maid, Maria, paying her, but he did not know that she was also working as a prostitute. Once, a Russian soldier stayed at Maria's place; he got drunk and started to smother her. She pulled away, attacked him and escaped. The soldier started to shoot around with an automatic rifle. We cowered in bed and by a miracle were not injured, the wall above us was covered with bullets. The soldier approached the window, and continued shooting randomly at the street until he was shot by a militiaman. He collapsed before our eyes.

After Father returned from the army he married Asya, who became our mother. We moved to Vilnius where Father began to work as a paediatrician, and he quickly gained popularity and respect. In 1958, by means of a fictitious marriage of Rut to a Pole, we obtained the permit to leave for Poland. One day before our departure, an officer of the NKVD came to our house. Father was out, but the officer waited for about four hours until he returned. When father saw the officer he went cold with fear, he was sure that he was to be arrested. The officer calmed him, telling him that there had been a denunciation: two Jews had informed the NKVD about Rut's fictitious marriage. The officer, possibly grateful to our father for the medical care he had given his children, told him he would delay the investigation, but that we should leave the USSR immediately. So we did and in 1958, via Poland, arrived in Israel.

In Israel, Rut worked for the rest of her life as an oculist; I became a microbiologist. We both married, established families, each of us with two children.

Petah-Tikva, Israel, June 2009

43. I Have Retained a Great Love of LIFE!

Gidon Sheftel

My mother, Chaviva Libaite, was born in 1915 in Lithuania in the small town of Varniai. In her youth, being pretty and lively, she had always been a centre of attention for many Jewish young men. Aharon Dambe, a young man from Varniai and one of Mama's admirers, made her a proposal of marriage. He was older than she was by six to eight years and she turned him down.

In 1938 my mother moved to Kaunas to start a job there, after she had had her application for a permit ('certificate'), to emigrate to Palestine turned down. She had been a member of the organization '*Hashomer Hatsair*' in Varniai.

Aharon in the meantime had set off to Palestine to seek his fortune there. In 1939 he had still not found his feet in Palestine and came back to Kaunas, where he met my mother again and once more started courting her. When he proposed for a second time, my mother accepted his offer of marriage. This time Aharon Dambe and Chaviva Libaite became man and wife; I was born on 6 February 1940. My father worked as the chief accountant in one of the town's large factories and my mother had an office job somewhere. My parents lived very well up until the war. They had a beautiful flat, opposite the Opera Theatre.

When the war began my parents tried to escape to Russia, but the train was bombed by the Germans. Half of the train moved off to the east, but they had been in the 'wrong' half. Lithuanians surrounded the remaining passengers, led the men off and shot them in the woods straightaway. To this day I do not know where my biological father's grave is. My mother and I were taken to the Kaunas Ghetto, but I do not know where we lived there or where she worked.

In 1943 a German soldier from the Wehrmacht, who had taken a shine to my mother, warned her about the 'Children's Action' and advised her to take me through the fence when he was on guard duty at the gate at night, so as to take me to safety.

I was taken in by a Polish family by the name of Wilkancas

Raimundas, living near the ghetto in the Slobodka district who also had a son and daughter of their own. My mother had previously given Wilkancas the key to our flat, saying that he could take all its contents including the bag of jewels that was hidden there. Since I had curly blond hair and blue eyes as a small child, nobody suspected that I was Jewish. I was taught to pray, while living with the Polish family, and became a proper little Polish Catholic boy.

Figure 69. Gidon Sheftel in the Ghetto, 1943.

After the ghetto in Kaunas was disbanded, my mother was taken to the Stutthof camp, which was eventually liberated by the Soviet Army. When my mother went back to Kaunas, she collected me from the family of my rescuers. After the war

Wilkancas became a People's Judge. His family was still living in the same house in Slobodka. In the spring of 1947 the Neman and Vilija rivers both broke their banks and there was a serious flood, which affected a large part of the city. My parents offered the Wilkancas family the opportunity to come and stay with us, but they declined. One night, when Wilkancas had not been at home, the whole of his family was drowned. Wilkancas subsequently married a second time. My parents helped him and his family a good deal, and Wilkancas even attended my wedding. Unfortunately he was in the habit of drinking heavily and in 1968 he died.

At the beginning of 1946 Yakov Sheftel had returned to Kaunas from the war. In the past he too had been one of mother's group of friends in Varniai. From 1942 he served in the 16th Lithuanian Division, took part in many battles and made his way as far as the Kaliningrad region. There he had been severely wounded in the head near Tilsit. A detachment from a penal battalion came across him lying unconscious on the battle-field, where he had been abandoned, because everyone had thought him dead. My father-to-be was first sent to a field hospi-tal, where they did not start treating him but sent him as quickly possible to a hospital out of harm's way in the Urals. In a mili-tary hospital out there a Jewish doctor, despite everyone predicting the worst, braved all the risks and operated: he over-saw Yakov's treatment and saved him from certain death. Yakov Sheftel was invalided out of the army classified as a Group-1 war invalid – the most seriously injured. Soon afterwards he met up with my mother again, and after all that they had lived through and all the losses and suffering they had experienced, the two of them decided to marry and begin a new life. In April 1948 my sister Sara was born.

My father, Yakov Sheftel (all through my life I have regarded him as my father and called him 'Father') went on to open a factory and a shop to make and sell meat products, and succeeded in making 'a whole heap of money' at it; later his shop was nationalized. Yakov was a generous man and gave money to the Jewish Orphanage and kindergarten and helped many Jews, who used to pass through our flat between 1946 and 1948 before their final departure to Palestine.

I studied for four years in the Jewish school and when it was closed I moved to the Russian school, from which I graduated in 1956. I gained a place straightaway at the Kaunas Polytechnic, graduating from it as an electrical engineer in 1961. I was given work in the Kaunas Planning Institute, known as *'Promproekt'*, where I soon became a team leader and member of the *Komsomol* Committee.

In 1963 our family decided to apply for the papers needed for emigrating to Israel. Prior to that, my father, as a war invalid, had not dared to leave. I think that it was the first time that the municipal authorities, including the KGB, had encountered such a 'shameless' request of this kind from a young engineer and *Komsomol* member. Soviet bureaucracy demanded that, when applying to emigrate, I had to provide a character reference from work and even the request for such a document alarmed those in charge at *'Promproekt'*. Three *Komsomol* meetings were held at which the question of my exclusion from the *Komsomol* was discussed. It was only on the third occasion that I was finally excluded, but even then the vote had not been unanimous. I was one of the first young men at the time to pluck up the courage to apply for permission to go to Israel; inevitably, our request was turned down.

In 1967 I married Shulamith Levin, a very pretty Jewish girl. Shulamith had been born in 1945, after the war, in the town of Osh in Russia. Her mother had been evacuated there for the duration of the war. In 1967 our son Arik was born. In 1969 my wife's mother and sister emigrated to Israel, after which we, too, made a second attempt, and on 20 January 1972 we at last flew to Israel. Immediately after completing the Hebrew language school, I started to work in the profession for which I had been trained. My wife found a job as a translator. In 1974 our second son Alon was born and in 1985 our daughter Miri.

In 1987 my father died, and my mother died in 1995. It was not until a few years after her death that a family friend, Yakov Levin, a Jew from Varniai, told me all about my early years. After hearing all those details I started to recall how during my childhood, when visitors were present and I happened to go into the room where they had congregated, everyone suddenly used to fall silent for some reason.

Mother had kept everything secret and had never mentioned the name Aharon Dambe, or told me that Yakov Sheftel was not my biological father. I do not know whether I behaved correctly as regards my real father, but I decided 'not to go there' and let everything be, just as my poor deceased mother would have wished. I retained the very warmest of feelings towards Yakov Sheftel, the father who had helped my mother bring me up with affection and patience. Today, as a pensioner, I have four remarkable grandchildren and have retained a great love of LIFE!!

Kfar Sava, Israel, 2008

44. Who Am I?

Aharon Avidonis

In 1957, when I was about 16 years old, my mother, Malka Avidonis, passed away. Only then, for the first time in my life, I was told by our neighbours that Rouven and Malka Avidonis were not my biological parents. It appears that in 1945 I was taken by them, both Holocaust survivors, from the Jewish Orphanage in Kaunas. The same neighbour told me that she had heard that my family had lived before the war in the old city of Kaunas.

Figure 70. Aharon Avidonis with his adoptive mother Malka Avidonis, 1955.

My birth certificate states that I was born on 15 May 1941. Most probably I was born before the war, since I was circumcised, so I guess this is not my real date of birth. I tried in vain to find out what was my name and surname at birth, who were my parents, what happened to them, how and by whom I was rescued, and who had brought me to the orphanage. I deeply regret that I did not ask for more information from my adoptive father.

After my service in the Soviet Army, I worked as an electrical technician, got married and in 1967 our son was born. We emigrated to Israel in 1991 and I worked in my profession till retirement in 2008. I would like very much to find out about my roots, but I do not expect such a miracle will happen.

Haifa, Israel, 2009

45. I Don't Want Any More Mamas

Rina Badesh

My father, Itshak Badesh, was a lawyer and my mother Sonya née Kalmansky, was a bookkeeper. In 1937 they had a son called Izya. I was born in 1939. My pregnant aunt, Ema Shtok, and her husband were shot by Lithuanians during the first days of the German occupation.

My father and my young unmarried uncle, Yankale Kalmansky, had perished at the time of the so-called 'Intellectuals' Action', when about 500 young educated Jews had been lured by a promise of interesting work into a fatal trap. They had all been shot immediately in the Ninth Fort. Everyone quickly found out about it, including my mother, who was left in the ghetto alone with two children on her hands to care for.

Some scenes of our life in the ghetto are still clearly imprinted on my memory. I remember our room, the house, the shouting in the street, my brother worried that he would be punished after he had lost the keys to the flat, and how I comforted him. I even found a way of getting back into the house by climbing through a fanlight.

I cannot forget policemen beating up an old man on Mapu Street until he stopped moving. I remember how some Germans dragged a woman out of a hiding place in the ghetto as she shouted and begged them not to hurt her. I remember the shiny buttons on the uniforms of the Germans and the local Polizei, and ever since I have been unable to look at shiny buttons.

I remember Mother preparing a blanket to wrap me up in order to take me out of the ghetto to some woman. I readily agreed to go, and to this day I cannot grasp how a little girl of four and a half could understand how still and quiet she had to be. I even tried to persuade my little friend, Dvorale Murin, who was crying and did not want to go, when her mother told her that they would possibly have to live apart for a time. I said to Dvorale, 'If you don't go, Hitler will come and get you and you'll die.' Unfortunately, she refused to go.

One night my mother carried me wrapped up tightly in a thick blanket to the fence. I suddenly felt I was flying through the air and then I fell to the ground. A woman took me by the hand and started walking quickly away from the ghetto. When I took off my headscarf, I saw that it was Manya Beresniavichiene, my mother's pre-war maid. Her husband worked in my father's factory. They asked absolutely nothing for hiding me.

I began to cry, hitting out at Manya and biting. Manya brought me to her flat in 3 Mapu Street, not far from the house we had lived in before the war. For the first two days I would eat nothing; I just sat there crying. On the third day I asked, '*Vandens*' (water). That was the first word I used, as I started to remember the Lithuanian language, which I had known from the moment I had first started to speak.

Manya was very kind to me; she talked to me gently and affectionately and smiled at me all the time. I grew used to her and stopped crying and thinking about my mother. One day, out of the blue, Manya said that we were going back to my mother. She took me to another flat, where a woman I did not recognize opened the door and said she was my mother. At that moment I believed her. It turned out that Manya was afraid to keep me with her, because her brothers were collaborating with the Germans. That was why Manya entrusted me to Bronya and Antanas Karaliauskas, who did not have any children of their own. They gave me the name Renate Karaliauskavichiute in the hope that my mother would not survive.

At the beginning Bronya and Antanas treated me well. Mother came to visit me from time to time, but Bronya used to make sure that I should not see or hear my real mother. Once Mother came by when I was at home on my own, but I did not open the door, saying that we were afraid of thieves and did not open the door to strangers. After the war Mother told me that she had been taken aback by my answer, but on the other hand she had been happy to hear my voice.

However, later, when Antanas was taken by Germans for some service from which he never came back, things had changed. Bronya began drinking heavily and forcing me to drink vodka as well: it was revolting. If I refused to drink, she used to force my mouth open and pour the vodka in. It was terrible; I tried to spit it out without anybody noticing. Ever since, I have been unable to bear even the smell of alcohol.

But the most awful thing was that Bronya used to abandon me, a girl of 5, leaving me on my own for several days. During that time I would feed on bread and butter, which I used to spread in thick layers on my bread and then sprinkle with sugar. If my behaviour was not to Bronya's liking, she would beat me or make me kneel on dried peas in the corner. That used to hurt a great deal. I don't know what crime I had committed, although I was quite a mischievous child. I used to think that God was punishing me.

Bronya had taught me to pray, and used to take me regularly with her to the Catholic Church. She believed that prayers would save me from death. Ever since then, despite this having no connection at all with religion, I love visiting churches and listening to church music.

At the end of the war I remember an incident when there was a lot of shooting. We were running to the shelter. I was ill with whooping cough and kept coughing and stopping to get my breath, unable to run any further. Bronya came over to me and smacked me hard on the face. Perhaps in that situation there was nothing else to be done, but I still remember that slap on the face.

When the fighting was coming closer to Kaunas at the end of the war, Bronya took me with her to the country where I played with the Lithuanian children. No one in the village suspected that I was a Jewish girl. One event from the time spent with Bronya in the village I will never forget. There was heavy shelling and a bomb hit some buildings. We ran to look what happened: there were bodies of children without arms or legs scattered in a field. I could not understand why one boy without a leg was so white and did not scream.

After Lithuania had been liberated from the Germans, we went back into Kaunas. Father's sister, Hiena Labensky, returned from Russia and went to see Bronya so as to take me back, but Bronya refused outright to let me go, saying that she would only give me back to my mother. A few days later my aunt's husband, an army doctor, Simha Labensky, appeared in the flat in his army uniform. My uncle offered Bronya money for having looked after me, but she demanded a huge sum and my uncle left. The next day I looked out of the window and saw some men in militia uniform. I said to Bronya, 'Let's jump out of the window.' At that moment Simha and his friend Liubecki, disguised as militiamen, came into the flat. My uncle placed a large sum of money on the table and picked me up and we all left together. Bronya fainted. My uncle was carrying me and, just as two years previously with Manya, I started shouting, biting and scratching.

I did not like 'Mama Bronya'. After the war when she used to come and visit us, I did not go up to her to give her a hug. Mother scolded me on more than one occasion for being so cold towards Bronya.

My uncle took me to my aunt, who hugged and kissed me and said that she was my real mother. I believed her. My uncle and aunt were living in a large flat belonging to a Jewish family who used to give temporary shelter to Jews from different backgrounds. All those Jews with long beards I found frightening and ugly. When they used to come to the flat I would hide under the table saying, 'Another *Jid* is coming'.

Later I was taken to Vitebsk, where there was a military hospital in which my uncle worked. I did not feel comfortable there and was afraid of everyone and everything. Children in our yard, sensing my fear, used to taunt me. My uncle told the chief doctor at the hospital about me; his advice was to teach me to give as good as I got. That was what my uncle did, telling me I should stand up for myself. The next day I punched a boy on the nose, which started to bleed. I thought I had killed him. I could still remember from the ghetto that when people began bleeding that meant that they were dying. It turned out that the boy I had punched was the son of the chief doctor, who after shaking my uncle's hand said that everything would be all right now. That was indeed how it turned out; I stopped being frightened, slept calmly at night and went out into the yard without a care in the world. When the war was over, we moved to Vilnius.

My energetic mother had also succeeded in sending my brother to a village to what she had thought was a good family. Apart from my brother, the family was also sheltering a few other Jews for short periods and an escaped POW. Someone informed on them and the Polizei came to look for him. When the POW caught sight of the Gestapo people, he ran into the shed and set himself on fire. The head of the household was arrested and never returned. His wife was warned by the Gestapo that the same would happen to her if she went on hiding POWs or Jews. Terrified, she took Izya back into Kaunas where she abandoned him in front of the Catholic church. My brother, Izya, disappeared forever. My mother was told that people saw Gestapo men arresting a Jewish boy at that place.

Figure 71. Izya Badesh, 1937.

After the war some Jews in Israel managed to obtain the status of one of the 'Righteous among Nations' for this woman. An article was published describing the rescue of a small child with the surname Badesh, whom they had to hand on to another family, but who survived. Someone telephoned me one day and said that my brother was alive. You can imagine how agitated we all were, but it turned out that they had simply read an article about that woman full of ridiculous assertions and lies.

I even went to Kaunas so as to meet with her and ask what had really happened to my brother. For a long time she refused to see me, until eventually I was able to obtain a meeting with her daughter through a lawyer. She kept contradicting herself, saying that her mother had seen Izya after the war, working in a garage; she did not admit that her mother had abandoned Izya to his fate.

Mother was transferred to Stutthof and survived. After the liberation she worked for nine months in a barracks in Germany. She sent a letter to Bronya, who told my mother that I had been taken away from her; my mother was in despair, thinking that I was no longer alive. Nevertheless she went to Kaunas to look for me. At the station in Vilnius, by chance she bumped into an acquaintance, a person called Kibarsky, who told her that I was living there with my aunt.

Meanwhile I had been settling down and had started to call my aunt 'Mama'. I was very fond of my uncle; it was a real 'love affair'. Then all of a sudden, yet another woman appeared saying, 'I am your real mother'. I got angry and said, 'I don't want any more Mamas. My Mama was young and beautiful and well dressed, and you...' Mother naturally looked terrible, dressed in a makeshift smock sewn together from soldiers' greatcoats. She refused of course to give in, and with a great deal of patience, perseverance, presents and loving care managed to win over my heart.

Mother married a second time. We lived in Vilnius where I studied medicine. I married Wolf (Zeev) Sharas. In 1971 we arrived in Israel. Here I immediately started working in a health centre as a paediatrician. I have two children and four wonderful grandchildren. Mother worked as a bookkeeper. She is 93 now, mentally alert and blessed with a wonderful memory. She lives in a flat on her own.

To this day I have not forgiven the Germans for their evil deeds and I have always refused to go to Germany.

Kiriyat Ono, Israel, 30 August 2008

46. A Little Girl with Three Mothers

Gita German-Gordon-Frances

It is the early morning of 28 October 1941. Today is my birthday. Gita'le is 2 years old. It was a rainy and foggy day. My parents woke me up early, and all the other family members were dressed up and ready to go. Somehow I felt festive being surrounded by my two grandmas, my parents, my uncles, Aunt Rivka Gordon and my cousin Sheinale. My father was in a wheelchair and I was sitting on his lap. My mother was pushing us. We were heading towards Democracy Square in the Kaunas Ghetto. What is awaiting us? What were the thoughts that crossed the mind of a 2-year old girl? What were her impressions? Did she feel the horror in the air?

From bits and pieces of early memories, and mainly through stories of the few who survived the 'Great Action' in the ghetto and through reading testimonies, I succeeded in reconstructing some of my feelings on my second birthday. The square was overcrowded with around 30,000 people. At first I probably felt secure being surrounded by all the members of our family. Hardly could I have imagined the scale of the tragedy that day when Gestapo master sergeant Helmut Rauca presided over the massive, day-long selection in Kaunas Ghetto, at the end of which 9,200 women, men and children were sent 'to the right' to be shot by the next day at the Ninth Fort. I had never been told that such horrible events can take place, not even in children's tales with their evil heroes.

I learned much later in my adulthood that my father, Yona German, was sitting in a wheelchair because he was mobilized by the Soviets to dig ditches before the German invasion, and he had become very sick. My mother, Fruma Lonshtein, moved with my father and her mother to the apartment of Aunt Rivka (Father's sister), in Slobodka, where all Kaunas Jews were ordered to move. My aunt's husband, Pesach Gordon, was a deputy of Chaim Yellin, the anti-fascist organization's leader of the ghetto resistance movement against the Germans. In the cellar of their house, which was situated on Ariogolas 36, partisans were trained to use weapons and planned various activities against the German forces.

Back to Democracy Square on 28 October. Suddenly my family was split into two parts. My grandmothers, my parents and my uncles were sent to the right, and only Aunt Rivka and her 4-year-old daughter Sheinele, who was sitting on her mother's shoulders, were sent to the left. Pesah was out of the ghetto that day, purchasing ammunition with a German passport. I found myself running towards my aunt who caught me in her arms. Never will I know why I ran to her, and who told me to do so. I probably wondered where my parents had disappeared, since they had never ever left me before. Wasn't this a terrible shock for a tiny and vulnerable little girl?

Those who were sent to the right were gathered for the night in the 'Small Ghetto', and marched the next day to Ninth Fort, forced to undress and brutally shot. The terrible scenes which took place there, about which I learned much later, persist in my mind and do not leave me. Human lives did not count in those days. I visited the Ninth Fort only in 2004, accompanied by my family, and a terrible chill went through my body as soon as I entered the gate. Only a second separated me from being a part of that massacre.

After the 'Great Action', Aunt Rivka became the centre of my world. I was told that the shock of losing my parents so suddenly turned me silent. I stopped talking. I have a photo of Sheinele and I participating in a Purim celebration in the ghetto kindergarten (see Figure 12), but my natural childhood cheerfulness had left me forever.

'Each man has a name that his parents gave him and God gave him', states Zelda's poem.[1] This is not my case. I was born as Gita German on 28 October 1939. Only in 2004 did I obtain a copy of my original birth certificate from the Vilnius Archive. My aunt Rivka had changed my family name and my birth date to 17 August 1941, and this is my official birthday to this date in my ID. The Germans closed the ghetto on 15 August 1941. I was proclaimed as Rivka's daughter. Since I was very tiny, it was no problem to claim that I was born in 1941. It was also easier to find an adoptive family for a younger child. So, it was as though I was reborn on 17 August 1941. Aunt Rivka became my official mother.

After the 'Children's Action', it was decided to hide me and my cousin/sister with Lithuanian families outside the ghetto. Thanks to the connections of the partisans with the outer world, two families were located. Sheinele together with some other grown-up children was taken to one family, and I was adopted by a childless Lithuanian family, who hoped to keep me forever, if my mother Rivka did not return from the forest, where she had joined the partisans.

I was hidden in a potato sack and taken out of the ghetto by the partisans: I have a sense that to this day I can smell the odour of that potato sack. The adopting family was told that I was just 2 years old, and that I did not speak. I remember that I was taken out of the sack and placed on a kitchen table; the feeling was of being in a warm and secure environment. Suddenly I started to count in Yiddish: *Eins, Zwei, Drei*. I believe that my adopting parents were in shock, but had to overcome it. I was reborn again with new parents, and my name was now Genuta, after Saint Genuta. I remember when I was baptized in the church and the feeling of cold water touching my forehead. I learned very fast to chat in Lithuanian. I had a new mother who loved me, and I loved her.

I remember her washing my hair with rainwater and chamomile to lighten its colour and make it look healthier. Every Sunday I was dressed up with festive clothes, with a large ribbon in my hair, and I went with my new parents to the church. I learned all the prayers, and seem to remember that I liked the ceremony.

Since my adoptive parents lived across the road from the Gestapo headquarters, German soldiers and officers used to visit the house and drink tea with strawberry jam. During these visits I wandered freely around the house, trying to attract the attention of the new visitors. I have a photo in which I am sitting on the lap of a Gestapo soldier, taken with my Lithuanian mother and some neighbours. When times became more risky and the Germans began to raid houses looking for Jewish children, I was sent to relatives in a nearby village. My cousin, Sheinele, was discovered in one of these raids and shot.

Aunt Rivka survived the war. Her husband was killed in January 1944 in a confrontation with German soldiers. I learned later that according to the agreement with the couple that

Figure 72. Gita German-Gordon sitting on the left knee of the SS officer and her foster mother is standing in the middle, 1944.

adopted me, if only the father survived (they were told that my aunt's husband was my father), they would have me forever, but if my mother survived, then they would return me to her.

One day, Rivka appeared at the door and presented herself as my mother. By then she was a total stranger to me, and also found it hard to communicate with me in Lithuanian. My adoptive family refused to give me away. For Rivka, I was the only family member to survive the war. She had lost her mother, daughter, husband and brothers: she was utterly determined to take me and raise me as her daughter. She returned with a cousin who was a high-ranking officer in the Soviet Army. They took me out of the house. It was a real drama. I did not want to go, and cried and screamed. So too did my Lithuanian mother who called her husband to return from work. They ran after the car in which I had been placed, and I remember them waving their hands and crying.

Again, Rivka became my mother, and she was to remain so until 2001, when she died at the age of 89. She separated me from the Lithuanian family and moved to Vilnius. From one perspective, I can understand her fear that I would be taken from her, but at the same time, I feel to this day a great frustration that I do not know the names of the Lithuanian couple who adopted me. Nor do I know what their destiny became, and I have not had the chance to thank them and reward them for their love and devotion, which they deserve. I only remember that they came to Vilnius once to visit me and told me that they were going far away. Most likely, they were deported to Siberia, or this was their way of telling me that we would never meet again.

The officer who helped Rivka to reclaim me from the Lithuanian family was named Kurecky. His wife, Tatiana Kurecky, was a famous singer. Once, when I was ill, they took me to recover in the countryside and I stayed with them for about three months; I loved being with them, and they were very fond of me. They did not have children of their own and decided not to give me back to Rivka. Only after a trial and with the birth certificate as proof that I was registered as Rivka's daughter was I returned to her.

Rivka remarried in 1947, to Judel Gerbajevsky, and he became my father. During the war he had lost all his family while he himself was serving in the Soviet Army. The maiden name in my ID appears as 'Gita Gerbajevsky'. He was a most loving father, reading me children's fairy tales, taking me to the cinema, writing songs for me, and putting toys and other surprises under my pillow. My sister, Sarah, was born in 1950, and we grew up as sisters.

In 1957 we moved to Poland, from where it was possible to migrate to Israel. We stayed in Poland eighteen months, and there I received my graduation certificate. We made our *Aliyah* (migration) to Israel in 1958. I joined the Israeli Army, but since my father had died and my mother was sick and there was no income, I had to start working. I became a laboratory technician and, after my studies, I started teaching at the ORT school. I became involved in the management of the school, and by the time I retired I was administrative director.

For many years it was a secret in the family that Rivka was not my biological mother. I knew the truth, but Rivka and I pretended I knew nothing. It was only when I was 19 years old that Rivka told me the whole story. Then, when my sister Sarah was in the Israeli Army, a mutual friend told her that I was actually her cousin: Sarah was desperately upset with our mother for lying to her. Sarah and I currently live very close to each other, we meet often and we are now a close-knit family.

Ramat Gan, Israel, 2008

NOTE

1. Zelda Shneerson-Mishkovsky, 'Everybody has a Name', in *Zelda's Songs* [Hebrew] (Tel Aviv: Kibutz Hameuhad, 1985).

47. Twenty-Six Years of Expectation

Rut Latzman-Peer

My father, Jehoshua Latzman, and my mother, Frida Peleryte-Latzman, met in the Jewish Gymnasium at Kaunas; they were both teachers. My father was a writer as well. His first book of poetry in Yiddish was published before the war. He was one of ten children: two of his sisters, Rochale and Henia, survived the ghetto and the camps and emigrated to Israel, all the other brothers and sisters were killed.

Father's marriage with Frida was his second; he had two children from the first marriage, Lili and Daniel. Lili spent the war years in an orphanage in Kazakhstan; 9-year-old Daniel Latzman perished in Kaunas Ghetto. Mother's parents were killed by Lithuanians in the town of Plunge. All I have of my mother is several photos given to me by her friend, Rocha Zacharovich.

Figure 73. Frida Peleryte-Latzman, Ruth's mother, 1940?

I was born in Kaunas in April 1941. On the first day of the German invasion my parents joined the crowd hastily leaving Kaunas and heading towards the east: my sad story was about to begin. As I slept peacefully in a pram I could not have known how my future was to unfold. Suddenly a lorry stopped and a driver shouted to the people in the crowd, 'Women and children only!' Father helped my mother to climb into the lorry, lifted the pram with me in it, and the lorry rolled forward. They thought the truck would take us east where we were heading. Nobody even suspected that after several kilometres the driver would turn 180 degrees and drive back directly to Kaunas. My father, together with many other men, continued his very long journey until he reached Kazakhstan.

My mother and I spent about two years in the ghetto, where we lived in one flat with my Uncle David and Aunts Rochale and Henia Latzman. Meir and Chaim Elin, the head of the anti-fascist underground, were my father's close friends. They decided to rescue me. Meir's wife, Busia Elin, found a place for me in the orphanage of Dr Baublys.

Figure 74. Dr Petras Baublys. In Baublys' managed orphanage at least thirty Jewish children were rescued. From the personal Sofia Ligija Makuteniene archive.

Naturally my mother did not want us to be separated, but she was persuaded to agree. I was given a shot of Luminal, wrapped in tattered garments and put on a sledge. Sonia Novodzelskyte (later Lupshisiene), a 17-year-old member of the underground organization with Aryan looks, was entrusted with carrying me out of the ghetto. After passing through the gates among the groups being led to work, she slipped away and reached the orphanage safely. She left me on the porch of the orphanage and fled. Sonia managed to survive. I remained in close contact with her until her death in Vilnius several years ago.

I stayed in the orphanage for quite a long time. I was a blue-eyed, blonde-haired girl, so nobody in the orphanage, except Dr Baublys, knew I was Jewish. I carried a small tag on a necklace with the name Irena Baltadonyte written on it; nevertheless Dr Baublys felt they should find me a home as quickly as possible. So a Lithuanian couple, the Urbonas, arrived looking for a child to adopt, and I was offered to them.

Figure 75. Ruth Latzman with her adoptive mother, Maria Urboniene, 1944.

My adoptive parents lived in the small town of Simnas. Since I did not speak Lithuanian at all, gossip spread among the Urbonas' neighbours suggesting that I was not really a Lithuanian girl. They called me 'Zhydelka' or 'Sorke'. I didn't know they were calling me a Jew and I ran to my mother, Maria, to ask her what this meant. I remember how neighbourhood children mocked me and pushed me into the river and how again I ran home crying. My adoptive parents felt it was dangerous to stay in Simnas, so we very promptly moved to a different part of Lithuania, to a small village called Butrimonys, which was nothing more than a number of houses around a church. We didn't leave anybody our new address. When I was 4, I asked Maria where my real parents were, and she told me they were not alive.

Figure 76.
Ruth Latzman in
the countryside,
1945.

After the war we moved to the town of Alytus where I grew up until I was 16. I graduated from a vocational college in Vilnius and specialized as a bookkeeper. I was sent to work in the town of Prenai and after several years I returned to Alytus, where I worked in a bookshop for the next thirteen years. Throughout all those years I felt I was Jewish and expected to be found by my biological parents.

My father spent the five war years in Kazakhstan; it was a time of difficulty and deprivation. There he met Lina, who became his wife. They returned to Lithuania, where he was informed that his wife Frida had died in Stuttoff and that I had survived. Father looked for me everywhere, but he could not trace me. I was told that a young man named Shmuel Peipert had come to our village looking for hidden Jewish children, but we had already left.

My father's new family lived in Vilnius where my half-brother Leopold (Lev) was born. Father continued to write and to publish poems in Yiddish; during the period of Stalin's persecution of Jewish intellectuals, he was arrested and spent several years in jail. There his health was badly damaged. He was released after Stalin's death. When Leopold reached the age of 18, my father told him about me and about his failure to find me.

Leopold initiated a search, but nobody knew the name that was given to me when I was smuggled, or what my name was now; Leopold asked our sister Lili to help him. She worked as a solicitor. While attending a conference she told colleagues about her search for me. By chance, a client of mine from the bookshop was also participating at this conference. She knew my story and approached Lili and thus they succeeded in tracing me. Lili and Leopold contacted me and I invited them to come see me in Alytus; Lili said that she immediately recognized me.

By then, I was a mother myself. My son Gil was already 6 months old. So, in 1967, after twenty-six years of separation I was reunited with my father, and the return to my Jewish roots and to my family began. Father and his family emigrated to Israel in 1971: he was a Zionist and had fought for his right to go to Israel for sixteen years! I joined them in 1973 with my son Gil. I did not want to leave Lithuania; in fact, it was my adoptive mother, Maria Urboniene, who encouraged me to leave. She came to visit us in 1989, and we were all so happy to meet again. Two years later she died; I have visited her grave several times. May this wonderful woman rest in peace.

My aunts and my father's wife Lina warmly embraced me into the family. My father died in 1984. Lina and I remained friends until she too passed away. In Israel, I quickly realized that I needed to change my profession. I went to nursing school in the Kaplan Hospital in Rehovot. I remember wondering how I would juggle my studies and bring up my son. I was told that many of the nurses' children were being taken care of at a boarding school while the nurses were studying for their qualification. This solution was absolutely out of the question for us, after what I had been through: I would never consider sending my child away from me.

After graduation I worked in the Kaplan hospital for six years. Then I married and we moved to Tel Aviv. I worked in Beilinson hospital till my retirement several years ago.

Tel Aviv, Israel, December 2008

48. Finally I Found My Roots

Rina Gilde-Rubinstein

One of my earliest memories of childhood: I am in a small country house with Yulia, a kind-eyed woman. A bespectacled stranger in a black coat and with a stick in his hand enters the room. He smiles pleasantly, talks with Yulia and caresses my head. Shortly after, I am in a military car riding along country roads. Eventually we arrive at a different house. The man in the black coat carries me into a big kitchen. I am sitting there, a little girl in a white fur coat and *valenki* (winter boots) on a big oven. I am embarrassed by the presence of strangers around me.

From this moment my life completely changed. I had grown up in Vilnius; we lived in a nice apartment in the centre of the city; I had my own, private room. My new father, Victor Micelmacher, was a highly respected professor of medicine and my new mother, Anna, was a chemist. My new parents always employed a housekeeper.

I remember an old, bearded doctor often visited me there. Now I know it was Dr Baublys. I was a skinny girl with a big belly; obviously I was suffering from rickets. We were three children in the family: Tolik, Gena and I.

The mother was responsible for our education since the father was always busy. We were treated very well by both our parents, but I was especially fond of Father. I will never forget one special day, when I was 8 years old. We were playing outside, and a boy from our neighbourhood told me that my parents were not really my Dad and Mom. I burst into tears, ran into our apartment and shut myself in my room. My parents asked what was wrong with me, and I asked them what the boy's words meant. Instead of an explanation, I was told that the boy would be punished. After that, one thought constantly bothered my mind: I am an adopted child, where are my real parents?

One particular woman from Kaunas used to visit us quite frequently; she always came with lots of presents for all the children, but especially for me. She was a mysterious person, but

I could feel her affection towards me. She and my father used to talk privately for hours. I remember that I was very much upset after one of her visits. I could not understand the reason for my mood. I liked her, but I also felt some uneasiness: I did not know her identity. After this visit, she disappeared for a long time. Later I learned it was at the request of my parents; I felt there was some secret surrounding me, but nobody talked about it.

Several years later, I went one evening, deeply frustrated, to my father's room, and demanded that he should tell me the truth: who were my parents? He became very emotional and told me that my parents had perished in the Kaunas Ghetto. He said he was a friend of my biological father, so he had resolved to find and to adopt me. Ever since I have felt profound gratitude to the Micelmacher family for their love and care, and the education they provided me, that enabled me to achieve what I have.

Figure 77.
Eida Gilde-
Judelevich in
'Matate' theatre in
Tel Aviv, 1937.

Figure 78.
Dr Max Gilde, 1937.

I was accepted. When I was a student in the Kaunas Medical Institute, I discovered that the mysterious woman who visited us for many years was my paternal aunt, a well-known paediatrician, Fruma Gurvich. Although she became my very close friend, we never talked about my past or my parents' fate.

In 1962 I married Reuven Rubinstein. His family had been deported by the Soviet authorities to Siberia on the eve of the war, returning to Kaunas in the late 1950s. Just before the wedding, I received a present from Israel from my aunt, Fruma Hasman, my mother's sister. She also sent me my mother's photos. Mother looked very much like I had imagined her in my dreams. I didn't even know of Fruma Hasman's existence, so her appearance was a complete surprise to me. It was my future mother-in-law, who after hearing my story, wrote letters to my aunt in Israel. Much later, Fruma told me that in 1950 she made unofficial inquiries at the Israeli Embassy about the possibility of taking me to Israel: there was of course no chance that the Soviet authorities would permit this.

Fruma Gurvich introduced me to my rescuers, Yulia Vitkauskiene and her son Arejas, very fine, pleasant people. During our first meeting, Yulia did not talk much, but only looked at me with affection. It turned out that for many years Yulia had corresponded with my aunt Fruma in Tel Aviv, who had supported the Vitkauskas family by sending parcels from Israel. Later I also did my best to maintain our relationship, and to express my love and gratitude to these wonderful people who saved my life.

It is mainly from my aunts and Yulia that I have learned what happened to my family in the Holocaust. My parents, Max Gilde and Eida Judelevich, were born in Shauliai. In 1935 my mother, who later became a singer and actress, moved to Palestine, where she acted in the '*Matate*' theatre. My father graduated from the Kaunas Medical Institute. In 1937, after completing his training in gynaecology, he followed my mother, and they married in Tel Aviv.

Conditions in Palestine at that time were very difficult. Father could not find work as a physician, and Mother lost her work in the theatre as well, so in 1938 they decided to return to Lithuania temporarily. I was born in Kaunas on 16 April 1940 and was given the Hebrew name Rina. From the letters my mother sent to her sister in Tel Aviv before the war, I learned that my parents' dream was always to return to Palestine.

On the first day of the war my parents tried to escape from the Germans and join a partisan detachment. Unfortunately I had whooping cough and so it was difficult for my parents to hide me and to pass through multiple checkpoints on their way. After two weeks, tired and exhausted, they knocked at the door of Yulia, a Lithuanian woman who had been their neighbour before the war. They had nowhere to live; their apartment was already occupied by the chief of the Lithuanian police. Yulia led them to her relatives in Vilijampole. On the second day, the house where we were staying was surrounded by barbed wire and became a ghetto.

Yulia had always been very friendly to our family, and she started helping us in the ghetto. Sometimes, when my father was taken for hard labour work in the city, he escaped from the convoy and went to meet Yulia. Secretly, she would put food into my father's pockets, and sometimes a bottle of milk for me.

Figure 79. Yulia Vitkauskiene, rescuer of Rina Gilde-Rubinstein and Pesah and Chanale Joselevich.

During the 'Children's Action' my father sedated me, together with other children, to keep us quiet in a hiding place. Immediately after this 'action', my mother arranged to meet Yulia outside the ghetto. Tired and suffering, she begged Yulia to save me: 'You would be rewarded with God's blessing for it,' she told her. With the consent of Arejas, her 16-year-old son, Yulia decided to help us. After some failures and in great danger, my father put me, certainly sedated, in a sack of potatoes on a cart and took me, with assistance from the bribed German guard, to Yulia, who was waiting for us at a meeting point. When I was taken out of the sack, I asked immediately, 'Where is Mom?' The German soldier looked at me with his penetrating eyes, then looked at Father and mumbled, 'What a pretty girl.' It was obvious he wanted an additional award. My father gave him his gold watches. The German was pleased and said, 'Let's get moving, we must return to the ghetto.'

Yulia had to change apartments regularly because of me, a typical Jewish-looking child. I spent a lot of time just sitting under the bed, neither eating nor drinking, out of fear that I would be discovered by the Germans. Warnings appeared on the walls of Yulia's house: 'People helping Jews will be punished by death.' Despite this, Yulia helped to save two more children: Pisinka (Pesah) and Chanale Joselevich. When there was a shortage of money and food, Yulia left her house and took us, three Jewish children, to her parents in the countryside, good and kind people. Arejas remained in Kaunas and took over Yulia's responsibilities in their publishing business.

We learned that we had to run whenever we heard the word 'Germans', the three of us, and hide under the sofa. We could sit there for hours, silently and without asking for food or even water. The neighbours in the village did look at us with some suspicion, but Yulia kept us till the end of the war.

Yulia and her son were real heroes. They both were awarded the title of 'Righteous among the Nations'. Unfortunately, they died before the ceremony was held in Yad Vashem in Jerusalem.

My parents were burnt alive, when the Germans liquidated the ghetto.

In 1973, after a long struggle with the Soviet authorities, we emigrated to Israel with our daughter Ilana. In 1975 our son Eitan was born. I worked in Israel as a paediatrician until my retirement.

Haifa, Israel, 2008

49. I Pretended that I did not Know She Was My Aunt

Rina Zupovich-Kaplan-Wolbe and Simon Wolbe

RINA

When my father, Meir Zupovich from Jonava, and my mother Mira, née Strashuner, were forced into the ghetto, my mother was expecting me, her first child. I was born on 16 August 1941. In the ghetto my parents lived with my grandmother, Chaya Hinde Strashuner, my mother's twin sister Frida and Aunt Rosa Strashuner.

My uncle Leibke Strashuner was a soldier in the Soviet Army. His paratroop unit was sent to join a detachment, and Leibke was killed in battle. Uncle Yehuda (Juda) Zupovich was a deputy of the Jewish police in the ghetto, and my father and his other brother Moshe were also members of the police; all three cooperated with the anti-fascist underground. It was Juda Zupovich who organized my rescue operation.

Figure 80. Zupovich with his wife Dita (Judith) Zupovich, today Shperling. Dita risked her life in rescuing Rina Zupovich-Kaplan.

Juda's wife, Dita (Judith) Zupovich-Shperling, recalls in her memoirs:

Rina was 1 year old, a sweet blonde baby, with rosy cheeks. Before the war Juda worked with the architect Count Vladimir Zubovas, who helped us now, risking not only his life, but also that of his family. He put us in contact with Dr Baublys. On a mild winter day we decided to smuggle Rina out of the ghetto and to lay her down on the steps of the Baublys orphanage. Rina was given a shot of Luminal so that she would asleep. On her little wrist we fixed a band with the name Irena Krikshchiukaite.

In my mind's eye I can see again the gate of the ghetto. It was getting dark. The street in front of us was full of ghetto inhabitants, coming back in columns from enforced labour. The Lithuanian policemen were busy at the gate searching people and rummaging through their small bundles. We chose the right moment to slip unnoticed through the narrow gate, which the Jewish Polizei had opened for us. Together with me was Frida, who would help me carry the child.

We walked on the sidewalks prohibited to Jews, hiding the yellow stars. In front of us there was a long road, ending in a bridge. There were no lights because of the air raids, no moon, only greyish snow. People hurried carrying sacks, bags and baskets, coming back from work. Nobody paid attention to two women with a child in their arm and the darkness concealed my Jewish appearance.

As soon as we were on the busy street, we felt more secure. But soon we left the suburb and reached the appointed place. We were now in a little wood. Suddenly the clouds parted and the full moon lit the white snow. It was like daylight. We walked on, the atmosphere was eerie. I was becoming more and more frightened.

It had been agreed that I put the child on the entry step of the institution. Dr Baublys was already waiting for us. But the way to the house led through a very narrow passage between the wall of the house and a high fence. From the passage it would be impossible to escape if we were noticed. In our anxiety we decided to lay the child, who was warmly wrapped, down on the snow near the gate, hoping that somebody would find her. Then we ran away, looking back once more. Rinale woke up from the cold snow and began to crawl. Fortunately, she could not yet walk. For us there was no return, we had to get away and reach the ghetto.

The next morning my Aunt Dita went to the town with the work brigade in order to see Zubov. To her great relief she learned that a Lithuanian policeman had been passing near the orphanage by chance; he found me and carried me into the orphanage. He was married, but did not have children of his own, and asked Dr Baublys to let him adopt the child. Baublys was happy to accept this offer, and arranged all the necessary papers. When Dita returned to the ghetto to report the news to my parents, to her surprise she found me lying in my bed. It appeared that when I woke up with my new Lithuanian family, they gave me a candy. '*Kecke*', I said, which means 'sweetie' in childish Yiddish: the policeman immediately realized my background. He swiftly brought me back to the ghetto gates and handed me to the Jewish Polizei. Fortunately, there were no Germans or Lithuanians guards around at that moment.

I was in the ghetto when the 'Children's Action' took place. My grandmother hid me in the attic of our house, where other children where hidden as well. I was given sleeping pills, but I woke up and began to cry, exactly when policemen were around. Grandmother was forced to shut my mouth with her hand, almost suffocating me: it took my grandmother some time to get me breathing again after the danger had subsided.

Frida carried me out of the ghetto for the second time and handed me over to a Polish woman. I do not know her name but I remember her daughter-in-law was called Vanda and Vanda's daughter's name was Janina. My name while I was with her was Irute Neshukaityte ('Do not look for me' in Polish). This second attempt to rescue me did not go smoothly either: a neighbour informed the police that a Jewish child was being hidden. Lithuanian policemen came to investigate, but my saviour managed to bribe them, and they left as they came. Much later I went with my husband to look for this woman, but we could not find her home.

My father and Juda Zupovich were shot in the Ninth Fort with nineteen other Jewish Polizei for refusing to disclose where some of the ghetto children were hidden during the 'Children's Action'. My mother, Rosa and my grandmother perished shortly before liberation. They were burnt alive in the '*malina*'. Dita Zupovich was sent to Stutthof; she was lucky to survive. Today she lives in Tel Aviv and at 86 she is well, both physically and mentally.

Frida managed to escape from the ghetto a day before its liquidation. She married Yakov Kaplan. Yakov had lost all his family in the mass killing of Raseiniai Jews by the Lithuanians during the first days of war. He himself slipped out at the last moment from the pit where the corpses of Jews were thrown by the murderers, and after hiding under a horse carriage, escaped unnoticed into the woods. Frida and her husband found and adopted me.

Frida did not want me to know that she was not my biological mother; for this reason she even avoided meeting Dita Zupovich. I knew from a very young age that she was actually my aunt; everyone around me knew the truth, and I heard the whispers of women in the synagogue, saying that I was adopted. But I always called Frida 'Mama' and Yakov 'Father.'

While escorting me to a hospital for my first delivery, Frida asked me if we had chosen a name for the baby. I told her that if it was a boy, we would call him Marik, and if it was a girl, Mara, both very similar to my parents' names. Frida later said to my husband that she was very happy with my choice. Even so, we never touched this subject, until her last days.

My adoptive parents migrated to Israel with their two sons. Frida died in 1979, and now I have a very close relationship with my step-brothers, Mark and Daniel.

SIMON WOLBE

Frida Epstein and Haim Wolbe fell in love and married sometime around 1928, and I was born in 1933. My father was a metal-worker in Kaunas. In 1941, my parents, with my 10-year-old brother Moshe, 13-year-old sister Haya and myself were ordered into the ghetto. I remember quite a few episodes from our life there. We used to play in the cellar of our house with the neighbour's children. We kept dogs and rabbits in the cellar, left behind when all the ghetto inhabitants perished. I will never forget how, one day, the neighbour's daughter killed a rabbit, skinned and cooked it for us. She was under 10 years old.

There was an attempt to organize a school in the ghetto. I remember I attended the first class for only one day. The next day we were sent home, teachers were afraid we would be rounded up all together and killed.

Mother was the first to perish. She was sick, and hospitalized in the ghetto hospital, where she was burnt alive with all the patients and staff.

I remember clearly the day of the 'Children's Action'. I was outside with my brother. We saw lorries gathering near the ghetto fence and we understood immediately that something bad was going to happen. We ran to the attic of the house, which was full of garbage. There were many other children. We hid behind old broken furniture, empty boxes and other garbage. A couple of German soldiers came to search the attic. They did not find us (or did not want to find anybody) and left.

From the broken roof of the attic I saw how the Polizei led an old man and woman carrying a child out of our house. The Polizei tried to take the child from the mother's arms. She resisted and the Polizei hit her, dragged the child from her and threw him into the lorry. The lorry drove away and the woman and the old man were left standing helpless on the street.

A day before the liquidation of the ghetto my father decided to escape with all of us from the ghetto. We left with the column of workers. We walked down Ponaru Street towards the house of a Lithuanian farmer who had agreed to hide a Jewish family. Suddenly a German soldier on a motorbike appeared and noticed Moshe, who was lagging behind us. The soldier stopped him, asked for documents and eventually arrested him. Despite Moshe's pleas for release, the German soldier took him away.

In terrible despair we reached the farm in Vilijampole. The owner of the farm, Petras Andriuskevichius, had agreed to hide us. My father promised this farmer his house as payment. His wife Joana and daughter, Eugenia Andriuskevichiute-Zhemaitiene, helped him in providing for our needs. After the war he visited us; my father wanted to keep his word and offered him money, but the farmer refused to take it. He was recognized after his death by the independent Lithuanian government and awarded the Life Saviour Cross.

We were hidden in the cellar of a barn covered by stacks of wood for two days. To our misfortune, the Germans arrived and ordered the farmer to leave, since they needed the house for an artillery defence unit. The farmer removed some planks from the fence to enable us to escape in the darkness. We ran to the fields. My father dug a pit, covered it with the old rusty lid of a pan and we hid there for another four days. Father went out in search of food and managed to find a peasant who supplied us with water and food. The next time my father crawled out of the pit, he was stopped by a soldier, who to our relief, spoke Russian.

Immediately after the liberation of Kaunas we went to the ghetto in the faint hope of finding Moshe there. We were among the first to see the burnt ruins and corpses. The defaced corpse of a boy was laid on the street near the place which was once our home in the ghetto. German POWs were ordered to pick up the bodies and to bury them. Father thought this was Moshe's body. But later, people who returned from the camps told us they had seen Moshe in the American hospital, wrapped in a blanket; he was very sick. We never saw or heard about him again.

My father resettled in Kaunas, he married Zlate, née Mashkantz, who lost her husband and two children, Riva and Israel, in the ghetto. They had a son, my youngest brother, Itzchak. My father died at the age of 90 in Israel.

For four years I attended the Jewish school, then the Lithuanian gymnasium, and went to the Soviet Army to serve in the Black Sea Navy. After my release I married Rina Zupovich in 1960. Like my father, all my life I worked as a metalworker.

We emigrated to Israel in 1972 with our two children. We have five grandchildren here in Israel.

Kfar Sava, Israel, February 2009

50. Kamochka, Come with Your Whole Family and I Will Shelter You Again

Kama Ginkas[1]
(As Told to John Freedman)

I was 6 weeks old when, as my mother always said, Hitler came to kill me. Hitler killed six million Jews. Thirty-five thousand lie in the ground beneath the Ninth Fort near Kaunas. Hitler killed my grandmother, Liza Zingman, my grandfather, Avraam Gink, my uncle, Khesya Zingman, and my uncle, Lyolya Gink. But he was not able to kill me, even though I was only 6 weeks old and quite helpless. To this day I live in defiance of Hitler. To this day I remember the people who rescued and sheltered me, my mother and my father, because for twenty years and more after the war I daily heard stories about what happened in the ghetto and, on occasion, I would meet people who had sheltered my parents and myself. I remain grateful to every one of them and I continue to do everything in my power to remain alive in defiance of Hitler.

These people are remembered not only by me. There are no statues and monuments erected to their memory, but there is the enormous historical museum, Yad Vashem in Israel: this means 'Memory and Name'. That is astonishing. It means every single name must be remembered. And the list is not yet full. Every Jew who perished must be named there. Every person who sheltered or rescued Jews must be named there. In some cases this means names cut into stone walls. There is also the 'Garden of the Righteous'; Sofija Binkiene, an amazing woman about whom I will say more, is represented there. In the Soviet era, when it was dangerous for any Soviet citizen to have dealings of any kind with Israel, she travelled there as a state guest in order to plant a tree in her own name.

I often ask myself: Could I have done what they did? Could I have risked my life to hide total strangers in my house? These people were not sheltering relatives or friends. They sheltered strangers, people who might even be considered alien to them. Because we, Jews, are alien almost to everyone. We are different. As the Lord is my witness, I do not know if I could have done what these people did.

The night the war began my father, Miron, who was 29, was in the little town of Taurage, situated exactly on what was then the border with Germany. Father had just graduated from the medical institute at the university and had been appointed a staff doctor at the hospital there. His wife, my mother, and I, his newborn son, were in Kaunas. Taurage was some 150 to 200 kilometres away. The particular night in question was a Sunday, and since everyone in the senior staff had weekends off, my father was on duty. That night the bombing began. Since the German border was right there, the town was overrun by German soldiers within hours and the casualties among the soldiers of the Lithuanian border patrol were heavy. As the sole doctor on duty that night my father took in waves of injured soldiers on his own. And he was forced to operate on them. Now, my father had no experience whatsoever of performing serious operations. So he laid the surgeon's manual in front of him and did everything just as it was written there. He removed bullets embedded in people's bodies, amputated limbs and closed catastrophic wounds. He literally did it 'by the book'. That quickly came to an end, however. The Germans entered the hospital and shot all the wounded soldiers that my father had just been attending to.

It did not take Father long to realize that this was no place to be, and he set out for Kaunas on foot. He moved only at night, keeping to side roads because during the day columns of German tanks and infantry were heading down the main road towards Kaunas. Kaunas, in fact, was seized within the week. If I remember the stories correctly, it took Father two or three days to reach us at home.

In all I spent two years in the ghetto and something just short of a year being passed from place to place after we escaped; I know three or four of those places for certain. How many places and how many people there were overall, I cannot say. I know about the Binkis family. I know about Antonina Vaiciuniene. I know my family spent one night with strangers who lived by the bridge that led from the ghetto to Kaunas. I know I was with some people in the country in Panemune.

My parents visited me wherever I was being sheltered. At one of these places I came out as dirty as sin and with my face covered in pimples. This was because I was being hidden in a pig sty. I boldly brandished a stick and marched around the yard, declaring in a loud voice, *'As Kaziukas, lietuvis! As Kaziukas, lietuvis!'* That is, 'I am Kaziukas, a Lithuanian!' And with my stick I whacked away at the nettles or other weeds towering over my head. This probably happened in Panemune.

Figure 81. Kama Ginkas with unknown girl that perished, the Ghetto, 1943.

MY MOTHER MANYA GINKAS

My mother would have been 24 at the time that we were forced to move to the ghetto. There was nothing to eat there, but she had me to feed. I know that I love potatoes and peas to this day because they were delicacies in the ghetto. The German soldiers discarded potato peelings and Jews salvaged them to create a variety of tasty dishes; they even gave them names. For example, 'fish' – although there was no fish in those potato skins; 'meat' – although there was no meat there, whatsoever; 'Sirloin steak', names like that. And there were peas. That is, the Jews salvaged and ate the black peas that the Germans discarded. People got sick on this food. My mother said she breastfed me until I was 2 years old, by which time I already had my teeth. She could only feed me from herself and with a few stray scraps. I had constant stomach aches and I cried all the time. This was on top of the high-strung disposition that I come by naturally. I gave no one peace in that tiny room full of so many people, all of whom had to get up early in the morning to go to work. Then they would return home in the evening, tired, hungry and irritable. And I wouldn't let them sleep again. My father would take me down into a cellar and leave me where I could scream to my heart's content and bother no one. He used to tell about the time he came back down to get me and saw an enormous rat that was either licking my ear, or preparing to.

Father first met mother when she was still a schoolgirl and he was a grown man studying at the university. She was very much in love with Father. He was Mother's first, last and only love. With Jews everything is always in extremes. If a Jew is smart, he's a genius. If he's a fool, he's a damn fool. If he's not handsome, he's plug ugly. If he's handsome, he takes your breath away. My mother was a beauty like that, a true Jewish beauty with distinctive, classically proportioned facial features. She was relatively short, very fragile, beautiful and coquettish. My mother had gorgeous, thick, well-formed, black, Jewish eyebrows and huge, beautiful black eyes beneath long eyelashes. That was something she had to hide after we escaped from the ghetto, because it was quite clear she was not Lithuanian.

When my mother became pregnant with me, Aunt Sonya shrugged her shoulders. 'How can you possibly have children when a war is about to begin?!' she asked. 'That is simply savage.' But Mother went ahead and had me. In 1945, while the war was still going on, my mother gave birth to my brother Zhenya. Aunt Sonya was beside herself. 'Every thinking person knows the war will not end when the fascists are defeated!' she said. 'Giving birth to a child at a time like this is irresponsible.' My mother simply smiled. 1950 was still a difficult, hungry time.

The post-war chaos had not yet settled; there were international crises of all kinds. But my mother gave birth to my sister Alisa that year. The most important thing for my mother was to be a mother and a wife.

When we were still in the ghetto, word came that the deportation of children was about to begin. That meant they were going to begin exterminating children, and I would have been among them. I do not know how it happened, but someone informed my parents that a childless German couple was prepared to adopt me and take me to Germany. This would have guaranteed my salvation. But Mother said, 'Never. I will never allow my child to be a German. I will never allow him to grow up hating Jews. He will share our fate.'

When I was an adult, my mother mentioned something that astonished me. She revealed a small problem she had to solve while living in the ghetto: she was compelled to have an abortion. This was not a matter of choice; it was forbidden to give birth in the ghetto. This news stunned me. Not the notion of the abortion per se, but the notion that such a thing would be necessary. Somehow it never registered fully in my mind that my parents were young people in love. The conditions in which they lived were inexpressibly horrendous. From time to time, without warning, a new group of people was taken to be shot. But even there, in that living hell of a place, nothing could stop a loving man and woman from sharing their love. Family relations, in all of their complexity, continued unabated.

Children went to school; they followed their studies. Old men celebrated religious holidays; they observed *koshrut* (kosher). Doctors treated their patients and the local Jewish policemen kept things in order. True, they also had the responsibility of seeing to it that everyone who had been marked for extermination showed up at the necessary place and at the proper time.

One photo of the Kaunas Ghetto astounded me more than any other. The ghetto was enclosed on three sides on land by a barbed-wire fence. On the fourth side the barbed wire ran parallel to the River Neris. In this photo you see young women on the shore in their bathing suits; people continued to live their lives. They continued to love one another. They tried to dress well. They raised their children. They prayed. They made plans for a better life: they sought to remain human in inhuman conditions.

This was a stunning revelation for me. Because long into my adult years I imagined the ghetto as a horrendous place where people, crushed in spirit, did nothing but sit and tremble and wait for death. Of course they were crushed in spirit. But they lived their lives.

MY FATHER MIRON GINKAS

I do not know exactly how we left the ghetto because I have heard numerous variations of the story. But this is the basic tale as it has taken form in my imagination. I was given a sleeping pill to calm me down. After I fell asleep on the chosen day or night, my parents wrapped me in a sack of potatoes and tossed me over the barbed-wire fence. After paying the guard to look the other way, my parents walked through the gates of the ghetto. At some point an arrangement had been made that we would stop at a small house located just before the bridge on the ghetto side of the river. Perhaps the idea was for my mother to change her clothes. The upshot, however, is that we ended up spending the night there.

Now, for a moment, let's leap forward in time. In 2005 I took my production of the play, *Rothschild's Fiddle* on tour to Kaunas. I was eager to go back to that small city for the first time as a professional theatre director. When we arrived we were greeted cordially by the tour organizer in his spacious office. After a while the door to the office opened and a man and woman about my age entered. I smiled at them. And then the woman asked, 'Do you realize who you are speaking to?' I laughed sheepishly and said, 'I must admit I have no idea.' That is when she said, pointing to the man next to her, 'You were spirited out of the ghetto in his baby carriage.'

This man's mother lived in that little house before the bridge. And she had recently given birth to a baby boy. He was not yet a year old. She and her husband, Mr and Mrs Grenda, opened their home to us that night to give us shelter. The next morning she put me in her son's baby carriage and walked me over the bridge with my father and mother. Of course, that was no easy task because of the German guards who were stationed on the bridge.

From there, avoiding the centre, we travelled all the way across town to Green Hill where Sofija Binkiene lived with her family. I had never before heard anything about these people we stayed with for one night; after all, it was just one night of many. But their family remembered it.

Figure 82. Sofija Binkiene. From the personal
Sofia Ligija Makuteniene archive.

After escaping from the ghetto, my father bided his time as a *batrak*, a hired labourer. He had blue eyes and a face full of freckles, so he looked every bit the typical Lithuanian worker. Father always loved to tell comical stories about the problems and dangers that constantly arose. One day he had a high temperature and lay naked in bed sweating profusely beneath a thin sheet. Suddenly a German burst into the room and began shouting at him. 'What are you lying around here for, you lazy bum? I need a horse!' And in his anger he yanked the sheet off my father. There lay my father in all his Jewish glory: that is something you cannot hide. That German must have been very angry at that moment not to notice.

Or here is another story I remember hearing. As many often did, Father once stepped out of the column of people being driven to or from work, took off the yellow star and headed towards the city to trade some possession for something to eat. A German soldier approached him and demanded to see his papers. Of course he had none. He was caught red-handed, a circumstance that could easily have fatal consequences. But before the soldier could arrest him and lead him away, the Lithuanian guard of the column saw what was happening. He ran up, cursing at my father furiously, and he began beating him over the head with his stick. Then he chased my father back into line. My father always used to say, 'I am grateful to that man. He saved my life.'

I have always loved the stories of how my father came to retrieve me after the Germans fled from the city. It was an early summer morning and the city was eerily quiet. The Russian army had not yet entered the town, but the Germans were already gone. My father emerged from wherever he had been in hiding. In order to reach me, he had to walk all the way across the entire, utterly empty, city. Perhaps it was five or six in the morning. There was not a soul on the streets. Suddenly, Father sees a person emerge from around a corner. And these two strangers – my father and a man I know nothing about – embraced each other. They knew that at that hour and at that moment, only Jews would have come up out of hiding in basements and other places.

Father continued on across the city. He arrives at the hospital for handicapped children, the last place where I was sheltered; Father begins to search for me. But there is no one there. The hospital has been abandoned. At this point someone approaches my father and says, 'The Germans deported the entire staff and all the patients of the hospital to Germany.' The story at this point grows fuzzy, with different variants crowding in on my impressions. But what is certain is that, at some point, someone says, 'You must be looking for a dark-haired little boy.' My father says, 'Yes.' The other person says, 'He's over there,' and points. Wherever and whatever it was, my father went there. And there he found me. Everyone had been deported. But Antonina Vaiciuniene had succeeded in moving and hiding me before she was taken away with the rest of the hospital staff. Papa scoops me up and takes me back home.

I have other memories created from stories I heard my father tell. In one, I apparently do not recognize him very well when he comes to take me home. Perhaps I don't want to go with him. Or perhaps there is another reason why Father is compelled to 'bribe' me by giving me a pair of shoes. I was barefoot. And he offered me my first pair of shoes in my life – shoes with wooden soles. I didn't really want to go with this man I hardly knew anymore. But I certainly could not pass on that new pair of shoes.

Or here is another memory created by my imagination mixed with stories my father told me. After having walked across the city, we arrive at whatever place was being called home that first night. Darkness falls, and I say, 'Papa. Be careful. The Jews will come and cut us up.' That apparently is what Lithuanians around me sometimes said. Or, perhaps, it was something they taught me to say so that I, with my black eyes and guttural speech, would be taken for a real Lithuanian.

I think about this now and I realize that Father really had his work cut out for him. For in order to calm me down, he must inform me that, to a certain degree – unfortunately, perhaps, but there's nothing to be done about it now – he, my father, was, so to speak, a Jew. I can only imagine my reaction to that. How could it be that my own father, this man who just gave me a splendid pair of shoes with wooden soles, could be such an awful person, a Jew? Can you imagine how difficult it must have been for him, and how much painstaking diplomacy it must have required for him then to inform me that my mother, too, as embarrassing and disheartening as it might have been, was also, to some extent, a Jew?

Of course, the most difficult task he had was to advise me that the horror of it all was, as a result of everything else he had already had to admit, that I, myself, was also a Jew.

My father was unique and extremely creative. At the same time that he undertook to restore the Kaunas health system (it fell to him, an inexperienced, 30-year-old doctor, to do that immediately after the city was liberated), he also organized a choir of medical employees. Let's have people sing! When he assumed control of the ambulance service in Vilnius – an organization that possessed two ambulances and occupied two rooms at the time – he not only began creating one of the most advanced ambulance services in the Soviet Union, he had the bright idea of creating a mandolin orchestra of ambulance employees. My father played the mandolin beautifully, and he saw no reason why his staff of doctors, attendants and drivers should not learn to play this fine Italian instrument too. It made all the more sense because it was about time for him to get his children started on a musical instrument. But that was still not enough for him. Now he organized a ping-pong competition. These guys weren't going to sit around idly if my father had anything to do with it. Within less than a year, he organized a puppet theatre, which, as it so happened, was the first ever created in Lithuania. We children were obliged to perform.

My father did all this without ever missing a beat as he updated and upgraded the service provided by his ambulance crews. His was one of the first ambulance brigades to use walkie-talkies in their vehicles, cutting down the time it took to respond to calls. He was one of the first in the Soviet Union to incorporate the use of statistics about illnesses in the city in order to speed up treatment. He created one of the first mobile, fast-response cardiology teams in the Soviet Union.

Father had a mission to educate people. This is very common among us Jews; we are always ready to teach anyone and everyone, even if they don't ask for it – in fact, especially if they don't ask for it. He always used to say to me, 'You must not merely study, you must examine things to their core.' I used to hate that.

Like any educated person of that time he did not believe in an afterlife, but believed only in human progress and the creative nature of mankind. He always used to say, 'I do not fear death; I have already seen it.' And he truly did not fear death. He did not believe in God, either, although he venerated science. He believed in the omnipotence of medicine with the kind of zeal that most reserve for their faith in God. Still, in his final days when he was wracked by terrible pain that no painkillers could ease, he would shout, 'What is wrong with medicine that it can't help a man die without pain?!' That's what my mother told me. I wasn't there to hear it.

MY UNCLE LEV GINK

The day my father came to Kaunas he learned what had happened to his brother and his family. His brother's wife worked as a dentist in the military garrison. As such, she had the right to be evacuated with her mother, her child and her husband. But my uncle refused to leave without saying farewell to all the members of his own family. By the time he got back his wife and child were gone. Every second was of the essence. No one waited for stragglers. But this was a crippling blow for my uncle. His interpretation of the event was that his wife had abandoned him, that she had betrayed him in the worst of ways.

My uncle Lev Gink was an extraordinary man. He might well have been the most talented of the six Ginkas children of that generation. He was a gifted mathematician and an excellent chess player. He was the liveliest and most spirited of all those children. But luck was never on his side. He married as a young man but was divorced within a year or two because his wife was unfaithful. Shortly before the war he married a second time and he was the happiest he had ever been.

He fathered a child in this happy marriage with his beloved wife – but now she abandoned him, or at least that's what he thought. He received this news as if it were a message from destiny. He had never been religious before, but now something happened; religion became the central focus of his life. He began rigorously observing all the Orthodox laws and commandments and spent hours upon hours in prayer. From then on, as happens to people who believe they are doomed, he constantly ran into problems. This was especially true after he was herded into the ghetto with the rest of the Kaunas Jews.

When Jews were led out of the ghetto and into town to work, they often exchanged some of their belongings for food. Under their clothes they would sneak the food back into the ghetto past the guard at the gate whose job it was to search people coming in. Almost everybody would get past him all right, but my uncle always got caught. They would beat him, take his food away and that was that – he went hungry. He was alone in the ghetto, having no family or children of his own. My parents tried to convince him to escape, but he always rejected the idea, preferring to put himself in the hands of God and Fate.

When my parents resolved to escape from the ghetto they came to say farewell to him. But he was praying at that moment. There are Jewish prayers that cannot be interrupted for any reason. My parents tried to get his attention to say goodbye, but he refused to acknowledge their presence. He had no right to break off his prayer.

Deportations were constantly being carried out in the ghetto. For some reason my uncle never fell victim to a single one of those deportations. Tens of thousands of people had already been exterminated, but my uncle, although he was there until the very end, was not among them. As the Russian Army entered Kaunas, the Germans hurried to destroy evidence of the atrocities they had committed. My uncle was assigned to the unit given the responsibility of burning and burying the corpses in order to conceal the truth of the ghetto. When this was done, my uncle and other survivors were packed onto a freight train and sent to Germany. When the train was approaching Poland or had just crossed the border, a small band of prisoners escaped. My uncle, of course, was not among them. He had put himself in the hands of God and Fate. The Germans, as a punitive measure in response to the escape, pulled one person from each car and shot them on the spot. That is when my uncle met his fate. He was pulled from his freight car and shot.

SOFIJA BINKIENE

My very first memory in life is of silver spoons. More precisely, it is an impression of silver spoons. I once asked my mother why I might have this memory. She thought maybe it was a memory of being in the Binkis home and that may be true. Before then I could not have known anything so beautiful and elegant. I was moved to the ghetto when I was 6 weeks old and from the ghetto I was moved to the Binkis home. This was a home that had been occupied by many generations of highly cultured, relatively wealthy people who knew the value of beauty and aesthetics.

The Binkis home was already full when our family arrived from the ghetto. Sofija lived there in this small house on Green Hill, one of the more privileged sections of Kaunas, with her husband Kazys Binkis, the great Lithuanian Futurist poet, who lay dying in one of the rooms. Also living there were Sofija's daughters, Lilijana and Irena, with their husbands and baby children. It must have been a madhouse, and one of the most sophisticated homes in the city. Sofija was a former actress. Her husband, although at death's door, was one of the country's great poets. Lilijana was an actress. Her husband, Vladas Varcikas, about whom I will say more later, was a violinist; Irena was a harpist. On top of that, a Jewish girl about 8 or 9 years old lived there as a member of the family. The official story was that she was a distant relative visiting from the country. Incidentally, this neighbourhood of charming homes and cottages attracted the officers of the German military, SS and Gestapo. Many of them set up residence on all sides of the Binkis home.

A stream of people escaping from the ghetto kept coming directly to this house, where they would stay until Sofija could find another place to shelter them. My parents moved on to other places fairly quickly – each to a different location – but there were difficulties placing me, and so I spent quite some time with the Binkis family. I was kept there in the crib of Iga, Sofija's grand-daughter, who was about 6 months old at the time. Astonishingly, no one seemed concerned by the fact that I had whooping cough, a contagious and deadly disease for young children; I was accepted into the home, and into Iga's crib, as readily as everyone else was. Iga later became one of my best childhood friends.

One of the first things I did after I married Henrietta Yanovskaya in 1964 was to take her to Lithuania and introduce her to all of the people who had sheltered my family. Because these people were family too. Henrietta became a witness to how conversations about these people, and the events involving them, took place almost daily in our home.

When Iga got married – the girl in whose crib I slept when I had whooping cough – she fairly quickly became pregnant. And it was discovered that she had Rh negative blood. This is very dangerous for the mother and the child. One or both might easily die at the time of birth. Naturally, my father remained in constant attendance beside her in the hospital when it was time for the baby to come.

During the German occupation Sofija Binkiene and her family took enormous risks. They sheltered my parents, they sheltered me, they sheltered that young girl who lived with them, they sheltered everyone who came into their home from the ghetto until better, more permanent places could be found for them.

Many years later I asked Sofija Binkiene why she did it. She said, 'I considered it my duty to prove that not all Lithuanians were killers. There were other kinds of Lithuanians, too.' She was moved to defend the nation's honour.

VLADAS VARCIKAS

Vladas Varcikas, an elegant young Lithuanian musician, would pin a yellow star on his breast and come to the ghetto to persuade Jews that they must, and could, escape. For two years my parents could not bring themselves to believe him. They were afraid to leave.

If you wanted to run, you could do it. The problem was that there was no place to run to. Most Lithuanians were not willing to hide escapees. On the contrary, they would turn them over to the authorities. Perhaps they thought this is what they were supposed to do. After all, Hitler had given the order to do so, and they were law-abiding citizens. Perhaps this was an expression of their attitude toward Jews. Because Jews always irritate others. We irritate people because...because we are Jews. We irritate by the fact that we pray with headwear on, while a good Lithuanian Catholic removes his hat when he enters church. We irritate by speaking a language no one can understand, leaving the impression that we are covering up some malicious plot. We irritate by coming so quickly to each others' defence – thus meaning we are ganging up on the Lithuanians. And we are so damned cunning because, as a rule, we don't drink vodka, and some of us are even wealthy. At least we are wealthier than most drunkards. In short, we Jews irritate because we are 'others'. In fact, we are 'others' in an aggressive, energetic, conspicuous way.

And, as if that was not enough, we Jews – sons of bitches that we are – welcomed the Soviet occupation forces with open arms. Not every Lithuanian wanted to understand that the German occupation meant death to the Jews. There was no grey territory. You were either for or you were against. Not surprisingly, perhaps, it was primarily the Lithuanians who carried out the executions. The Germans themselves rarely did that. In Eastern Europe the executions were almost always carried out by the local populations – Lithuanians, Estonians, Ukrainians, Poles and Latvians. Most of all, however, people probably turned in escapees because it was dangerous not to. So what was the point of a Jew escaping from the ghetto? Anyone caught was shot. If you were not caught, you had to put yourself in the hands of someone willing to risk helping you. If you were an honest, self-respecting person, how could you come into someone's home and ask them to risk their own life for yours? This was the dilemma that the Jews faced in the ghetto.

Again and again Varcikas would come to the ghetto to persuade Jews that they must escape. He explained that there were Lithuanians willing to shelter them. This was an opera violinist, a tall, energetic, handsome man, who loved life. And he convinced my parents to overcome their doubts. He is the one who brought our family to the home of his mother-in-law, Sofija Binkiene. For this, Varcikas occupied a special place in our 'extended family'.

Time passed. The war ended. My family went to Vilnius. Varcikas's family fell apart, and his former wife remarried. Varcikas became the managing director of the Kaunas opera theatre; he was an excellent manager. He ran that place with discipline and vision. And whenever he would travel from Kaunas to Vilnius, where we then lived, he would always stop in to visit us. When I last saw him in Kaunas four years ago, he was still teaching violin. He was well into his 80s. We had a fabulous conversation, going over photos and stories. He had gone grey, but he is not an old man at all. He was handsome, courteous and had a way of remembering the past with an incisive sense of humour.

'BROLIUKAS'

A man whose real name was Bronius Gotautas was known to our family as 'Broliukas'. He was an amazing and very strange person, a monk and absolutely illiterate. He acted as a liaison between Sofija Binkiene and others who sheltered refugees. It is entirely possible that he is the one who went out and found people willing to accept Jews into their homes, explained to them why it was necessary and convinced them to do it. He appears to have been something of what we call a holy fool. But I do not know for certain. I heard various stories about him. My parents, for example, did not consider him a real monk. Antonina Vaiciuniene insisted Broliukas was a real monk, who, in order not to attract attention to his monastery among the occupying Germans, told everyone he was not a monk.

Now, if Sofija Binkiene risked her life to shelter people in order to prove that not all Lithuanians were killers, Broliukas engaged in this activity for purely religious reasons. By saving bodies he was saving souls. As such, he christened many of the Jews he saved. These were the conditions he attached. I do not imagine it was a categorical demand; rather, it probably was his wish. I know he did not christen my parents, but he did christen me.

My father's name according to his false papers was Jonas Mironas. His name, Miron, was turned into his last name, and he was given the Lithuanian name of Jonas. My mother was given the name of Maria, the diminutive of which was Maryte. My name was Kazys. Both of my parents carried false passports with these names in them. Chances are it was Broliukas who delivered these passports to them.

He invariably went barefoot. It did not matter whether it was winter or summer. He was always a little dirty, and he looked as if he were homeless. He would carry his batch of passports to be delivered in his coat pockets. But because he could not read, he did not know which passport was to be delivered to whom. To make it easier, he would put all the women's papers in one pocket and all the men's papers in the other. He would approach a man and would pull all the passports out of his 'male' pocket and say, 'Look through these and see if there isn't one for you.'

My mother always related this story with a mixture of affection and amusement. Broliukas himself was deadly serious about it. There was nothing funny in what he was doing. He was arrested just as the German occupation was ending. To his good fortune, this happened so late that the Germans did not take the time to execute him and, instead, shipped him off to Germany. The Jews of Kaunas, when they found out where fate had flung him, took up collections and sent him money. They did this knowing full well that entering into contact with anyone from a country that was considered enemy territory by the Soviet government could bring down heavy punishment. But what is really interesting about it is what we learned only much later – that all this time Broliukas would send the money he received to his sister who lived just outside of Kaunas. Perhaps at the end of the 1940s or the beginning of the 1950s, my father received a letter from West Germany. Broliukas wrote that after the war, he had ended up in the American sector of Berlin and, thus, had been saved. But he did not like life in Germany, and he wanted to come home. He asked my father to help him do that.

This was a horrible dilemma for my father. How could he tell Broliukas that he had no business returning to Soviet Lithuania? The best-case scenario would be that the instant he crossed the border he would be arrested and exiled to Siberia. The worst-case scenario would be that he would have been shot on the spot.

I do not even know if my father ever wrote back. But he never did anything to help Broliukas to return. I suspect Broliukas was extremely offended and considered my father an ingrate for that. I would say there is no way of determining who was right and who was wrong. Of course, my father was right. But I am sure Broliukas thought nothing of the sort; he would have considered that a betrayal on my father's part.

ANTONINA VAICIUNIENE

Antonina Vaiciuniene reappeared in my life absolutely unexpectedly nearly half a century after I had been in her care. I received a letter, a semi-literate letter, in which she asked if the person she had just read about in the newspaper was the same Kama that she had sheltered. I almost immediately travelled to Lithuania to meet her.

Later she would often send me letters. The handwriting on the envelopes was very childlike. And when I would open the envelope, a small, dried flower would invariably fall out of it. Each letter would begin with the phrase, 'Can that really be you, the little boy who used to cling to my skirt and now has become a famous director?' After there was a sharp rise in anti-Semitic threats in Russia, and pogroms were expected to begin any day, she wrote, 'Kamochka, come stay with me with your whole family. I have already planted potatoes and pickled the cabbage and I will shelter you again.' I wanted to bring Antonina to Moscow, but she never consented.

I originally came to Antonina when the German occupation was nearing its end. On the banks of the River Neris, across from the ghetto, there stood a hospital for handicapped children. The hospital was staffed by nuns who were charged with taking care of children in need, sometimes children who had been born of syphilitic mothers. This meant they were severely stunted in their development or were paralyzed in some way. Some had Down's syndrome. This was the last place I was sheltered. As Antonina later told me, she would occasionally go out and find a Jewish child abandoned by his or her mother along the fence or by the gate. These were probably people who knew they were going to be executed and they somehow found ways to leave their children to be cared for at this hospital. I do not know the details. Whether people were marched past the hospital on their way to be shot, I do not know. But from what Antonina told me, she understood that these were children from the ghetto.

It is necessary to recall that Hitler's policy was to destroy all handicapped children. Not just Jews and Gypsies, but the handicapped and the insane as well. In other words, this hospital should have been closed. Antonina explained that one of the doctors, a Lithuanian, raised the question, 'Why, in this time of war, was a hospital being maintained for handicapped children? There's nothing to feed the soldiers with and we're giving food to these sick children. This place must be destroyed.'

Then a marvellous group of Lithuanian doctors and professors responded by organizing a 'scholarly discussion'. They could not say that they were opposed to Hitler's ideology. So they organized a 'scholarly, professional seminar' to determine whether or not it would be proper to destroy this specific hospital. Perhaps it would not; perhaps there was some useful future for such handicapped children? This group of doctors found the funding to print a report – that is, an official document – proving that a professional discussion had been conducted on the matter and that a resolution had been passed, stating that, despite all arguments to the contrary, this hospital indeed had reason to exist.

Although this had nothing to do with why that 'scholarly discussion' was held in the first place, the result was that, in addition to handicapped Lithuanian children, Jewish babies could continue to be brought and abandoned at the hospital gates in the hope that they might live.

Naturally, I remember nothing whatsoever of my time in this hospital. And I heard virtually no stories about it. My father visited me there rarely, so my parents knew almost nothing of what went on there. Decades later, after I was reunited with Antonina, she told me that my father would come and criticize her. He was unhappy because I had grown so close to her. I would cling to her skirt and not let her go. Knowing my father, I can imagine these conversations. So I can see him scolding Antonina, 'You should not make the child so dependent on you. This may have an adverse effect on his psychological state in the future.' For Antonina to have remembered this for nearly half a century, I can imagine how my father must have said it. Instead of saying, 'Thank you for sheltering my child', he scolded her for conducting herself improperly.

I know from Antonina that the Germans would come from time to time to run inspections; they suspected there might be more children at the hospital than was officially reported. These children, the ones unaccounted for, would hastily be hidden in the beds of the real patients, often children who were sick, could not control their bowel movements, or who urinated in bed. Then the nurses would quickly close the door to the ward and hang a sign on it: '*Typhus abdominalis*'. The Germans would fear getting infected, and they would pass that ward by.

Antonina told me she was extremely thin at that time. I asked her if that was because she had nothing to eat. She said, 'Yes, of course. But that wasn't the main thing. The real reason was because it was so terrifying. We knew they could discover what we were doing at any moment. And if they did, we would have been shot right there. This was so frightening that one day I could not bear it any more, and I went to see my mother in the country.' I should add that Antonina's mother was a simple, religious woman who lived in the countryside. Her daughter was a nun and her son was a priest, who, in another region in Lithuania, also spent the war sheltering Jewish children, christening them and creating false identification papers for those who needed them. And so Antonina said, 'Mother, I could be killed at any minute because I am sheltering Jewish children. I'm so frightened I don't know what to do.' And this is what her mother told her: 'In that case you'll at least know what you are dying for.'

NOTE

1.   Kama Ginkas is a prominent theatre director in Russia.

References

Arad, Ytzhak, 'The Murder of the Jews in German occupied Lithuania (1941–1944)', in A. Nikzentaitis, S. Schreiner and D. Staliunas (eds), *The Vanished World of Lithuanian Jews* (Amsterdam and New York: Rodopi, 2004), pp.175–204.

Atamukas, S. *Lietuvos zydu keliais* (The Way of Lithuanian Jews) [Lithuanian] (Vilnius: Alma Littera, 2001).

Atamukas, S., 'The Hard Long Road towards the Truth: On The Sixtieth Anniversary of the Holocaust In Lithuania', *Lituanus. The Lithuanian Quarterly Journal of Arts and Sciences*, 47, 4 (Winter 2001), pp.16–45.

Beasley, N.W., *Izzy's Fire. Finding Humanity in the Holocaust* (Richmond, VA: Palari Publishing, 1977).

Binkiene, S. (ed.), *Ir be Ginklo kariai* (Unarmed Fighters) (Vilnius: Mintis, 1967).

Bliutz, B., *The Fate of the Jewish Doctors in Lithuania* [Yiddish] (Tel Aviv: The Society of Lithuaninan Jews and 'Sela', 1974).

Bubnys, A. 'Holocaust in Lithuania: An Outline of the Major Strategies and their Results', in A. Nikzentaitis, S. Schreiner and D. Staliunas (eds), *The Vanished World of Lithuanian Jews* (Amsterdam and New York: Rodopi, 2004), pp.205–21.

Chrust, J. (ed.), *Keidan Memorial Book* [Hebrew] (Tel Aviv: Keidan Association in Israel, with the Committees in South Africa and the USA, 1977).

Dubnov, S. *History of the Jews in Russia and Poland. From the Earliest Times until the Present Day*, translated by Israel Friedlaender (Philadelphia, PA: Jewish Publication Society of America, 1916–1920).

Eilati, S., *Crossing the River* (Tuscaloosa, AL: University of Alabama Press, 2008).

Elin, M., 'Kaunas Death Forts', in V. Grossman and I. Erhenburg (eds), *The 'Black Book' on Atrocities of the Nazis against the Jewish Population* [Russian] (Vilnius: Yad, 1993), pp.279–90.

Elinas, M. and Ghelpern, D., *Kaunas Ghetto and its Fighters* [Lithuanian] (Vilnius: Mintis, 1969).

Elinas, M. and Ghelpern, D., *Kaunas Ghetto Partisans* [Yiddish] (Moscow: Der Emes, 1948).

Elkes, J., *Doctor Elkhanan Elkes and the Kovno Ghetto* (Brewster, MA: Paraclete Press, 1999).

Encyclopaedia Judaica (Jerusalem: Keter Publishing House; New York: Macmillan, 1971–72), 'Kaunas', Vol.10, pp.846–50.

Encyclopaedia Judaica (Jerusalem: Keter Publishing House; New York: Macmillan, 1971–72), 'Jews in Lithuania – State of Lithuania 1919–1939', Vol.11, pp.361–74.

Faitelson, A., *Nepokorivshiesia* (Not Defeated) [Russian] (Tel Aviv: DFUS Ofset Israeli Ltd, 2001).

Faitelson, Aleks, *Heroism & Bravery in Lithuania 1941–1945* (Tel Aviv: Gefen Books, 1996).

Ghelpern, D., *Kovno Ghetto Diary*, translated by C. Bargman (Yiddish–Russian), Robin O'Neil (Russian–English, JewishGen, Inc., 1996) (Moscow: State Publishing House, Der Emes, 1948 [Yiddish]).

Gilbert, M., *The Holocaust* (London: Collins, 1986).

Ginaite-Robinson, S., *Resistance and Survival, the Jewish Community in Kaunas 1941–1945* (Canada: Mosaic Press and The Holocaust Centre of Toronto/UJA Federation, 2005).

Grossman, V. and Erhenburg, I. (eds), *The 'Black Book' on Atrocities of the Nazis against the Jewish Population* (Vilnius: Yad, 1993).

Hands Bringing Life and Bread, vols 1–3 (Vilnius: Vilna Gaon Jewish State Museum/Zara, 2005).

International Commission for the Evaluation of the Crimes of Nazis and Soviet Occupational Regimes in Lithuania, Jews in Lithuania (Vilnius, 2000).

Kwiet, Konrad, 'Rehearsing for Murder: The Beginning of the Final Solution in Lithuania in June 1941', *Holocaust and Genocide Studies*, 12, 1 (1998), pp.3–26.

Levin, D., *The Litvaks. A Short Story of the Jews in Lithuania* (London and New York: Berghahn Books, 2001).

Levin, D., 'Lithuania', in *Encyclopedia of the Holocaust* [Hebrew] (Tel Aviv: Sifriyat Hapoalim, 2006), pp.636–9.

Levin, D., 'Kovno', in *Encyclopedia of the Holocaust* [Hebrew] (Tel Aviv: Sifriyat Hapoalim, 2006), pp.1071–4.

Levinson, J., 'Foreword', in J. Levinson (ed.), *The Shoah in*

Lithuania (Vilnius: Vilna Gaon Jewish State Museum and Vaga Publishers, 2006), pp.11–16.

Levinson, J., 'The Shoah and the Theory of Two Genocides', in J. Levinson (ed.), *The Shoah in Lithuania* (Vilnius: Vilna Gaon Jewish State Museum and Vaga Publishers, 2006), pp.322–53.

MacQueen, Michael, 'The Context of Mass Destruction: Agents and Prerequisites of the Holocaust in Lithuania', *Holocaust and Genocide Studies*, 1 (1998), pp.27–48.

Nikzentaitis, A., Schreiner, S., and Staliunas, D., *The Vanished World of Lithuanian Jews* (Amsterdam and New York: Rodopi, 2004).

Oshry, E., *The Annihilation of Lithuanian Jewry* (New York: The Judaica Press, Inc., 1995).

Porat, D., 'The Holocaust in Lithuania. Some Unique Aspects', in David Cesarani, *The Final Solution: Origins and Implementation* (London: Taylor and Francis e-library and Routledge, 2002), pp.159–74.

Ro'i, Y., *The Struggle for Soviet Jewish Emigration 1948–1967* (Cambridge: Cambridge University Press, 1991).

The Association of Lithuanian Jews in Israel, *Lithuanian Jewry. Vol. 4. The Holocaust 1941–1944* [Hebrew] (Tel Aviv: Reshafim, 1984).

Tory, A., 'The Great Action in the Kaunas Ghetto', in J. Levinson (ed.), *The Shoah in Lithuania* (Vilnius: Vilna Gaon Jewish State Museum; Vaga Publishers, 2006), pp.78–93.

Tory, A., *Surviving the Holocaust. The Kovno Ghetto Diary* (Cambridge, MA: Harvard University Press, 1990).

Truska, L., 'Lithuanian History: Did the Jews Commit a Crime against Lithuania in 1940', *Akiraciai*, 7 (1997).

Truska, L., 'Preconditions of the Holocaust. The Upsurge of Anti-Semitism in Lithuania in the Years of the Soviet Occupation'. Research Work Database of the International Commission for the Evaluation of the Crimes of Nazis and Soviet Occupational Regimes in Lithuania, Jews in Lithuania (Vilnius, 2000).

Truska, L., 'Contemporary Attitudes toward the Holocaust in Lithuania', *Jews in Eastern Europe*, 2, 3 (2001).

Truska, L., 'Preconditions for the Holocaust in Lithuania', in J. Levinson (ed.), *The Shoah in Lithuania* (Vilnius: Vilna Gaon Jewish State Museum and Vaga Publishers, 2006), pp.361–80.

United States Holocaust Memorial Museum, *Hidden History of the Kovno Ghetto* (Boston, MA: Bulfinch Press/Little Brown and Company, 1997).

Vareikis, V., 'Preconditions of the Holocaust. Anti-Semitism in Lithuania. 19th Century to Middle of the 20th Century (15 June 1940)'. Research Work Database of the *International Commission for the Evaluation of the Crimes of Nazis and Soviet Occupational Regimes in Lithuania, Jews in Lithuania* (Vilnius, 2000).

Venclova, T., *Forms of Hope* [Translation from Lithuanian] (Riverdale, NY: Sheep Meadow Press, 1990).

Venclova, Tomas, 'Jews and Lithuanians', in J. Levinson (ed.), *The Shoah in Lithuania* (Vilnius: Vilna Gaon Jewish State Museum; Vaga Publishers, 2006), pp.443–50.

Vildziunas, L. (ed.), *Mano seneliu ir proseneliu kaiminai Zydai* (My Grand and Great Grand-Parents' Neighbours were Jews) [Lithuanian] (Vilnius: Garnelis, 2002).

Wolpe, David, *The Destruction of Keidan* (Johannesburg: The Keidaner Sick Benefit and Benevolent Society, 1950).

Zilber, Eliezer, 'A List (Incomplete) of Jewish Children Saved at the Kaunas Ghetto', in J. Levinson (ed.), *The Shoah in Lithuania* (Vilnius: Vilna Gaon Jewish State Museum; Vaga Publishers, 2006), pp.311–14.